CATHEDRALS OF BONE

CATHEDRALS OF BONE

The Role of the Body in Contemporary Catholic Literature

John C. Waldmeir

Fordham University Press

New York   2009

Library of Congress Cataloging-in-Publication Data

Waldmeir, John Christian, 1959–
  Cathedrals of bone : the role of the body in contemporary Catholic
literature / John C. Waldmeir.—1st ed.
      p.   cm.
  Includes bibliographical references and index.
  ISBN 978-0-8232-3060-0 (cloth : alk. paper)
    1. American literature—Catholic authors—History and criticism.
2. American literature—20th century—History and criticism.   3. Body,
Human, in literature.   4. Body, Human—Religious aspects.   5. Catholic
Church—In literature.   6. Christianity and literature—United States—
History—20th century.   I. Title.
PS153.C3W36   2009
810.9'92128273—dc22

                                                                    2008053539

Printed in the United States of America
11 10 09   5 4 3 2 1
First edition

For Mary, Louis, and Helen

The family as body
blessed

Contents

Acknowledgments

Early conversations with Giles Gunn led me to reconsider and reorganize my thinking about the relationships between literature, religion, and denominational identity. A final reading of the manuscript by Susan Hill helped to make it a clearer text for, I hope, a wider audience. I thank them both.

I am deeply indebted to three readers who spent considerable time with the book and improved its style, content, and argument. Joseph J. Waldmeir, Douglas O. Wathier, and Richard A. Rosengarten shared their wisdom and expertise with great patience and goodwill, and I only hope they know how much I appreciate their insights and detailed readings.

My thanks to Loras College for its ongoing assistance. A 2004–5 appointment by the College to the John Cardinal O'Connor Chair for Catholic Thought provided me with essential time and resources for writing. Two presidents, John Kerrigan and James Collins, as well as Provost Cheryl Jacobsen, supported the project on its academic merit, a shared commitment that I deeply appreciate. Thomas Jewell-Vitale opened his remarkable portfolio of artwork and allowed me to select the piece that graces the cover. Finally, my colleagues within the Division of Philosophy, Religion and Theology—and others across the College—persisted in their interest and encouragement, making the otherwise lonely task of writing a much happier experience.

We Catholics are very much given to the Instant Answer. Fiction doesn't have any. It leaves us, like Job, with a renewed sense of mystery. St. Gregory wrote that every time the sacred text describes a fact, it reveals a mystery. This is what the fiction writer, on his lesser level, hopes to do. The danger for the writer who is spurred by the religious view of the world is that he will consider this to be two operations instead of one. He will try to enshrine the mystery without the fact, and there will follow a further set of separations which are inimical to art. Judgment will be separated from vision, nature from grace, and reason from imagination.

—Flannery O'Connor

Introduction: The Body, Flesh and Bone

Thus ignorance of literature among students of theology can give Christianity a bad name. Since by nature we learn only by proceeding from sense experience to higher truths (there is nothing in the intellect that does not come via the five senses), so only by means of poetic imagery and sensitivity to language do we grow in understanding and intelligence. This adds strength and a certain fittingness to the art of writing. Hence a particular native elegance in speech moves and invites men to hear and read it. Thus it so comes about that men are more easily moved to hold with greater conviction truth which is illustrated by the beauty of Literature. Liturgy and the worship of God has a certain likeness to this.

—Pope Leo XIII, letter to Cardinal Parrochi, 20 May 1885

It is as clear for the writers to be discussed here as it was for Leo XIII that, when one brings the strongest attributes of imaginative literature to bear directly upon Catholic faith and practice, liturgy becomes the primary site of interaction. Moreover, when that literature is dedicated to representing the body, the possibilities for a sustained and compelling correspondence increase significantly. During the drama of the Mass, individual bodies join symbolically and actually with each other and with the body of Christ. As the novelist Ron Hansen says, Catholics

> have three yoked concepts in *Corpus Christi*: Christ as human being, Christ as Host or blessed and consecrated bread, and Christ as mystically embodied in the Church. We were saved in a mysterious way by Christ's crucifixion and physical death on the cross; we are helped and preserved and sustained through the real presence of Christ in the Eucharist; a Church inspired by the Holy Spirit keeps us from harm or loss through wise precepts and ordinances; and we share in Christ himself when we join together a Church in his name.[1]

Hansen's summary of the term "body of Christ" defines the *corpus* by the way believers experience it: as human, Host, and Church. His words also emphasize the purpose of this experience: that is, union with God and one another. All of the writers in the following chapters recognize and value the Catholic understanding of the term "body of Christ" because of the relationships the term both connotes and stimulates. However, it is crucial to recognize that, amid all of these relationships, one point persists: each author imagines those relationships primarily in terms of fleshly existence. Even the ultimate union between human and divine is construed as a relationship between human and divine "bodies." Moreover, in each case, these authors find Catholic liturgy to be the source and summit of their faith, because it is in the liturgy that the sacred is called forth from the mere proximity of flesh to flesh.

Consider, for example, Sebastian Taggart, Alfred Alcorn's reluctant protagonist of his novel *Vestments*, as he watches Mass unfold from the back of the church:

> Transubstantiation. It changed bread and wine into the body and blood of God; it meant union, communion, with God and God's essence. But what God? What essence . . . ? It made sense to him now . . . that we are, individually, all a small part of the Godhead.

Sebastian reaches this conclusion while he witnesses two events: the priest before him acting *in persona Christi* and "the faithful who rose to approach the railing for communion. . . ."[2] In this scene, Sebastian's reluctance to join the congregation at the communion railing results in his "envy" of their ability to act in ways that demonstrate the essence of a Eucharistic experience, a moment when believers accept and enact an analogy between their approach to the rail and an advance toward God. Fellowship during the meal, Sebastian discovers, proves Jesus' point that he will be present when two or three gather in his name.

This same analogy operates when the central character of Louise Erdrich's novel *The Last Report on the Miracles at Little No Horse*, a priest named Father Damien Modeste, tastes the wafer in the midst of his first consecration. Looking out from the other side of the altar in a wintry, bone-chilling Objibwe reservation church, Father Damien sees around him the pinched faces of those starving nuns who live and work at Little No Horse, and as he lifts the bread to his lips two experiences follow. In one, he tastes God "in his mouth. Real and rich, heavy, good," and with "startled shock" he

realizes that the flesh is "Real! Real!" In the other, which is almost simulta-
neous with the first, he longs to know if the experience has been communal.
Had the sisters on the reservation before whom he prays also felt "full . . .
satisfied and calm?" When the Mass is finished, he cannot be certain what
has been shared, only that the sense of community persists in every member
of the congregation as they stumble back to the convent, "holding one another by turns. . . ."[3]

As both Alcorn and Erdrich emphasize, the relationships created by liturgy are indeed tangible: real bread and real people. The movements that
Sebastian Taggart envies and eventually will perform are the movements
that Father Damien leads with no less fear and trembling. Like all good
drama, the liturgy of the Eucharist prompts an exchange between action
and thought. Liturgical theologian Aidan Kavanaugh emphasizes one direction in this exchange when he writes that "worship conceived broadly is
what gives rise to theological reflection, rather than the other way around."
For Kavanaugh, one of the finest liturgical theologians of this age, the correct order of the exchange is "first 'right worship' and only secondarily doctrinal accuracy." According to that order, a physical experience of the Mass
provides Catholics with a vocabulary that organizes and orders their theological reflection.[4]

But the exchange of course is more circular than Kavanaugh describes.
Catholics also understand liturgical actions according to a tradition that is
both intellectual and idealistic. Although the liturgical event is tangible, the
meaning Catholics ascribe to it is deeply influenced by a complex nexus of
ideas and ideals that are fashioned by a lengthy heritage and by the influence
of the present, historical moment. In the case of the contemporary authors
discussed in the following chapters, the significance of the liturgy—the
gravity of faith itself—depends upon the rhetorical impact of one defining
historical moment: namely, the Second Vatican Council. Each one of these
writers understands the importance of the Council; each refers to it, and
some, like Mary Gordon, J. F. Powers, and John Patrick Shanley, have relied
on it for topics, plot lines, and themes throughout their prose. Their fascination with the religious consequences of human bodies living out the tensions inherent to their physical, emotional, psychological, and spiritual
constitutions, and their willingness to examine those consequences in their
writings, is intimately connected to the way Vatican II produced documents
and codified practices that invited Catholics to consider the Church anew
and to imagine their relationship to it in terms borrowed from "bodily"
existence.

Vatican II Idealism

The rhetoric of the Council in this matter was far from uniform. Conflicts embedded in the documents have led to disagreements within the Church, fissures that, in their American context, have caused observers like Peter Steinfels to label the contemporary Catholic age—now forty years after the Council—a period of "crisis."[5] One need look no further than the writings of Joseph Ratzinger, now Pope Benedict XVI, to gain an immediate sense of how the choice of terms and words by Council theologians forced an uncomfortable moment of self-reflection upon the Church. Before he became the pontiff, Cardinal Ratzinger wrote that Vatican II had misunderstood the responsibility of the Church to answer "the fundamental biblical call for conversion and love of neighbor." According to Ratzinger, the "Council understood itself as a great examination of conscience by the Catholic Church" and "wanted ultimately to be an act of penance, of conversion." Those who gathered in Rome, he claimed, steered Catholicism "not only to uncertainty about the Church's own identity, which is always being questioned [in their writings], but especially to a deep rift in her relationship to her own history, which seemed to be everywhere sullied." For the future pontiff, the Council smacked of a "naïve optimism," an attitude he would strive to correct in his years as head of the Congregation for the Doctrine of the Faith.[6]

But according to Jesuit historian John O'Malley, that optimism—even in its most naïve form—actually defines the language of the Council. In a brilliant essay on the literary implications of Vatican II, O'Malley points out that the conciliar documents broke with the dominant genre of earlier Councils.[7] Previously, when the Church gathered, it produced largely canonical ordinances—brief, formulaic statements that set out regulations and described punishments for those who did not comply. Throughout the centuries, O'Malley notes, "the canon stands out for its recurrence and—if we take into account that in the sources it sometimes goes by other names—for its numerical predominance over every other form." These canonical statements are concise, and the certainty of their authors is evinced most clearly in the formula they follow: "If anyone should . . . let him be anathema."[8]

By contrast, Vatican II issued no canons, choosing instead a new genre to convey the import of its message. O'Malley insists that the genre "can be precisely identified."

It was a genre known and practiced in many cultures from time immemorial, but it was clearly analyzed and its features carefully codified by classical authors like Aristotle, Cicero, and Quintilian. It is the panegyric, that is, the painting of an idealized portrait in order to excite admiration and appropriation. An old genre in the rhetorical tradition of the West, it was used extensively by the Fathers of the Church in their homilies and other writings. It derives from neither the legal tradition of classical antiquity nor the philosophical/dialectical but from the humanistic or literary.[9]

This is the language of the Church Fathers and later of Renaissance Humanism. It is largely forgotten in the turbulent polemics of the Reformation but revived in the twentieth century as part of a renewed interest in the Fathers by key Vatican II theologians, most notably Jean Danielou and Henri de Lubac.[10] The language is marked by its attention to the interior life and by the way it links a plurality of human experiences to the persistent presence of the divine. It is, in other words, a genre marked by the kind of discourse imaginative writers tend to employ as they develop characters and explore in their plots the ramifications of new social arrangements.

As we will see, however, the rhetoric of Vatican II and the ways it shapes Catholic thinking about the world influence but do not overwhelm the prose and poetry under discussion here. For the most part, these authors do not organize their texts historically around the Council, nor do they analyze their subject matter in theological language taken exclusively from Vatican II sources. Rather, they dramatize the results of its rhetorical breakthrough, which they value precisely because of the resources it provides to a pilgrim faith.[11]

For this reason, it is important to note that none of the authors in this study adopt the rhetorical structures of Vatican II uncritically. Despite the deep, defining influence of the Council on each one, all would have understood J. F. Powers' remark that, after 1968, he always chose to sit in the balcony at Mass because "it's the one place in Church where I can't hear anything."[12] (Annie Dillard is just as cutting as she muses during a Sunday liturgy: "Who gave these nice Catholics guitars?"[13]) Typically, the tug these writers feel toward the pluralism implied by Vatican II is met with a second impulse characterized by a strong set of aesthetic reservations. Some writers like Powers, Mary Gordon, and Ron Hansen—who are old enough to draw upon their memories of a preconciliar Church—lament the loss of important formalisms in their faith; for example, they speak nostalgically at times about the structure and order of the Tridentine Mass. Others, converts like Annie Dillard and Mary Karr, express their surprise that, after the Council, the Church let go of so many traditions that seemed essential to Catholic insiders and Protestant outsiders alike: the use of Latin, Gregorian chant, Church architecture and design, even the habits worn by women religious.

The tensions these writers experience when they attempt both to welcome a plurality of voices and viewpoints and to regain the symbols of a unified past is matched by a similar set of tensions that appear throughout the conciliar documents themselves. The writings of Vatican II were forged in committees, often during heated debates, and as such they depict concession, compromise, and ultimately the kind of frustrating inconsistencies one would expect from such arrangements. The words selected by the authors of these documents describe the complexities at work in their texts; the recurrence of terms and phrases like "partnership," "dialogue," "human family," "brother and sister," "joy and hope," "grief and anguish" prove to be remarkable examples of how Vatican II was written under the pressures of corporate wrangling.[14] But notice that these same words also propose a solution to that complexity. "Partnership" and "dialogue" imply a need for both phenomena. Human families—perhaps especially brothers and sisters—do spend a lot of time arguing, yet their bonds also indicate resources for overcoming conflicts. The tensions that demand dialogue may be resolved through conversation; arguments between brothers and sisters, which carry the marks of joy and anguish, can only find their resolution by confronting (even if to reject) family ties and contexts.

As O'Malley notes, this situation is not surprising given the rhetorical structure of these documents. The "penchant of the [panegyric] genre to focus on big issues," he claims, and thus the language of these texts, signal both the problem and a way out of the dilemma. "The council was about persuading and inviting," writes O'Malley, and with those motives it crafted a style (and ultimately a resource) that called for groups "to rise above all pettiness" and for individuals to overcome their internal divisions in the name of both "an expansive vision and a generous spirit."[15] One way to read the writers discussed in the following chapters is as Catholics who share the frustrations and ideals of the Council and at the same time are captivated by the manner in which an influential conciliar rhetoric described the combination as essential to understanding humanity in the twentieth century. Thus Mary Gordon writes with clear reference to *Gaudium et Spes* when she insists: "The second Vatican Council emphasized the importance of the Church's coming to terms with the modern world by being open to it."[16] Ron Hansen echoes Gordon's reference (and borrows terminology from John XXIII) when he says that "Vatican II sought an *aggiornamento*, a renewal or updating of the institutes and practice of the Church."[17] Annie

Dillard explores the ideas of theologians who were not only important to the Council but notorious for the way the proceedings lifted the veil of suspicion from their works. Dillard writes of her familiarity with the "big" ideas of Karl Rahner and, more specifically, of Teilhard de Chardin, the Jesuit writer and paleontologist whom "Vatican II calmly endorsed" after years of marginalization by the Roman hierarchy.[18] Even those writers like Louise Erdrich and John Patrick Shanley, who offer more personal testimonies of their relationship to the postconciliar Church, describe their encounters in terms borrowed from postconciliar Catholicism. Although Erdrich can joke about the fact that, "after Vatican II, I got to join the God squad," she also speaks idealistically of the broad carapace that defines the tradition and permits her to "write about the kind of Catholicism that exists in these little pockets here and there." Shanley sets his Pulitzer prize–winning play about clergy sexual abuse, *Doubt*, in the midst of the Council—1964—at a parish in the Bronx that he would replicate on stage for the Broadway production.[19] Replete with references to a changing Church, the play reveals the conflicts and hopes that become the lot of this and other institutions as they open themselves to the dilemmas of a modern world poised to enter a postmodern age.

Shanley could be speaking for other writers in this study when he professes the belief he sought to dramatize in his play, that "to be an adult . . . is to live with the paradox that you can never know for sure, to live with doubt, ambiguity, contradiction." To grasp that belief, he insists, is to discover "part of the experience and dilemma of being human."[20] In the end, for Shanley, Erdrich, Gordon, Hansen, and other writers, human experience cannot be untangled from the facts of physical existence. As I will try to show in the chapters that follow, Catholicism leads all of these authors to discover in words and actions involving the body a set of metaphors and descriptions that express both the discord of human existence and the means of transcending that variance. As the body in all its physical specificity—desire and pain, aroma and sweat—becomes for these writers a source for mediating God's presence to the world, it takes shape as a sacramental reality. In fact, in this postconciliar literature, the body may be the quintessential sacrament to a world (and a Church) that needs to heal.

Conciliar Ambiguity and Postconciliar Certainty

In his encyclical *Fides et Ratio*, Pope John Paul II indicates that, when reason explores the mysteries of faith—especially the liturgical mystery of the Eucharist—it should begin its inquiry with the physical experiences associated with the Eucharistic celebration. The "knowledge proper to faith," writes John Paul, reveals something about "people's lives" and discovers "truth . . . immersed in time and history."[21] In one of the most profound moments of this encyclical, the late pontiff chooses to quote Pascal's *Pensees* 789: " 'Just as Jesus Christ went unrecognized among men, so does his truth appear without external difference among common modes of thought. So too does the Eucharist remain among common bread.' "[22] The passage is significant for two reasons. Not only does it locate the sacred within profane experience, it also challenges Christians to cultivate a fresh sense of wonder for the everyday realm of life. "God comes to us," writes John Paul, "in the things we know best and can verify most easily, the things of our everyday life, apart from which we cannot know ourselves."[23]

If it is true for the Catholic sense of sacramentality that the natural world mediates the supernatural to us, then postconciliar Catholicism positions the body as a powerful mediator. This fact becomes apparent to anyone who attends a contemporary Catholic service or "Mass" and observes, even casually, his or her surroundings. One phenomenon that distinguishes the Catholic liturgy from other Christian gatherings is the movement of bodies. During the Mass, the body sits, stands, kneels, listens, speaks, tastes and, perhaps most important of all, touches other bodies.[24] The poet Mary Karr interprets those actions and interactions as crucial to the way she recast her life when she joined the Church:

> through the simple physical motions I followed during Mass [*following* something?], our bodies standing and sitting and kneeling in concert, I often felt my mind go quiet, and my surface differences from others began to be obliterated.[25]

As it will be for other authors examined here, for Karr the obliteration of "surface differences" involving people in the pews implies a corresponding shrinking of differences between the poet and God.

In *Fides et Ratio*, John Paul asserts that "Human beings are not made to live alone."[26] His successor, Benedict XVI, develops that very assertion in his first encyclical, *Deus caritas est*, when he identifies the Church as "God's family in the world" and insists upon the "parable of the Good Samaritan" as "a standard which imposes universal love towards the needy whom we encounter 'by chance.' " Benedict interprets the parable with a degree of physical, even "bodily" specificity that would appeal to the authors discussed in this volume. For the Pope, my "neighbor" is "anyone who needs me, and whom I can help. The concept of neighbor," he goes on to state, "is now universalized, yet" through the parable "it remains concrete. Despite being extended to all mankind, it is not reduced to a generic, abstract and undemanding expression of love, but calls for my own practical commitment here and now." According to the Pope, the Church is called to lead in this regard: like the good Samaritan, it "has the duty" to attend to the body—"the actual daily life of her members."

Benedict insists that the Church must "interpret ever anew" the parable for what it can tell us about "this relationship between near and far," the profane world of contemporary experience and the sacred realm of God's kingdom. Each of the writers studied here would agree, but they also would point out, I think, that Benedict and the Church are not exempt from this call: they too must continue to examine the tale. How one responds to the person in need constitutes but half the challenge Jesus places before his Jewish listeners. The other portion involves how one accepts help when in need. As John Dominic Crossan demonstrates, this parable is not just about how we should be nice to others. "The point is not that one should help the neighbor in need," writes Crossan. "In such an intention the naming of the helper as a Samaritan before a Jewish audience would be unnecessary, distracting, and, in the final analysis, inimical and counterproductive."[27] If this were its single message, the parable would have reversed the roles and made the Samaritan the victim, enabling Jesus' Jewish audience to see one of their own coming to the aid of the otherwise "unclean" Samaritan victim. Rather than describe only our obligation to assist others, however, Jesus' story also depicts the way people create community with their neighbors by accepting help. In this respect, the parable shares certain motives with the panegyric form that organizes so much Vatican II prose. In both, a new, expansive ideal is proposed, not only to embrace tension and conflict, but to reorder it. There is no doubt that, for many, this challenge is far more difficult. When good (clerics) and bad (Samaritan) become, "respectively, bad and good," Crossan maintains, "a world is being challenged and we are faced with polar reversal." In the parable, the question becomes: can Jesus' Jewish listeners truly *hear* this story of debt owed to a Samaritan and change their ways? For the Council, the question took a similar form, namely: how can the Church describe and embody a reality that is always "more" than what the institution can represent, forever in excess of the experiences it offers? The "Church already on this earth," the authors of *Lumen Gentium* insist, "is signed with a sanctity which is real although imperfect." This "pilgrim Church in her sacraments and institutions," the authors go on to write, must dwell "among creatures who groan and travail in pain until now and await the revelation of the sons of God."[28] Although it is an extremely difficult place to reside, such a dwelling permits the institution to find and accept aid from its own "Samaritans."

The implications of this position for every follower of Christ are far-reaching. As Pearl Meyers discovers from her hospital bed in Mary Gordon's novel by that same name, "weakness . . . is at the same time a force," and to refuse assistance and "choose death because you are unforgivable" is to "dishonor" the body.[29] Quite simply, Gordon's character concludes, "this cannot be done," and so she admits she will have to accept the aid offered her by two estranged friends, Breeda and Joseph, and her otherwise distant and domineering mother, Maria. She also will have to accept the kindness offered by the physician who treats her as she lies dying, and she will have to live according to the insight she gains in realizing "She is trusted. Forgiven. Once again."[30]

Other characters accept a similar conclusion. In Erdrich's *The Last Report on the Miracles at Little No Horse*, Father Damien agrees when one of the patriarchs of the reservation, Nanapush, gently removes the bottle of poison from the priest's hand; Sebastian Taggart capitulates when he awakes suddenly from his dream of suicide to discover himself alive on the floor beside his couch and filled with "a marvelous feeling of peace and purpose, which he took to be grace."[31] The voice of Mary Karr's poet admonishes readers "only to surrender" and thereby to give in to God and his creation; in other words, to ourselves and one another.

> . . . open both arms to the inner,
>   the ever-present hold,
> out-reaching every want. It's in the form
>   embedded, love adamant as bone.[32]

Open yourself this way and you may enter, with another poet, Annie Dillard, the "land of the living . . . time, this hill of beans" where you suddenly find yourself heavy with "a backload of God" (perhaps in the person of a Samaritan) and shedding "light in slats through [your] rib cage."[33]

Can the Church also hear the rhetoric of assent that is constitutive of its tradition? As the body of Christ, can it accept the help of those who lend it assistance? This is perhaps the greater challenge facing Catholicism as the twenty-first century begins, one that authors from Mary Gordon to Mary Karr find themselves placing before their faith. The challenge constitutes what postmodern thinkers have come to identify as the problem of "the other." Michael A. Fahey explicates one dimension of this problem in his theological reflections on the Church, when he writes:

> Another contextual factor that bears upon how one begins to reflect theologically upon the nature of church is the fact that growing numbers of people in the church, speaking primarily but not exclusively from a Roman Catholic perspective, have an acute sense of their own marginalizations by those in charge of the church. They see themselves as, practically speaking, irrelevant in the way church leaders establish priorities or shape pastoral strategies.[34]

According to Fahey, the Church since the Council has worked to promote a " 'restoration' of cultural Christendom in which theological formulations and their philosophical suppositions are clear and distinct."

Despite the sensitivity shown to human fallibility and uncertainty captured in encyclicals like *Fides et Ratio* and *Deus Caritas Est*, the tendency in writers who increasingly represent the public face of the Church, especially in the United States, is toward a more rigid doctrinalism. A pervasive confidence in the authority of the hierarchical Church to discern, for instance, the correct intellectual and liturgical center for God's presence is part of a much broader certainty on the part of a new generation of Catholic apologists. Not necessarily theologians or even scholars in the broadest sense, these spokespeople appear regularly on the Eternal Word Television Network (EWTN) and seem to have captured the minds and hearts of American bishops. As Richard Gaillardetz points out, these "new apologists evince a peculiar kind of Catholic *romanticism* that speaks easily of the transcendent truth and beauty of the Catholic Church and its teachings but fails to acknowledge its pilgrim status as a human community."[35] Gaillardetz cites the popular work of a speaker like Scott Hahn, who makes the outlandish claim on one of his many audiotapes that the Vatican II document *Dei Verbum* simply restates the teachings of Pope Leo XIII on Biblical inerrancy (*Providentissimus Deus*, 1893).[36] Gaillardetz could just as easily have cited the work of Christopher West, whose commentary on John Paul II's *Theology of the Body* carries the rather presumptuous title *Theology of the Body Explained*. Or he could have referred to the writings of several contemporary bishops, such as Thomas G. Doran, Bishop of Rockford, Illinois, who states with both certainty and relief that the Church has moved beyond those days when, in seminaries and parishes, "the breath of fresh air that was the Second Vatican Council's reformulation of the Church's traditional doctrine became a malaria or for some even a miasma which infected where it did not obscure."[37]

Gailladetz's skepticism of such apologetics leads him to an argument that each of the authors discussed here could accept, namely: "Belief in the indefectible holiness of the church does not preclude one from also holding that the church itself, understood as the whole people of God, the *congregatio fidelium*, is always only more or less faithful to its call to holiness."[38] The basis of that conviction has less to do with defining precisely and irrefutably what the Church is and more to do with living in the midst of what it hopes to become.[39] For the new generation of apologists Gaillardetz quotes, the criterion for precise definitions seems to be an anthropology that privileges the cognitive domain of human experience, specifically, human rationality. According to this outlook, the compulsion to define the essence of the Church springs from the basic conviction that, as one current Catholic educator, Robert Sokolowski, asserts, "We are distinguished as human beings by our ability to think. Our reason is the specific difference that makes us human and thus differentiates us from other animals."[40]

By contrast, the willingness to live with the uncertainties of a Church always in transition would appear to grow out of a very different set of anthropological assumptions, most basically that human beings are physical creatures and subject to "feeling" in all the connotations of that term. Such assumptions are crucial to understanding the content and style of Vatican II documents, but the notions are not limited to those writings. As another Catholic educator from an earlier generation, Miguel de Unamuno, wrote:

> Man is said to be a reasoning animal. I do not know why he has not been defined as an affective or feeling animal. Perhaps that which differentiates him from other animals is feeling rather than reason. More often I have seen a cat reason than laugh or weep. Perhaps it weeps inwardly—but then perhaps, also inwardly, the crab resolves equations of the second degree.[41]

For Unamuno, the view of humankind as distinctly emotional emerges from the anthropological view that humans are, as he writes, "flesh and bone." That he would begin with this fundamental assumption is no surprise, given the lines of interest that tend to intersect across his writings. Philosopher, novelist, and poet, Unamuno is a writer whose interests range far and wide, in each case beginning with his passionate commitment to explicating the self in all its various dimensions. In that respect, he is part of a collection of writers who, as Merold Westphal writes, search for ways out of "a metaphysical tradition that extends from Anaximander to Nietzsche and includes Aristotle and Hegel as high points."[42] Westphal describes the consequences of this tradition as "onto-theology": a mode of thinking that posits "a Highest Being that is the key to the meaning of the whole of being" so that it then can assert its hegemony, "can occupy the divine perspective on the world, or at least peek over God's shoulder."[43] The line of writers Westphal examines as sources of resistance to such an onto-theology includes Kierkegaard and Heidegger, Emmanuel Levinas and Jean-Luc Marion.

But Unamuno's commitment is not exclusively to the line of thinking that runs from Kierkegaard to Marion but also to the type of lived experience essential to a form of Catholicism evinced in the works of writers represented in this book.[44] Moreover, its importance is not limited to discussions of the self but includes the body of Christ, the *congregatio fidelium*, which displays to these authors its own need for a theology that is serious about the mysteries of the flesh. Recent apologists concerned with reasserting the hierarchical structures of the Church in the face of an otherness they view as threatening prefer to imagine the Church in terms first announced by the deutero-Pauline letters to the Ephesians and Colossians. In those documents, the authors argue for images of the Church as God's "body" and Christ as its "head" (Eph. 4:15–16; Col. 1:18). Pope John Paul II develops this metaphor in his ambitious but ultimately problematic *Theology of the Body* and follows its connotations where Ephesians leads him, namely, toward the twin comparisons of the Church's "body" to that of a "bride" and of Christ's "head" to the role of a "groom." For the late pope, and for those who have been shaped so deeply by his theology, the metaphors suggest that the "union of the body with the head is above all of an organic nature."[45] The difficulty many Catholics have with this conclusion is that, once reached, the notion of "union" often becomes the first step toward a hierarchy of distinctions: the head rules the body as the groom rules his wife, as priests, acting *in persona Christi Capitis*, rule the laity. Throughout this sequence, bodies both real and provocative become not only neglected but sanitized. Those apologists who draw their conclusions from the metaphors introduced in Ephesians, for instance, rarely speak of the extraordinary physical detail in that letter—of its references to circumcision "done in the flesh by human hands" [2:11], of its call to stand fast with "loins girded in truth" [6:14], of the "odor" emitted because "Christ loved us and handed himself over for us as a sacrificial offering to God for a fragrant aroma" [5:2].

Although Catholic novelists, poets, and playwrights from the late twentieth and early twenty-first centuries seem unable to discover in the head/body dichotomy of Ephesians or Colossians resources for their art, they do find compelling theological bases for their thinking about the Church in two other New Testament letters, both of which were essential to Vatican II texts. In Paul's correspondence with the churches at Rome and Corinth, letters that proved to be essential to the conciliar documents *Gaudium et Spes* and *Sacrosanctum Concilium*, writers discover the apostle describing a relationship between Christ and the *ekklesia* that does not depend upon a dichotomy but upon images of physical integration. To the Romans, Paul writes: "For as in one body we have many parts, and all the parts do not have the same function, so we, though many, are one body in Christ and individually parts of one another" [Rom 12:4–5]. To the troublesome Corinthians he was more specific about the need to overcome the sources of so much dichotomous thinking, insisting that "As the body is one though it has many parts, and all the parts of the body, though many, are one body, so also Christ. For in one Spirit we were all baptized into one body, whether Jews or Greeks, slaves or free persons, and we were all given to drink of one Spirit" [1 Cor. 12:12–13].[46]

The new generation of Catholic apologists is fond of arguing that Paul's language on this point is too vague, for it leaves the postconciliar Church without a clear and distinct identity. Again, it is important to note that none of the writers in this study would disagree entirely with these assessments. No novelist, poet, or playwright discussed here could be called an unreflective ecumenist, that kind of reformer who is eager to dissolve the heterogeneous gifts of the Spirit into a homogeneous landscape.[47] Rather, each one of these authors retains a fascination with the unique beauty and art of the Roman Church precisely because it calls them to a special kind of reverence. Each one would agree with Paul's admonition to the congregation at Corinth that, when they gather for worship, no one should eat or drink without first "discerning the body" in all of its manifestations: natural and supernatural, individual and communal, self and other (1 Cor. 11:29). But for these contemporary Catholic authors who have fallen under the influence of arguments proffered by Paul in Romans and Corinthians, as well as by the conciliar texts these letters inspired, reverence for God comes not in spite of the body but because of it. Catholic Christians do not need to distinguish the "head" and all the reasoning faculties it connotes in order to retain a fascination with what God accomplishes through flesh and bone. These writers encourage the Church to accept the assistance offered by those who speak from within a broader history and wider culture.

Thus the writers gathered together here find in the topic of the body ways to challenge certain facile claims to truth that are based primarily on the simple hegemony of existing Church structures.[48] All of the authors in the following discussions are Catholic; all of them write about material that is recognizably Catholic. That is, their works use characters, terms, and events drawn explicitly from the tradition. But for these authors, the body becomes not just a way to describe and affirm the tradition but also a means to resist certain of its methods and assumptions.[49] In this way, these contemporary Catholics reach into their tradition and retrieve an understanding of the body as a source of questions for and even opposition to the status quo. Their writings echo the efforts of other Christians—those from the second century—who looked to their bodies and renounced sexual activity, not because it was inherently evil but because such a decision could challenge "the huge fabric of society" that the Roman Empire had fashioned. Deny Rome its future citizens and, as the great scholar of late antiquity, Peter Brown, notes, the society "would crumble like a sandcastle" touched by "the ocean flood of the Messiah."[50] None of the writers in this volume would flood the Church with change. Each one of them, however, would challenge it to look more closely at itself, to consider change in the light of the ways it has, at times, honored the body and, at times, abused it. Most do it with a remarkable sense of innocence that speaks of their hope. They are like the child in Mary Karr's poem "The Toddler as Cathedral," who positions himself before the kitchen table and "pounds and croons," hoping somehow to "take this ocean of wood / in his mouth where he can chew it whole." "How boldly he stands," Karr notes,

> in his solid cathedral of bone,
> slapping his shadow, which spreads
> large across the table's surface.[51]

Like the child, these authors will never ingest the wood, but they will continue to see their outlines on its surface. And ultimately they will consecrate not the shadow but the flesh and the bone.

1. *Discovering the Body: Catholic Literature after Vatican II*

Because the panegyric discourse of Vatican II strives to embrace such a broad vision of the Church, it tends to laud the social dimension of the faith. Of course, Catholicism has a long and rich tradition of social engagement. Nevertheless, this council emphasized the tradition in new ways. Consider that the Tridentine Profession of Faith in 1564 had characterized the Church as not only "holy, catholic, and apostolic" but also as "mother and teacher."[1] It had insisted that salvation depended upon "true obedience" to one individual: "the Roman pontiff, successor of the blessed Peter, chief of the apostles, and vicar of Christ."[2] As a profession of faith, it assumed what the Council of Trent had asserted when it opened its proceedings eighteen years earlier—that the Church was most effectively imagined as an individual—mother, apostle, or, according to another rhetorically charged image, "soldier." Such an assertion permitted Council participants to describe the Church in personal terms—that is, as one who carries the "shield of faith," dons the "helmet of salvation," wields the "sword of the spirit," and braves in battle the "flaming darts of the evil one."[3]

In contrast to this rhetoric of individuality, Vatican II emphasized a second set of terms that encouraged believers to imagine the Church as essentially social. *Lumen Gentium*, which was released in 1964 as part of the Doctrinal Decrees of the Council, began by insisting that the mission of the Church was not to distinguish among individuals but to build a social entity, "the Kingdom of God." Confident that this emphasis joined ecclesiology more closely to the Gospel message, the document chose to reveal the "inner nature of the Church," not only through the measured discourse of theological argument but also "through a variety of images." Most of those images would prove to be social and would provide the authors with occasions to employ and cultivate rhetoric that valued a social dimension of faith. Using this approach, *Lumen Gentium* asserted that "the Church is the sheepfold," "the estate" of God. It called the Church "God's building" and, moreover, his city "the Jerusalem above." "In the world," the writers flatly asserted, the Church is "set up and organized . . . as a society."[4]

This shift in rhetorical emphasis resulted in a much greater sense of uncertainty about what it means to be Catholic.[5] In the West, democratic cultures in particular have struggled with the consequences of this shift. As Clarke and David Cochran point out, for most of its history the Catholic "ideal was the confessional state, where Catholicism was the official state religion and Catholic values were the law of the land." In this environment, the Church "remained largely hostile to both democracy and pluralism," and few imagined the institution in ways that would give it multiple voices or various, perhaps even competing, perspectives.[6] The choice of a social rhetoric by the participants in Vatican II, a type of discourse full of images that required thoughtful discussion, interpretation, and even a new imagination, pushed Catholics to examine anew the ways they committed themselves to the institutional Church. A historical moment that could have promoted a more consistent view among many as they considered the interaction between faith and the formation of democratic forms of government instead resulted in greater confusion about what value to place upon either of those realities.

Nowhere does this predicament seem more pronounced than in the works of those who have tried to use these rhetorical systems to create imaginative literature. Three recent critical studies of Catholic fiction have drawn attention to just this point. In *The Catholic Imagination in American Literature*, Ross Labrie claims that, after "Vatican II with its strong social emphasis," Catholic writers found themselves faced with "the problem" of how to reunite "the social apostolate of the church with its transcendental consciousness." This task, as Labrie points out, was especially difficult as writers found themselves faced with new interpretations of the ancient acts and symbols that had established this union originally and, as a result of that establishment, had inspired a rich artistic tradition. Could the new practices surrounding "the sacraments and liturgy in particular" stimulate an aesthetic worthy of their significance?[7] Changes in the Church, that "imposing intermediary" in the "economy of grace," raised what Labrie correctly calls a "distinctively Catholic dilemma."[8]

The success or failure of writers who responded to that dilemma constitutes to a large degree the topic of two other recent studies. One of these, *Testing the Faith: The New Catholic Fiction in America*, by Anita Gandolfo, begins with a grim account of these fictional efforts. "From the evidence of fiction," Gandolfo writes, "postconciliar Catholicism seems mired in the residual ethos of the old paradigm while unable to effectively envision the emerging culture of the new."[9] Reestablishing the union between the social apostolate and transcendent consciousness, a union that Labrie ascribed to a preconciliar Church, will be extremely difficult, Gandolfo writes. Among the reasons for this difficulty is the continuing dependence of the Church on certain triumphal images from scripture. For example, "traditional Catholicism derived meaning from Matthew 16:18–19" and still depends upon it in a postconciliar age that has raised numerous questions about the passage, including whether Jesus ever uttered the rhetoric it inspires and elevates.[10] For Gandolfo, the hope of writers who seek to make a contemporary Catholic faith central to their fiction rests not with such traditional images and the paradigms they support, but rather with a fresh set of ideas and understandings promoted by the Council. In contrast to the triumphalism of a preconciliar Church grounded in the conversation between Jesus and his apostles in Matthew 16, Catholicism after the Council "locates the source of its meaning within the human" and tenders "an incarnational vision reflected in Luke 17:20–21."

> Asked by the Pharisees when the kingdom of God would come, he said in reply," "The coming of the kingdom of God cannot be observed, and no one will announce, 'Look, here it is,' or 'There it is.' For behold, the kingdom of God is among you."[11]

Although Gandolfo begins her study with a bleak summary of the role that postconciliar Catholic fiction has played in helping the Church articulate a new paradigm for evaluating its place in the world, she concludes in a more positive way. Her preference for Jesus' words in Luke 17 suggests that she sees more in the move from a preconciliar to a postconciliar Church than a shift in rhetorical strategies; it indicates that she finds in postconciliar Catholicism a source of creativity for writers and a reason to hope for the tradition generally.

Such is not the case with another critic who has examined the way Catholic authors respond to the dilemma of ecclesiological change. J. C. Whitehouse's book about the classic works of three outstanding preconciliar authors, Graham Greene, Sigrid Undset, and Georges Bernanos, provides the most succinct metaphor for helping readers understand and appreciate the consequences for literature of Vatican II. Preconciliar writing, Whitehouse argues, gave us a vision of "vertical man." Greene, Undset, and Bernanos created a body of Catholic fiction dominated by descriptions of the human "creature living in an individual relationship with his creator." Post-conciliar writing, by contrast, "has largely given way to a representation of the human being as a nexus of social relationships," and therefore, according to Whitehouse, it presents readers with a vision of human life lived primarily among the things of this world. To continue Whitehouse's metaphor, this fiction gives us not "vertical man" but "horizontal man."[12]

Contrary to Gandolfo's conclusions, this change, argues Whitehouse, does not arouse hope. Rather, it provides Catholics with one more example of a larger cultural malaise. Whitehouse links the change, and its corresponding shift in rhetorical emphases, with two anthropological views that, as he describes them, provide the bases for a stark contrast. Movement between these rhetorical strategies illustrates nothing less than the break that has erupted between traditional and postmodern forms of philosophy and theology. According to Whitehouse, an earlier rhetoric of individual value promoted the concept of "Man as capable of God, as an image of God, as a creature able to accept or reject a certain kind of relationship with his creator and sustainer." The language of social interaction, which is central now to a post–Vatican II Church, can offer only a vision of "Man as a social unit with no significant personhood, a conditioned operant existing in a horizontal continuum where all is relative, contingent and ultimately value-free."[13] For Whitehouse, this latter view "urges a narrower and narrowing view of human beings" while the former constitutes "the only hope left" for "the creation of a dignified moral and religious anthropology."[14]

The differences between the conclusions drawn by Gandolfo and Whitehouse result from their descriptions of the role individual and social rhetoric plays in Catholic literature as well as from the prescriptions they offer for how to interpret those differences. For Gandolfo, rhetorical strategies connected with ideals of individuality and social interaction need not compete. Vatican II may have fostered the distinction, but only so the Church could continue the process of negotiating the difference. Such a process aims at synthesis and involves, most basically, acts of imagination. "What is significant," argues Gandolfo, "is not that the process of re-imagining Catholicism *can* be documented in contemporary fiction but that the process of change in Catholicism is *best* documented in this fiction."[15] According to Gandolfo, Catholic literature does not have the choice to return to a time when the rhetoric of the self and of individual value dominated its fictional worlds; that option is gone. However, it did not disappear because the world fastened upon the Church an anthropology that required believers "to think of human beings as primarily a nexus of social relationships."[16] Rather, it ended because the Church leadership during Vatican II chose to end it. Quoting Jeanne Schinto's story "Before Sewing One Must Cut," Gandolfo concludes her own study with a prescription for Catholicism and Catholic writers. Growth and development, she insists, are possible only after "You . . . accept who you are and what has happened to you."[17]

Gandolfo's emphasis on the "process" that led the Church to its current state captures an essential feature of Vatican II deliberations. Pope John XXIII's preference for the term *aggiornamento,* or "updating," to describe the reason for the Council suggests this sense of process as an ongoing response to change. The Pope's call for *aggiornamento* corresponded well to his essential optimism about what the Church was undertaking. In his opening remarks to Council members, *Gaudet Mater Ecclisia,* the Pope distanced himself from those who "see in modern times nothing but prevarication and ruin. They keep saying," John XXIII went on, "that, as compared with past ages, ours is getting worse, as if in the time of preceding ecumenical Councils everything represented a complete triumph for Christian ideas and Christian life and for a rightful religious liberty."[18] Nothing could be further from the truth, the Pope points out. Those who would return to a golden age of Catholic imagination and literature, the kind of age Whitehouse seems to recall, delude themselves, for it is unlikely that such an age ever existed. The tradition endures because we imagine it anew—theologically, artistically, and rhetorically.

Rhetorical Tensions and the Council

Although the distinction between the rhetoric of individuality and the language of social interaction can help to explain differences between Catholic literature before and after Vatican II, ultimately the distinction reveals not a chronological or even a thematic break, but rather a persistent tension. That tension is notably present in the Council. It is there in John XXIII's earliest writings about what he intends to pursue—in journals that describe his personal "concern for the 'good of souls'" alongside his social awareness as a new pope who must "come to grips" with the "needs of the present time."[19] It is there in virtually all of the major documents of the Council, most emphatically in *Gaudium et Spes, The Pastoral Constitution on the Church in the Modern World,* which speaks of an "interdependence" between "person and society" and maintains that, "Insofar as man by his very nature stands completely in need of life in society, he is and ought to be the beginning, the subject and the object of every social organization."[20] Another major document, *Lumen Gentium*, translates that interdependence into a vision of the priesthood that is social yet grounded in the individuality of God incarnate. "Though they differ essentially and not only in degree," the document states,

> the common priesthood of the faithful and the ministerial or hierarchical priesthood are none the less ordered to one another; each in its own and proper way shares in the one priesthood of Christ.[21]

Ultimately, it would be *Sacrosanctum Concilium, The Constitution on the Sacred Liturgy*, that would offer perhaps the most powerful theological combination of these rhetorical strategies. Hoping to impart new "vigor" to the "most sacred mystery of the Eucharist," the Council juxtaposed these terminologies in new and imaginative ways. According to that constitution, "the Church earnestly desires that Christ's faithful, when present at this mystery of faith, should not be there as strangers or silent spectators. On the contrary," the document goes on to explain, the faithful

> should take part in the sacred action, conscious of what they are doing, with devotion and full collaboration. They should be instructed by God's word, and be nourished at the table of the Lord's Body. They should give thanks to God. Offering the immaculate victim, not only through the hands of the priest but also together with him, they should learn to offer themselves. Through Christ, the Mediator, they should be drawn day by day into ever more perfect union with God and each other, so that finally God may be all in all.[22]

Here references to the hope and duty of individual faithful and the presence of the solitary priest and single sacrifice blends almost seamlessly with talk of social "collaboration," togetherness, "union," and the binding quality of God, who ultimately is "all in all."

Passages like these frustrate attempts to find in Vatican II an explicit break from the rhetoric of individuality and an exclusive preference for terminology and vocabulary associated with the horizon of social relationships. In some of his comments about *Lumen Gentium*, Paul VI emphasized the complexity of this very interaction. Speaking about the reference in the Constitution to socially driven "collective action," the Pope seemed to appreciate the way such a concept could respond to contemporary challenges. Collective action, according to Paul VI, was "more complicated than individual action." However, as if he feared that his remark would be read as privileging one set of rhetorical terms over another (and establishing his preference

for new theological models), the Pope immediately added that, despite the ability of collective action to answer the complex nature of the modern world, individual action actually "corresponds better to the monarchical and hierarchical nature of the Church."[23] The theological consequences and ideological positions contained in such a remark are numerous, but in each case they depend upon the ability of the terminology to connote different meanings. The striking fact, of course, is not that the rhetoric of individuality and the language of social action are at odds but that the Pope could employ both and apparently recognize his combination to be essentially Catholic. His comments offer a telling insight into the way the Church maintained a tension between the two.[24]

That tension would persist throughout the proceedings of the Second Vatican Council and would become part of the fabric of its discourse. Consider, for example, the way the tension controls the key description of the Church in paragraph 48 from *Lumen Gentium*. Although the passage is indeed part of a unified narrative, it can be analyzed rhetorically into two sets of terms, one emphasizing the ideal of the individual and another stressing a more social value.

Christ lifted from . . . . the earth,
has drawn . . . . all men
to himself.

Rising from the dead
he sent his life-giving
spirit . . . . upon his disciples and
through him set up
His Body . . . . which is the Church as the universal
sacrament of salvation.

Sitting at the right hand
of the Father he is
continually active . . . . in the world in order to
lead men to the Church and, through
it, join them
more closely to
himself; and by . . . . nourishing them with
His own Body and Blood, ... make them partakers in
His glorious life.

The heart of the passage appears in the eighth line above. With the words "His Body which is the Church," the authors transform tension into a coherent vision. The equation permits the writers of *Lumen Gentium* to bring together not just two terms but two entire realms of discourse. The result is a metaphor that describes church society as a single body, and the authors use it time and again to articulate their sense of what is foundational to an "updated" understanding of the Church and its members. The metaphor bridges these terms so effectively that it allows readers to reverse the way they typically imagine entities and the manner in which they use words to describe those entities. According to this reversal, a "body"—even one that is made of flesh and blood—becomes something social; and a social unit, the Church, takes on a new life as an individual being. The consequences of this metaphor involve far more than just emphasizing one concept over another or reimagining what was "vertical" as now somehow "horizontal."

Ross Labrie underscores the theological value of the "body" metaphor for post–Vatican II Catholicism when he points out in the final pages of *The Catholic Imagination in American Literature* that "The doctrine of the Incarnation can be seen as the axis on which Catholic American literature in general rests and from which variances between particular authors can be measured."[25] The doctrine is particularly useful when "measuring" the differences between pre- and postconciliar fiction. More than any other topic, "the body" has occupied writers who have tried to create imaginative worlds that depend upon the facts, ideals, and beliefs of a post–Vatican II Catholicism. Writers have seized upon the topic and the metaphor it implies because they have recognized it as crucial to understanding what happened when a preconciliar tension between individual and society became a postconciliar tension, never lost but distinctively transformed. Jacques Dupuis refers to it when he writes about the 1974 Synod of Bishops held in Rome just ten years after the close of the Council and dedicated to the topic of evangelization. Dupuis reads the Synod as significant for several reasons, but perhaps especially because of its inconclusiveness. "The Synod did not altogether resolve that tension" between the competing impulses toward monism and pluralism, individual and society. But the unwillingness of the bishops to fall back on the deductive methods of neo-scholasticism announced, albeit indirectly, that "a worn out theological approach had failed and been rejected." In a postconciliar Catholicism, Dupuis argued, the Church would be unable to formulate convincing arguments "without reaching down to reality"—specifically, to the bodies that constitute the vastness and diversity of the local Church.[26]

The Examples of Georges Bernanos and Ron Hansen

A brief comparison between two imaginative works may help us explicate the difference between pre- and postconciliar tensions within the Church, especially as they pertain to changing perceptions of the body. In 1948, the year in which he died, the Catholic writer Georges Bernanos completed a prose-play that eventually became the basis of the film *Joy*. Published as *Dialogues of the Carmelites*, Bernanos' drama presents the story of eighteen Carmelite nuns living in a convent at Compiègne, France, in the aftermath of the revolution in that country. In his play, all but one of these nuns are executed by the guillotine. Significantly, the one to survive is not the protagonist of the play; that role belongs to Blanche de la Force, a young postulant who is the last one to mount the scaffold at the Place de la Revolution, Paris.

Although Bernanos is best remembered for his novel *The Diary of a Country Priest*, at least one critic, Erasmo Leiva-Merikakis, calls *Dialogues of the Carmelites* Bernanos' "literary and religious masterpiece." Blanche herself has been described as the character who constitutes "the main preoccupation" of the author's "spiritual life and work."[27] Both claims can be misleading. *Dialogues of the Carmelites* does synthesize many of the leading qualities of Bernanos' writing, but its force comes from its depiction of a nineteenth-century Catholic ethos. As an example of imaginative writing within the tradition, the play is a period-piece, steeped in the beliefs and ideologies of a Church that was still a century away from the reforms initiated under the leadership of John XXIII.

Its ability to capture and illustrate so many qualities of nineteenth-century Catholicism, however, does make *Dialogues* a strong candidate for general comparisons with post–Vatican II literature. Moreover, there are compelling reasons for comparing it with one specific text from that later period. Both *Dialogues of the Carmelites* and Ron Hansen's *Mariette in Ecstasy* (1991) depict nuns living together in cloister. Both works are historical, Bernanos setting his piece in the late eighteenth century and Hansen setting his in the early years of the twentieth. Both balance their stories of women's religious communities with tales of individual nuns—postulants who arrive in their respective convents and cause other characters to think and behave differently. Finally, both give us protagonists with similar backgrounds: Blanche de la Force and Mariette Baptiste are the youngest children of single fathers; their mothers dead, both women enter convents hoping to find someone who can provide the love and assurance of a surrogate matriarch, but both lose those surrogates when the prioresses of their respective convents die.

When compared, both works also challenge the claim of a critic like Whitehouse—that pre- and postconciliar writing divides neatly, if not exclusively, between contrasting calls for, on the one hand, a "vertical" connection between the individual and God and, on the other, a more horizontal union between God and the wider nexus of social interactions. Although *Dialogues of the Carmelites*, for example, is a preconciliar drama, it is indeed a work of social fiction. Without the context provided by the French Revolution, characters have no motivation, the plot has no climax, and Bernanos can create neither the sense of innocence nor the acts of heroism that are central to his theme. True, the transcendent hand of God is present throughout the narrative and will be one of the features that distinguishes this work from Hansen's; nevertheless, readers cannot claim that this play, which so thoroughly depicts what Whitehouse calls Bernanos' "instinct for orthodoxy," lacks those social elements that give it an appreciation for the sacred in life's more "horizontal" relationships.[28]

In a similar manner, Hansen's novel also challenges the assumptions behind the "individual/social" distinction. *Mariette in Ecstasy* is much more interested in locating the value of individual entities within creation than it is in studying the role of the sacred among social arrangements. If Bernanos' pre–Vatican II play depends upon social drama, Hansen's postconciliar novel ironically revolves around the "vertical" connection that the protagonist, Mariette, establishes with God. True, the phenomenon of Mariette's "ecstasy" invites us to consider her relationship to all other characters, but the mystery of her experience demands that we come to terms with her ability or inability to connect "upward" with a deity that is both transcendent and other.

Although *Dialogues of the Carmelites* and *Mariette in Ecstasy* challenge straightforward assumptions about the introduction of individual and social rhetoric in pre- and postconciliar writing, they are particularly illustrative of the roles each period assigns to the body. *Mariette in Ecstasy* represents the bodies of its characters in ways that are typical of Catholic literature written under the influence of tensions present in Vatican II documents and thought. When readers enter the world that Ron Hansen has created for the Sisters of the Crucifixion, they discover not just characters whose bodies are portrayed realistically but ones whose realistic bodies define their Catholic identity. The opening pages establish this relationship, beginning with lines that embed the physical detail of priory life into a world that clearly is charged with God's presence.

Upstate New York.
August 1906
Half-moon and a wrack of gray clouds.
Church windows and thirty nuns singing the Night Office in Gregorian chant. Matins. Lauds. And then silence.
Wind, and a nighthawk teetering on it and yawing away into woods.

Much is prepared for readers by these lines: scene, time, and place, but also (and most important) the interaction of all three. In this concise opening, readers sense immediately that Hansen seeks to connect the world inside the priory with the environment outside its walls. We simply do not know where the sound of one realm begins and the silence of the other ends. The "wind"—a word often joined to spirit—blows through both, and if outside the priory a goatsucker (the "nighthawk") yaws, inside a nun undoubtedly yawns.

The attention paid to such pointed, physical details in these lines announces a narrative technique that Hansen uses throughout his book. By the end of the first pages, he has begun to apply that technique to describe more than a bond between the convent and nature. He also has started to link the bodies of individual characters with images from a wider creation. For example, in these pages we witness the morning dressing ritual of Mother Saint-Raphael, which begins with her tugging a nightgown above her head to reveal not just "the great green-veined bowls of her breasts" but also "cuttings from the French garden's rosebushes" that she has wrapped around herself, mortifying flesh that is "scarlet with infection." The practice, which was not uncommon for Catholic religious during the older nun's formative years, is neither condemned nor praised in the text. Rather, it is recognized for what it is at its root: an occasion for physical pain (occasioned by mingling the outside world of the garden with the nun's dressing chamber). Thus, as Mother Saint-Raphael ties her habit with "a sudden jerk," she "winces and shuts her eyes." Meanwhile, readers discover that, outside, the same spirit that blows between the woods and convent also unites the bodies of otherwise separate entities. In the moment that the stinging pain of thorns bring tears to Mother Saint-Raphael's eyes, "waterdrops from the night's dew haltingly creep down green reeds."

The connections made explicit and implicit by Hansen's technique will develop in ways that depend upon his understanding of the pivotal relationship between Catholicism and the body. Although a series of smaller actions in the priory will help sustain this bond—such as the image of Sister Emmanuelle's hunched back and "quick hands tying off bobbins and pins as she creates lace periwinkles for the white corporal that the holy chalice will rest on"—one central action will establish the connection most effectively. It will involve the body of Mariette Baptiste, who disrupts life at the convent first as a postulant by all accounts "too pretty" to be there and then as one whose beauty appears to suffer from the wounds of stigmata.

Mariette's stigmata are the evidence of her "ecstasy," and Hansen's ability to represent them that way is essential to the "Catholic" character of this novel. Obviously stigmata are associated most explicitly with Catholicism—with the stories of figures from Saint Francis to Padre Pio. But the term "ecstasy" is more complicated. Its roots are not Latin but Greek. The term carries with it ideas from the Hellenistic traditions that early Christianity worked so hard to incorporate. In Greek, the word "*ekstasis*" means literally to "stand outside oneself." From this original description comes a series of meanings with various connotations, from "frenzy," "fear," and "passion" to "trance," "catalepsy," and "stupor." Mariette will exhibit many of the characteristics of "ecstasy" implied by the original Greek meaning of the word. She will, for example, kneel or lie for hours in a trance-like state. But Hansen will use the term in a second way that reflects its incorporation into Christianity, specifically Catholic Christianity. Unlike suggestions of "doubleness" that are part of the original Greek root, Hansen refuses to separate Mariette's ecstasy from her body. At no time, for instance, does Mariette find her "soul" separated from her flesh; in fact, the exact opposite proves true: Mariette's ecstasy is decidedly physical. It takes its most obvious form in the bloody marks that appear on her hands, feet, and side. She will feel them first as she listens to the swirl of the "winds outside" the convent, the same spiritual manifestation in the natural world that opens the novel.[29] They will begin as a "hot sting" that persists "like hate inked on a page." Other symptoms will follow, among them high temperature and irregular heartbeats, both of which occur before the "hideous" holes appear.[30]

The marks upon Mariette's body define her experience of ecstasy. Hansen will create suspense by allowing other characters to raise such intense doubt about the wounds that Mariette eventually will be asked to leave the community. But a final scene when she experiences the pain in her hands again years later implies that we are to accept the stigmata as genuine. Furthermore, we are to accept the marks as real *because* of Mariette's physical existence, not in spite of it. The wounds appear because of the intimacy she has sought with Christ, a kind of love that is not ethereal or idealized but, quite explicitly, sexual. We glimpse it first when she enters the convent and exchanges her clothes for those of the postulant. In a narrative that moves easily between time periods, this is the first memory Mariette's story gives us. It comes while she "uneasily gets out of her dress and underthings" in the cold changing room of the convent and gazes up at the crucifix on the wall. Suddenly she is transported back in time and "she is a girl again, four years old and staring at the Christ in her mother's room. She touched the pink mouth" of the figure hanging there, Hansen writes, "and then she touched her own. She touched underneath her skirt." This sexual attraction to the Christ figure persists until it consumes her in the physical onset of the stigmata.[31]

Hansen's insistence that Mariette's ecstatic, "out-of-body" experience must leave its mark upon her flesh is one of the most important ways that this novel establishes its link to the traditions and practices valued in a post–Vatican II Catholic Christianity. As we will see, Bernanos' depiction of "ecstasy" in *Dialogues of the Carmelites* leads to dramatic renderings of the experience nearly opposed to what Hansen crafts for his readers. Bernanos creates no link between ecstasy and the flesh; the out-of-body experiences he depicts leave no physical trace upon his characters, in part because the controlling theological models of his day avoided such connections. Dominated by a Tridentine ideal of the body in its "pure and spotless state like a best robe" (like a garment, Trent insists, decidedly not worn against the flesh but "carried . . . before the tribunal of our Lord"), Catholicism for the preconciliar generation Bernanos knew existed amid a tension between body and spirit, where the latter typically prevailed.[32] Perhaps the apposite example would be the theological proclivities of the popular *Baltimore Catechism*, which began by defining God as "perfect Spirit," without body and "above all creatures," and continued by representing the incarnation as the fruit of supernatural activity associated with a miraculous intervention into the life of the Virgin, not as a result of divine self-emptying as recorded in the ancient hymn from Philippians 2.[33]

In contrast to this nineteenth- and early twentieth-century emphasis, Vatican II interprets the tension between spirit and flesh in ways that understand the body as valuable because of its physical attributes, not in spite of them. *Lumen Gentium* stressed this point when it chose language from Colossians 2:19 to illustrate the relationship between the ideal and mysterious concept of the Church as Christ's body and the physical presence of the risen one within that ideal. According to the document, we do not understand how the postconciliar Church develops unless we conceive of it as "nourished and knit together through its joints and ligaments, [growing] with a growth that is from God."[34] Here is a notion of Catholic sacramentality carried to its remarkable conclusion. Not only do the physical and spiritual relate in mysterious ways, part of the mystery associated with their interaction is the astonishing claim that they share a historical context, one as fragile and resilient as the human body.[35]

As subsequent chapters will show, the Catholic response to this possibility is captured in the language associated with the sacraments—from the rites themselves to their cultural influence. The distinguishing feature of Catholic sacramentality has been the notion that sacraments not only represent God's presence, they also effect that presence. "Celebrated worthily in faith," the *Catechism* states, "sacraments confer the grace they signify." In this way, they are "efficacious" because, "in them Christ himself is at work" (1128). Hansen's narrative reflects the postconciliar fascination with the body in this process. A scene from early in Part 3 of the novel makes just this point. The setting for the scene is the infirmary in Our Lady of Sorrows. Mariette is "in ecstasy": she lies upon the hospital bed in a trance, her "eyelids fluttering in dream," her mouth "sore and cracked and welted purple by her own teeth." Keeping watch beside her is one of the young nuns who has been friends with Mariette since the beautiful postulant arrived. Sister Hermance regards the prone patient lovingly and, after hesitating for a second, "unwraps the torn strips of cloth from a hand that is as stained as a dyer's."[36]

Much comes together in the fascinating actions that follow. Sister Hermance bathes the hand and admits to a sleeping Mariette: "We were all wondering. We didn't think it would be so real." She then confesses what is deepest in her heart, that the love she has felt for Mariette is more than an ideal. "Ever since I first met you, I have loved you more than myself," she whispers. With Mariette's palm upturned, Hermance bends and "licks the blood inside the hand wound," saying to the body before her: "I have tasted you. See?"[37]

The actions are done "with reverence," and in no way do their lesbian overtones deter from the remarkable conclusion that Hermance reaches when she says finally to the sleeping Mariette: "You have been a sacrament to me." It is true, Mariette has been, and this moment is sacramental not in spite of the physical attraction the young sister feels for the postulant but because of it. In this scene Mariette's body reminds readers of the one experience that makes all sacraments possible: the incarnation.[38] Hansen helps readers understand this point when he contrasts Hermance's ability to experience the wounds—indeed, to feel them with her tongue as though they were as delicate as a wafer one must not chew—with the inability of others to witness them. In the final scene at the priory Mariette's hands again are unwrapped, this time for onlookers who include Mother Saint-Raphael, the priest in the priory, Père Henri Marriot, and her father, Claude Baptiste, the local physician. It is her father who investigates, touching the hand and washing it, and her father who discovers first that the wounds have disappeared. Mariette's explanation is simple: "Christ took back the wounds." Dr. Baptiste's is equally direct: "you all have been duped."[39]

Much more is at stake here than the contrast between traditional faith and modern skepticism, between healing and medicine. Dr. Baptiste in fact is unworthy to witness the wounds that Sister Hermance felt, not because he is an enlightened skeptic who knows how the body works but because he has chosen to neglect, even abuse, what is most important about the body. Sister Hermance's loving expressions of lesbian attraction stand in direct contrast to the strong suggestion that Mariette has been sexually abused by her father. In Part 2 of the novel Mariette encounters him for the first time since she has come to the priory. She stands with her back to him and remembers: "She feels his eyes like hands. Enjoying her. She knows their slow travel and caress."[40] In a novel tied so thoroughly to the consciousness of a character who can be "ecstatic," readers can question the accuracy of such a memory. Moreover, they can establish a string of psychological associations between Mariette's sexual experiences ("Weren't you going to ask if I'm a virgin?" she inquires of the nurse, Sister Aimee, when she was examined upon entrance to the community) and her religious beliefs and zeal. But none of those associations can explain the pain Mariette undergoes, nor can they negate the fact that, for sisters like Hermance in the priory, Mariette's body has caused God's mysterious presence. To the world Ron Hansen has created, Mariette has been a sacrament.

Despite their remarkable similarities in elements of scene and characterization, Hansen's novel departs dramatically from Bernanos' *Dialogues of the Carmelites* in the theme it develops and the conclusions it reaches. Mariette enters the convent to deepen a passion for Christ that seems to charge her entire being—body and soul. Blanche de la Force, the protagonist of Bernanos' drama, enters Carmel at Compiègne because she "cannot physically support" the world. "The world is simply for me an element in which I cannot live," she confesses. She cannot tolerate those features that occupy her body, especially those that bring her in contact with other bodies. "The sound of this great indefatigable city" frightens her, the "very bustle of the streets" with their "noise" and "restlessness" "stun" her.[41]

Blanche imagines that the solution to her fears is to learn to live "an heroic life."[42] Her first step toward that end is to assume the name "Sister Blanche of the Agony of Christ," a name that suggests a substantial literary and theological link between heroism and the body. The connection implied by the name gains additional support through the fact that the prioress who awards it, Mother Henriette of Jesus, once considered taking the name herself. After she confers the name upon Blanche, Henriette enters into the last moments of her life—sick and dying in the Carmelite infirmary. Curiously, the more she remains still and thinks about her decision, the greater the distance grows between her mental and physical states of being. She becomes "ecstatic" in the most traditional sense; she is separated from her body. "I have no more control over my tongue," she admits. She resolutely refuses to yield "to this harassed breast which I can no longer even feel."[43] Finally, in the delirium of sickness, she experiences God in the form of a vision. She sees the convent chapel "empty and profaned" by the revolutionaries who will storm the grounds and eventually martyr all members of the order. Though the vision refers to physical details—"the altar split in two, the holy vessels strewn on the floor, the flagstones covered in straw and blood"—Sister Henriette is quite certain that the source of the images is not tangible. "God has become a shadow," she says, employing a metaphor that is remarkably appropriate to a work that otherwise describes the relationship between divinity and bodily existence as close but not corporeal.[44]

God lives amid the shadows in *Dialogues of the Carmelites* and interacts with characters conceptually, not physically, with their respective imaginations and not their bodies. Although this situation is precisely what enables God to embolden Blanche in the end, it also creates tremendous anxiety for her. Throughout the drama, the very imagination that will bring her closer to God is also her undoing. "Blanche," the convent chaplain tells her, "your imagination always becomes inflamed too swiftly."[45] Such inflammation leaves Blanche in an almost perpetual state of fear. At times she herself moves "like a shadow" around the convent; at other times she imagines "phantasms" and fears the shadows that are cast upon the walls of her cell.[46] As the reality of the eighteenth-century revolution moves closer to her world, Blanche becomes increasingly agitated and afraid. When the sisters finally agree to take a silent vote on the "vow of martyrdom" that likely will be necessary when troops reach the convent, Blanche casts her ballot, but immediately "is seen to leave the chapel and run off."[47]

Despite her fear and physical cowardice, Blanche de la Force has an opportunity to meet a God who encounters people principally in their concepts and ideas. As long as death is foremost a concept that can be applied to different bodies, Blanche will be able to understand and accept her fate. Bernanos tries to make this point when he posits a supernatural situation in which Blanche seems to switch places with the sister who once considered taking her name, the ailing Henriette. It is Sister Constance who calls this to our attention when she claims that Sister Henriette's ecstasy—with its sense of bodily displacement—actually belonged to "someone else." "Yes, that must have been someone else's death," she says to Blanche, "a death which did not fit our prioress" because it was "too small for her." When Blanche asks Constance "what, in fact, does that mean?" she responds by claiming that some "other person, when the hour of death comes, will be surprised to find it so easy, to find death comfortable. . . ."[48]

Clearly it is Blanche who benefits from this "switch" in the story. When she finally overcomes her persistent state of fear at the end of the play and mounts the scaffold, she is calm, confident, serene. But the discovery of this "switch" is far less interesting than what it implies, namely, that Bernanos could conceive of death this way. Such a notion would be impossible in the world Ron Hansen creates for Mariette and her fellow nuns. By making death little more than a concept, Bernanos has made the body an afterthought, almost insignificant. One scene captures this distinction especially well. It is Christmas for Blanche and the Carmelites and, following a tradition at the convent, a small statue of the infant Jesus dressed as "a little king" is carried from room to room. When it comes to Blanche's cell, she reaches out for it and drops it. As it shatters, she cries out: "Oh! The Little King is no more! Now we have only the Lamb of God." Blanche's cry distinguishes "King" from "Lamb," but at the same time it calls attention to the way Bernanos separates objects and ideas in his drama. In this case Jesus as "King" is not just an idea, it also is a tangible object—the statue that Blanche breaks. The "Lamb," by contrast, is a concept with no "bodily" parallel. For that reason it is far more important to Bernanos than the body of the king. To demonstrate just how important it is, Bernanos introduces a topic familiar to readers of Hansen's novel. When the statue falls, Blanche is so "terrified" that, according to Bernanos, she wears "the expression of a stigmatist."[49] But it is only an expression. In the world of *Dialogues of the Carmelites*, it is the idea of the stigmata that so intrigues Bernanos. Just as the concept of "the Lamb" is more important than the objective reality of "the

King," the expression of the stigmatist is more significant than the wounds themselves.

There are many reasons Hansen and Bernanos differ on a range of literary attitudes and approaches, and enough explanations of their contrasting approach to the topic of the stigmata to fill the generational gap between them.[50] Hansen need not be read as a "postmodern" writer to reveal the influence of a postmodern sensibility upon his work. Postmodern thinking generally has been interested in both the role of the body in different cultural arrangements and the notion of "the trace," especially as it pertains to religious artifacts and the imaginations of those who legitimize their power. All three of the central categories of postmodern investigation—gender, race, and class—involve the body as a defining element. Feminist analyses like Paula M. Cooey's *Religious Imagination and the Body* make precisely this point when they submit that a " 'human body' apart from sexual difference as this is socially construed according to gender distinctions simply does not exist."[51] Other postmodern critics interested in race and class would make a similar point, claiming the same definitive status for their particular topic.

According to many religious thinkers and writers, one of the challenges put to human beings in a postmodern world is to discern traces of a divine otherness. Jacques Derrida sparred with Emmanuel Levinas over the meaning of the term in *Writing and Difference*, calling Levinas to task for failing to interpret such traces as anything other than "a metaphor whose philosophical elucidation will ceaselessly call upon 'contradictions.' "[52] Mark Taylor correctly interprets these "contradictions" as expressions of alterity, the "name we give to an unnamable Other" that is "never present without being absent," that "approaches by withdrawing and withdraws by approaching."[53] Taylor finds tangible expressions of this notion in works of postmodern art, especially those pieces that "disfigure" their medium in some way with tears, cracks, holes, etc. These acts of disfiguring "mark the trace of something else," writes Taylor, "something other that *almost* emerges in the cracks of faulty images."[54] The postmodern text that is "woven from these traces," he points out, "inscribes an Other it cannot represent."[55]

Mariette's wounds, which follow this very pattern of appearance and disappearance, are the traces of an unnamable Other. But postmodern theory does not provide the only framework for understanding their significance. Catholic history provides its own context for interpretation, one that not only feels the influence of postmodernism on its structures of meaning but also exerts its own pressure upon the postmodern situation. At the center of an exchange between postmodernism and Catholicism is the most important event in Catholicism during the latter part of the twentieth century: Vatican II. Novels like *Mariette in Ecstasy*, therefore, are indebted to a postmodern emphasis upon the body. But they discover that emphasis, as it were, through a Catholic orientation provided by the Council.

Hansen is explicit about this point. In a collection of essays entitled *A Stay Against Confusion*, he describes a twofold motive for writing *Mariette in Ecstasy*. On the one hand, he says, "I hoped to present in Mariette's life a faith that gives an intellectual assent to Catholic orthodoxy."[56] On the other, he says he wanted to show that genuine assent "doesn't forget that the origin of religious feeling is the graced revelation of the Holy Being to us in nature, in the flesh, and in all our faculties." The Catholic Church during Vatican II sought to link these two motives—the orthodox and personal. Despite all of its problems, this Church, Hansen insists, "sought an *aggiornamento*, a renewal or updating of [its] institutes and practices." Although such change took the Church through periods like "the sixties and seventies" when, Hansen writes, Catholics traded "secrecy and panoply and weird accretions" of the old rite for "the homely vernacular and folk guitar" of "roll-your-own liturgies," nevertheless the Council managed to accomplish its goal "like no other council had since Trent."[57] According to Hansen and many other Catholic writers and thinkers, the renewals that endured after the Council closed sprang from theological shifts that enabled believers to think about their faith in ways that were new yet also recognizable. For novelists like Hansen, John XXIII's *aggiornamento* permitted a retrieval of rhetoric about the body from within aspects of the tradition long neglected by the nineteenth- and twentieth-century Church Bernanos knew. This retrieval included a willingness to recall the "earthiness" of phrases and references that addressed not only concepts and ideals but also physical experiences. They are embedded within the tradition from writings as early as Irenaeus, that second-century exposer of Gnostic heresies, who challenged the followers of Valentinus precisely because they refused to recognize that "flesh is that which was of old formed for Adam by God out of the dust, and it is this that John declared the Word of God became."[58] Such references, Boethius argues ca. 520, become "a firm principle of our religion," that is, "to believe not only that men's souls do not perish, but that their very bodies, which the coming of death had destroyed, are restored to their first state by the blessedness that is to be." The principle of course endures as a theological tenet, but what began in the context of disputation survives as a rhetorical thread available to writers of different generations.

Thus the carnal implications of the principle will emerge at moments within the tradition: from the local Lateran Synod of 649, which spoke of "two nativities" for Jesus—one of God and one of Mary—through the Fourth Lateran Council of 1215, which detailed the crucifixion on "the wood of the cross" and reasserted the resurrection of all people "with the bodies, which they now wear," to the Council of Vienne (1311–12), which not only described Jesus "in the womb," "nailed to the cross," and "pierced by a lance" but also decreed "that the substance of the rational or intellectual soul is . . . essentially the form of the human body."[59] In each case, a certain rhetorical approach to the tangible references in the message was remembered and reasserted. So it was for those leaders at Vatican II and the deeply interested and committed Catholics who followed—theologians who strove to renew a relationship between the orthodox and the personal and novelists who sought to dramatize it for a world rapidly becoming "post" conciliar.

Vatican II and the Eyes of Faith

Vatican II would describe the relationship between orthodoxy and the human person principally in terms of faith. Prior to this gathering the Church had tried to mandate such faith. For example, the antimodernist oath crafted by Pius X, *Sacrorum Antistitum*, called for a personal testimony of faith in orthodox authority. The oath insisted that the speaker deliver it in the first person, testifying to the "absolute and immutable truth" of the Church and denying the possibility that faith might indeed spring, as Hansen suggests, from "the graced revelation" of God to us "in the flesh and in all our faculties." *Sacrorum Antistitum* demanded that the speaker of the oath deny the possibility that faith "burst forth from the recesses of the subconscious," that it might respond in any way to the rhythms of the flesh: "the pressure of the heart or the impulse of the will."[60]

By contrast, Vatican II documents repeatedly use language associated with the body and its senses to describe the kind of faith necessary to relate orthodox concerns to personal existence. The Church, according to *Lumen Gentium*, "already present in figure at the beginning of the world," took bodily form in Jesus.[61] The father sent him to serve as "bodily and spiritual medicine," according to *Sacrocanctum Concilium*.[62] Once here, he continually feeds believers "under the guise of signs perceptible by the senses"; those who refuse him suffer from "senseless hearts."[63] Instead of fearing the recesses of the self, Vatican II speaks of God's revelations "deep within . . . conscience." "For man has in his heart a law inscribed by God," the authors of *Gaudium et Spes* write, and in "his most secret core . . . his sanctuary," man is "alone with God whose voice echoes in his depths."[64]

Although God's orthodox "law" may at times be given a "voice" in these documents, it is much more likely to be given a shape that readers are asked to visualize. Seeing, not hearing, is the sense that most often provides Council writers with imagery to "embody" faith.[65] *Gaudium et Spes* describes the human predicament in these very terms: "Many . . . fail to see the dramatic nature of this state of affairs in all its clarity for their vision is in fact blurred by materialism."[66] True, *Dei Verbum*, the *Dogmatic Constitution on Divine Revelation*, begins with a call to "hear the summons to salvation" and, "through hearing," believe; but it insists that the power either to hear or believe comes from a Holy Spirit who "opens the eyes of the mind."[67] Once those "eyes" are opened, *Lumen Gentium* maintains that they should be able to see "the light of Christ, which shines out visibly from the Church."[68] According to *Sacrosanctum Concilium*, the Church "is essentially both human and divine, visible but endowed with invisible realities."[69] Those two realms come together in the figure of Peter's successor, the "Vicar of Christ," who should be recognized as "the visible head of the whole Church."[70]

The decision of Council theologians to adopt language related to the body, specifically to its sense of sight, was motivated in part by concerns that continue to influence Catholic writers. It was, to begin, a decision born out of theological resistance to Vatican hierarchy. Prior to the opening of the Council, the international bishops had received over 2,000 pages of documentation outlining how various existing Vatican offices and commissions felt the Council should proceed. These documents comprised seventy "schemas" for Council members. Four schemas were generated specifically by the Theological Commission at the Vatican, and they addressed topics such as the sources of revelation, the deposit of faith, Christian moral order, chastity, virginity, marriage, and family.

The schemas met with considerable resistance from participants who looked forward to fulfilling the mission of the Council as outlined by John XXIII. The pope had called for an "updating," but the schemas, many participants argued, indicated otherwise. As one young Council member, Joseph Ratzinger, said, the schemas produced "a certain discomforting feeling that the whole enterprise might come to nothing more than a rubber-stamping of decisions already made." Clearly this was not the intent of John XXIII when he called the Council, but rather the actions of the Vatican leadership that the Pope had inherited. Ratzinger and others feared that, unless plans for the Council were taken away from the authors of the schemas, participants would find themselves "impeding rather than fostering the renewal needed in the Catholic Church."[71]

Rather than challenge directly the concepts of Church authority that justified the schemas, theologians like Ratzinger, Karl Rahner, and Bernard Lonergan chose to question the presuppositions of the Theological Commission by raising an entirely different topic: anthropology. Like so many post–Vatican II Catholic novelists who would follow them, these theologians insisted that issues of human identity should determine the theological approaches taken by the Council. To fashion their appeal, they turned to several sources, including the insights of one particular theologian from an earlier generation of preconciliar thinkers, Pierre Rousselot (b. 1879).[72] Rousselot's writings, which centered around two groundbreaking essays composed for *Researches de Science Religieuse* and later published together as *The Eyes of Faith*, were instrumental in helping participants articulate a vision of the human person that would find its origins in Thomistic thought, yet demand nothing less than the *aggiornamento* called for by the Pope.[73] Maurice Nedoncelle calls *The Eyes of Faith* "beyond dispute the most stimulating work of the first half of the twentieth century."[74] As Gerald P. Fogarty has said, Rousselot's theology, combined with the work of others like Maurice Blondel and Joseph Maréchal, gave the Council "a dynamic and profoundly unified conception of man," one grounded in the "'natural' character of the desire to see God." When Rousselot placed this desire at the center of his anthropological vision, a series of traditional distinctions collapsed. Polarities of intellect and will, truth and good, even self and other began to disappear under the pressures of a desire so strong that, according to *The Eyes of Faith*, to love God would be to know him.[75]

It is evident that Rousselot's emphasis upon desire raised the topic of the human body in new ways for the Council and for the life of a Church living under its inspiration. By "joining love and knowledge," John McDermott writes, "Rousselot conceived knowledge as a tendency toward its goal and effectively rendered man connatural with that goal, specifically the First Truth, God Himself, and with all that led to that goal."[76] Such a unified approach could not deny the role of the body. In fact, Rousselot's approach would insist upon the value of the body through repeated references to its senses. Even the title—*The Eyes of Faith*—suggested to Vatican II theologians a range of rhetorical possibilities associated with acts of perception, especially as they manifest themselves in the physical work of seeing.

According to *The Eyes of Faith*, the Church "during the [First] Vatican Council . . . condemned two extreme explanations" of the relationship between orthodoxy and personal belief, what Rousselot called the "faith that believes with the faith that is believed." Vatican I rejected two types of rationalist explanations of faith, one sort that "attributed to reason all the specifications of our beliefs" and another—far more "sentimental"—which claimed that the "discernment of doctrines depends on an inner witness of experientially perceived grace." Neither option—nor the work of "modern theologians" who, Rousselot claimed, proffer psychological explanations of faith—proved to be acceptable to the participants of that council.[77]

In response to this condemnation, Rousselot would go on to propose a third alternative based on his concept of human life as more cohesive and more completely "unified" with God. Rather than begin with the experience of division between "the believer's conscious states" and "that which is represented," Rousselot suggested that believers should consider more carefully the *"synthetic activity of the intelligence,"* because this activity, by its very action, overcomes division. Although the content of his thinking would speak directly to those later Vatican II theologians who sought to negotiate theoretical and practical issues related to unity, it was Rousselot's use of language and imagery here that seemed to impress Council writers most. Of those who engage their full powers of perception, Rousselot writes that they may "have the whole of . . . knowledge or experience before the mind's eye." The phrase is used in the same manner in *Dei Verbum* when the author speaks of opening the "eyes of the mind" in order to realize a synthesis between "the interior helps of the Holy Spirit" and the "exercise" of faith. By contrast, the one who does not recognize such unity suffers from a lack of vision. *Dei Verbum* will speak of that person as being in "darkness"; Rousselot is more direct, stating simply that "He 'does not see.' "[78]

"The same thing holds true for faith," Rousselot writes, which he imagines as the source of vision, *lumen fidei* or the "light of faith." Once we are lit by this light, we see Christ. Fifty-four years after the publication of Rousselot's essays, Vatican II writers turned to his rhetoric to describe Christ as not only "the light of humanity" but also as the founder of a faithful Church that exists in this light as a "visible sacrament."[79] "Enlightened by the spirit of truth," this Church of the faithful "grows visibly through the power of God."[80] Its role is to "reveal in the world . . . however darkly, the mystery of the Lord" until that time when the mystery "shall be manifested in full light."[81] It awaits a time when "the glory of God will light up the heavenly city, and the Lamb will be its lamp."[82]

To value the world of sensible reality so thoroughly—to write of the "earthly liturgy" as "a foretaste of that heavenly liturgy"—Vatican II theologians needed to assume what Rousselot had argued: that "the natural and supernatural" are "neither opposed nor disparate," that in fact the one encompasses the other, "deepening and perfecting it from within."[83] Vatican II refused to describe this interaction in purely conceptual language. At the paschal banquet, it insisted, "Christ is consumed," the faithful are "nourished at the table of the Lord's body."[84] *Lumen Gentium* references not only Colossians 2:19 regarding the "joints and ligaments" shared by Jesus and his Church, but also 1 Corinthians 12:12 to explain and validate its claim that a plural Church constitutes God's one body.[85] Readers of the documents find similar language throughout. *Gaudium et Spes* insists that "man may not despise his bodily life" but should instead "regard his body as good and . . . hold it in honor since God has created it."[86] The authors of *Sacrosanctum Concilium* are perhaps most provocative when they write: "we must always carry around in our bodies the dying of Jesus, so that the life also of Jesus may be made manifest in our mortal flesh."[87]

The boldness of such imagery presumes an equally strong claim made earlier by Rousselot: that "the supernatural being we are speaking about is a natural being, but elevated." "In the final analysis," writes Rousselot, "the essence of natural being consists in its essential aptitude to serve as a means for created spirits to ascend to God, their final end."[88] The process of "seeing" and "synthesizing" culminates in "assent." But assent to the supernatural is always already assent to the natural. Therefore, for the Church to live out its mission it must attend fully to both realms. It must, in other words, do precisely what Ron Hansen implied throughout the drama of his novel *Mariette in Ecstasy*: provide an "intellectual assent to orthodoxy" while never forgetting that "graced revelation" comes to us "in the flesh, and in all our faculties."

The "processes" implied first by Rousselot's description of perception as a "synthetic activity," then by the claims of Vatican II that Catholics participate in a "Pilgrim Church," and finally by Hansen's dramatic rendering of revelation: these processes are absent from a work like Bernanos' *Dialogues of the Carmelites*. Given what Erasmo Leiva-Merikakis says about the "common theme" of Bernanos' work, that absence is not surprising. According to Leiva-Merikakis, Bernanos maintains a "deep conviction that what will save the world in the end is not intellectual achievement, or technological progress, or political effort, or genetic engineering, or theological acumen, but the heroism of innocence."[89] Neither the documents of Vatican II nor the novels of Ron Hansen place their faith and confidence in those technical or professional achievements that lead people away from memories of what is most human. But neither do they rest with an idealized vision of heroic innocence (especially a vision understood to be exercised exclusively in "vertical" relationship to God). The flesh, these texts insist, is rarely innocent; nevertheless, we find God in its persistent strivings over time, in the *aggiornamento* whereby it sees itself anew, as it were, by a light that has always been within. This discovery is surely part of what Pope John XXIII meant when, at the opening of the Council, he called for "a renewal, serene and calm acceptance of the whole teaching of the Church in all its scope and detail as it is found in Trent and Vatican I." The Pontiff illustrated what he meant by this breadth of fidelity when he made certain that the Church understood his position: this Council, he insisted, would not be an intellectual exercise. "So the main point of this Council will not be to debate this or that article of basic Church doctrine that has been repeatedly taught by the Fathers and theologians old and new and which we can take as read." Vatican II would call the Church through the idealism of epideictic prose to "ever great fidelity to authentic teaching" by recognizing the historical, tangible, lived conditions that stimulate and promulgate doctrine. "For the substance of the ancient deposit of faith is one thing," the Pope insisted, "and the way in which it is presented is another."[90] Such presentation can take many forms, among them the two shapes that intersect in the works of postconciliar Catholic authors studied here: bodies and the narratives created to represent them.

2. *Writing and the Catholic Body: Mary Gordon's Art*

> So to be a Catholic, or even to have been one, is to feel a certain access
> to a world wider than the vision allowed by the lens of one's own
> birth.
>
> —Mary Gordon, "Getting Here from There:
> A Writer's Reflections on a Religious Past"

Mary Gordon has said of that marvelous pre–Vatican II writer Flannery
O'Connor that "For O'Connor, the habit of art . . . began with the habit
of looking. It was," Gordon insists, "the peculiar habit of her genius." Several of Gordon's own critics have used similar terminology to describe the
role of "looking" in her art as well. Some have made their references to
highlight strengths in Gordon's prose. Kathryn Hughes, for example, praises
Gordon for her "minute observation."[1] Anita Gandolfo values Gordon's art
for its "prophetic vision" and its ability to bring Catholic issues into
"sharper focus."[2] Others have been less generous, noting that Gordon's preoccupation with looking at the world produces narratives that rarely move
beyond an interest in superficial qualities. According to James Wolcott,
Gordon employs Catholic imagery "decoratively" and is far too satisfied
with "ticky-tack symbolism."[3]

"If we accept the truism," as Gordon suggests we should, "that all writers
are voyeurs," then the "peculiarity" of O'Connor's genius relates less to the
fact that she looked at the world and more to the way she chose to look.
One could say it that it relates to the "lens" she used. According to Gordon,
O'Connor's line of sight was directed by her life as a "passionate, traditional" Catholic who scrupulously practiced her faith within a specific institution, the preconciliar Church.[4] "It must be remembered that O'Connor
was a strict Catholic" in a pre–Vatican II world, writes Gordon, one "who
believed all the dogma of the Church and obeyed all its rules, including the
one that demanded she ask permission of a priest before she read a book on
the Index." According to Gordon, when O'Connor looked at the world of

the 1950s and early '60s, she saw the Church as "a visible symbol of order," "invaluable to her, particularly in the context of modern disorder."[5]

Although she could never follow O'Connor's strict Catholicism, Gordon nevertheless would refuse to disparage that path. Part of the reason is what she knows from reading O'Connor's own words: that her preconciliar counterpart never accepted the Church uncritically. "It seems to be a fact that you have to suffer as much from the Church as for it," O'Connor once wrote, "but if you believe in the divinity of Christ, you have to cherish the world at the same time that you struggle to endure it." Gordon likes the quote and uses it in her essay on O'Connor that appears in the collection entitled *Good Boys and Dead Girls*. To it she adds another from O'Connor: "nature is not prodigal of genius, and the Church makes do with what nature gives her."[6]

Although the words provide an interesting counterpart to O'Connor's orthodoxy, Gordon still does not give them the final say. Her essay on the writer from Milledgeville, Georgia, avoids the image of the author as renegade. Rather, it celebrates O'Connor as a Catholic whose "cardinal virtue" is her "courage" to resist easy explanations and simple categories. Gordon's O'Connor sees reality through lenses that admit, indeed insist upon, a world that is never just one thing. For Gordon, O'Connor is a fascinating collection of impulses and motives: "funny, relentless, deeply touching"; her prose is full of "irony and formality" and her voice is both "a deep pleasure" and "harsh." In Gordon's description these disparate, even contradictory qualities do not remain at odds. We can name them, she insists, for together they comprise "an edification."[7]

This choice of words constitutes something that, as Gordon reminds us, "Catholics used to say." She borrows the term from a preconciliar world that she knows is gone. Yet she allows it to be the last word of her essay on O'Connor, even though the choice says more about Gordon than it does O'Connor, for it is indicative of Gordon's own contradictions and the struggles she undertakes to understand and live with the way faith fragments both her life and her prose. No contemporary Catholic writer has sought access to a wider world, yet none has insisted more ardently upon wearing the lenses of her pre–Vatican II Catholic upbringing to view the post–Vatican II reality. Much of the drama in Gordon's prose comes from repeated realizations that, despite the attractiveness of those pre–Vatican II lenses, the world is more complex than the light they admit.

Metaphors of "seeing," for example, describe not only the relationship of both writers to their respective worlds; they imply a sense of distance that reveals the origins of their fictions. The worlds these writers create frequently are seen from the outside. Even the titles of their works imply such remove: Gordon writes of *The Other Side* and of *Seeing Through Places*; O'Connor searches for someplace apart where she might hear witness to the fact that *Everything That Rises Must Converge*. From a distance, both seek to view their Catholicism. Furthermore, as they look to establish their view, both seem to follow a method that the American critic Kenneth Burke called "perspective by incongruity"; that is, they attempt a "merging of categories once felt to be mutually exclusive." O'Connor is quite clear on this point. "I can write about Protestant believers better than Catholic believers," she states, "because they express their beliefs in diverse kinds of dramatic action which is obvious enough for me to catch."[8] Her fictions become exercises in what Burke calls "planned incongruity," "guided by a principle of inappropriateness" and demonstrative of a kind of "methodological misnaming."[9] How else could one explain O'Connor's assertion that the Bible-thumping preacher of "The Violent Bear It Away," Old Tarwater, is a Protestant "and his being a Protestant allows him to follow the voice he hears which speaks a truth held by Catholics"?[10]

Gordon shares O'Connor's purpose and methodological incongruity, but for her the terms are different. She writes almost exclusively about Catholics. For Gordon, Catholicism has its own "obvious" actions to capture on the page, and therefore it functions in her prose much as Protestantism operates in O'Connor's. To use Catholicism this way, Gordon must see it as "double," as both the subject she hopes to illuminate and the light she will use to bring out its features.[11] The Second Vatican Council makes that possible for her, for it marks a break in the tradition and divides it in two. Gordon's fiction, essays, and autobiographical writings consistently explore the implications of this break. What Protestantism allows O'Connor to accomplish as she employs its characters and settings to examine the depth of her own faith, Catholicism enables Gordon to perform as she dramatizes transitions between the pre- and postconciliar periods. And just as the result in O'Connor's work is a combination of fear and insight—what Richard Rosengarten calls an "unremitting intimacy of violence and vision"—the combination in Gordon's texts also appears as a disturbing juxtaposition.[12] For Gordon, however, the paradox does not involve violence and vision as much as it does freedom and constraint. It is as though Gordon is permanently haunted by moments like the one she experienced in the confessional at the height of the Council when a young priest told her she "shouldn't worry" about her adolescent acts of "private impurity." "It was as if he had demolished the walls of the confessional," she writes, "leaving me, an animal whose habitat had been the lightless cellar, suddenly exposed to the light, a light which hurt my eyes and rendered everything they fell on unrecognizable."[13]

True to the paradoxical nature of the juxtaposition, it is not clear which period offers freedom and which constraint; or, for that matter, if one is preferable to the other. The "light" Gordon experiences when the metaphorical walls of the confessional collapse is painful but, as her choice of words suggests, she could never return to the "darkness" of a preconciliar Catholic world. She makes that point more directly in a work written for *Harpers* entitled "More Catholic than the Pope." In this piece she recounts her flirtation with the conservative Catholic movement begun by Archbishop Marcel Lefebvre. She describes her trip to the Long Island Chapel, rectory, and seminary organized by Lefebvre's fraternity, the Society of St. Pius X. She tells of her conversations with one of the resident priests, of being "pulled in by the priest's discussion of 'the Catholic spirit' " as something "sublime" yet "universal." The movement, she writes, "engages my imagination," for it offers the hope of an aesthetic alternative—"all the beauty of the ages" available to all: "Chaucer and his Miller in the same pew."[14] There is a part of Gordon that hopes she has found a replacement for the "new," post–Vatican II liturgy, which, she insists, is "piecemeal, tentative, on the whole a botched job."[15]

Ultimately, the hope fades. In the midst of her tour of Lefebvre's Long Island seminary and its grounds she realizes "our honeymoon is clearly over, and . . . I am out of love."[16] Ironically, her hopes begin to dissipate with the growing awareness that the movement fails severely in the very realm where she most expected it to succeed: the aesthetic. The seminary, for example, has converted an indoor tennis court into a huge storage room and has chosen to fill it with some of the most "tacky" Catholic art still available: it "is full of those mass-produced, entirely undistinguished, entirely undifferentiable, statues that adorned every church built in America before 1955," she laments. "Virgins on globes stand with serpents between their toes. Christ fingers his bleeding heart. It was precisely this kind of mediocrity," she says, "that gave anyone with an eye second thoughts about the church."[17] Even her attendance at the Tridentine Mass disappoints her. "I had forgotten one of the features of the old Mass: its inaudibility." Looking at the priest's back and hearing only the mumbling of altar boys who "spend most of their time, it seems, with their foreheads to the floor," Gordon writes that she is "not bathed in a bath of bittersweet nostalgia; rather, I feel vaguely frightened."[18]

In the end her interest in Lefebvre's movement dies because "the image of a prelate who cannot love his age" simply "will not do." Ultimately, it is not Lefebvre's aesthetics that discourage her but his "view of history, a highly fanciful conviction that the world before the Enlightenment was an orderly, harmonious family of colorful but always essentially docile children over which Holy Mother Church ruled, firmly, but benignly."[19] Gordon remains keenly aware that this image is constructed, built from a combination of fact and ideology, memory and metaphor that is far more complex than the fraternity of St. Pius X presumes. Yet, although she cannot accept the invitation of one of the Lefebvre priests to "come back to the True Church," neither can she completely deny its appeal. It speaks to her conviction that some view of history is essential, for without such perspective we risk losing our connections to physical reality. We are threatened with exile, not only from our actual homes but also from our physical selves; from our bodies.

Body to "Body"

"I'm in a queer position," Gordon writes; "the Church of my childhood, which was so important for my formation as an artist, is now gone." "There is," she says, quoting Gertrude Stein, "'no there there.'" Her remedy for this loss, her way to overcome this particular exile, however, is not to find another church but to practice a vocation. "So what do I do? I write my fictions. And my relation to the 'there' that is not there," she says, "I make up each day, and it changes each day as I go along."[20]

This admission joins more than Gordon's fiction with her faith. It describes both as personal acts. Significantly, this personal quality counters much of what is "Catholic" about Gordon and her writing. Elsewhere, for example, she is quite clear about her attitude toward certain forms of highly subjective, personal piety: "what makes me even more nervous than the word 'spiritual,'" she writes, "are the words 'evangelical' or 'charismatic.' The religious impulse unmediated by reason," she continues, "terrifies me."[21] Despite this deep suspicion of the subjective side of religious experience, Gordon finds that her position demands she cultivate it. Without a fully adequate community in either the pre- or postconciliar Church to help her "reason" through her faith, she is left largely to her own devices. She begins by avoiding the "twin dangers of religious life," "abstraction and dualism." The first, she argues, denies the physical world; the second "calls it evil and commands that it should be shunned."[22] She concludes by holding fast to that part of the tradition that O'Connor valued when she called the Church a "visible symbol of order": its miraculous ability to "hint of matter turned to spirit or eternal life."[23] What keeps Gordon's otherwise "personal" approach true to her Catholic compass, therefore, is the fact that both her faith and her fiction are rooted firmly in the physical details of reality.

The most important of those details for Gordon is the body. Nothing else reminds her so forcefully of her problematic connection to Catholicism. In many respects, she seems to remain a Catholic because, as she says, "the body must not be left out."[24] That sense of commitment is present when she writes autobiographically about the Church as a physical reality, represented most keenly by its priests, those flesh-and-blood men who stand *in persona Christi* and are, for Gordon, "erotically charged yet unreachable figures." It is present as well when she writes fictionally of the pull of the Church toward the senses, when the nameless narrator of her novella *Immaculate Man*, for example, describes priests and laity dancing together at a Marimba concert: "the beautiful, the unbeautiful, the lucky, the unfortunate," all coming together in rhythm and exertion to bring people "to faith."[25] It is present when Gordon returns to her own voice and recounts with both sadness and resolve the funeral of her uncle, where a member of her family approached her to assert that the deceased "loved you very much" but that "he thought your books were very dirty."[26]

Gordon's compact with Catholicism depends upon the various roles that bodies play in her life and work. "I was fourteen when the second Vatican Council began," she writes. "Virginia Woolf tells us that on about December 1910 the world changed," Gordon continues. "Well, the great changes of the Church coincided—unfortunately perhaps—with the great changes in my body." With this very suggestive insight, Gordon places her body at the intersection of the pre- and postconciliar Catholic worlds she writes about so extensively. To the dialogue between the Church and faith Gordon adds a third element, the body, and the "perspective by incongruity" that she develops as she studies the pre- and postconciliar worlds comes to depend upon references to this particular physical reality. "I became at puberty properly irreligious," she explains. The Council made her disdain for the faith even easier. After all, most Catholics she knew "were confused and angry and outraged" at the whole process. "They felt that the rug had been taken out from under them." But the era of the Council produced other results in Gordon as well. "It was at that point that I began to think of myself as a poet, as an artist," she writes. This change, of course, came with additional consequences for her body. "I had no more interest in being a saint," she says, "and I stopped putting thorns in my shoes."[27]

The coincidence between Vatican II and changes in Gordon's own body is even more specific than these general observations suggest. To be more precise, the relationship Gordon goes on to explore in her writing involves two particular entities: her body and the conceit that runs throughout Council documents, the one that describes the Church itself as a "body," visible and invisible, singular and communal. The possibility of a relationship between those "bodies" is what enables Gordon to imagine her characters interacting with the Church in very physical ways. Thus the narrator of *Immaculate Man*, for instance, seeks to maintain her tenuous relationship to Catholicism through her love affairs with two priests. Her first is a sexual relationship with the young Father Clement, her second an equally physical but asexual love for the dying body of Clement's aging mentor, Father Boniface. In both cases, as the narrator points out, love "was centered in our bodies." But the "flesh" of the priests' bodies is both literal and figurative; it is the flesh of men and of the "person" they represent when they stand before the altar or sit within the confessional.[28]

The association of physical and metaphorical bodies continues into other examples of Gordon's fiction. In Gordon's second novel, *The Company of Women*, Father Cyprian struggles to end a relationship with an institutional church that is described in very physical terms. Enraged at the hierarchy after changes introduced by Vatican II, Cyprian's rancor is described as the revulsion of one body toward another.[29] With sexual overtones, Cyprian describes the postconciliar Church as "a new breed," "'effeminate and womanish,'" one that he would, if possible, "vomit . . . out of my mouth."[30] A similar frustration exists for young Joseph Kaszperkowski, the protagonist of Gordon's short story "Temporary Shelter." Joseph wants nothing more than to begin a relationship with the Church, not for himself, however, but for his childhood sweetheart, Maria Meyers (who would "grow up" to become the mother of Pearl—pun intended—in Gordon's novel by that title). Maria wants to be a nun—giving to Christ "the body . . . that always did what she told it." Ultimately Joseph's hope for Maria ends because Maria's body betrays her. The daughter of converts who have come to Catholicism from Judaism, Maria will be kept out of all orders "because of her blood." For her, the union of physical and metaphorical flesh will never happen, and Gordon's story ends with Joseph dreaming of the only alternative that remains for him: "He would make her want to marry him before they went to college."[31]

In their efforts to begin, maintain, and end a relationship with the Church as "the body of Christ," Gordon's characters typically reflect some aspect of the author's biography. Father Cyprian, for example, seems to be based on a priest Gordon refers to as "Father D." in her autobiographical essay "The Architecture of a Life with Priests." Although Gordon nowhere speaks of having an affair with a member of the clergy, she does write openly about their bodily desires. Father D., for example, was someone who was part of a "triangle" with her mother and father: "friend" to her mother but, in all likelihood, a man in love with her father.[32] Like Maria Meyers, Gordon had hoped as a child to consummate her own love affair with Catholicism by becoming a nun, a vocation she would have struggled to adopt if she had pursued it for, like Maria, Gordon also suffered from bad "blood" (she is the child of a Jewish father who converted as a young man to Catholicism).

As these autobiographical connections suggest, the relationships that Gordon dramatizes between her characters and the Church tend to involve her own relationship to her parents, especially, as it turns out, to her father. Two works best represent the complexity of this interaction. The first is the novel *Final Payments*, which Gordon published in 1978 when she was just twenty-nine years old. Her initial book, it laid a foundation for much of what followed in Gordon's *corpus*. It introduced the topic of women in the Catholic Church and began her artistic scrutiny of faith as an embodied experience. The second work is the autobiographical memoir *The Shadow Man*, a text that Gordon completed in 1996. Separated from *Final Payments* by genre and by almost twenty years, *The Shadow Man* nevertheless is a remarkable continuation of what Gordon began in the late seventies. Like the earlier work, *The Shadow Man* studies Catholicism as a religion that both invites and repels the body. In this case, however, Gordon raises the stakes considerably, putting her own face on the character of her narrator and exposing the pain and regret experienced by a body that is unmistakably her own. First, however, *Final Payments*.

Final Payments *and the Body as "Home"*

In *Final Payments* Gordon tells the story of Isabel Moore, a thirty-year-old woman who must begin the process of living an independent life after eleven years of caring for her invalid father. The novel opens in 1973 with the death of that father, Joe Moore. A professor of medieval literature at St. Aloysius College in New York City, Joe Moore practiced an extremely conservative form of Catholicism, disdaining all things Protestant and even "polishing Joe McCarthy's speeches" so that he could help fight that most godless of all political scourges, communism.[33] He has been bedridden since he suffered a stroke in 1962, and throughout his long convalescence Isabel has been his only caretaker. They have lived together in the house that is part of a blue-collar, Irish Catholic neighborhood, the type of area that New York Catholics frequently referred to as "the parish."[34]

In its heyday the house held three people: Isabel, Joe Moore, and a housekeeper named Margaret Casey, whom Isabel's father hired sometime after her mother died (Isabel was only two). Almost all of the themes in the novel involve Margaret in some way, even those that emphasize the body. She is the "other" female vying for the attention of Isabel's father. Her heaviness lumbers on "feet flat as fish" past the developing teenage body of Isabel, and Isabel can only view her with disgust. "All of her clothes seemed damp," Isabel remembers, "as if her body were giving off a tropical discharge. I believed it to be contagious. . . ." She convinces her father to fire Margaret, and in a moment of despair for the housekeeper and triumph for the daughter, Margaret breaks down and confesses her love to Joe Moore. The professor puts "his hand to his mouth" and rushes out the backdoor, leaving an exceedingly confident thirteen-year-old Isabel to state coldly: "I think you'd better leave now."[35]

Seventeen years later Isabel wonders, "How did I become, at thirteen, such a monster of certainty?"[36] The question is especially apt because, at thirty, Isabel has lost that confidence. Its source had been her father and his own unwavering orthodoxy. His total commitment to the Catholic Church had given him, in her eyes, "the purest and the finest and the most refined sense of truth against the slick hucksters who promised happiness on earth and the supremacy of human reason." It had enabled him to project an image of himself as an angel whose finger "points in the direction of hell, sure of the justice of the destination of the souls he transports."[37] Despite momentary lapses such as the one where he flees a love-struck Margaret, his authority remains largely intact and, for Isabel, contagious.

When Joe Moore suffers his stroke, however, a number of items in Isabel's life begin to fail her, including her faith. "I had ceased to believe," she admits, and as a result of her loss of faith she stops attending Mass. Of course, she never tells her father, for her apparent trips to church to fulfill her Sunday obligation constituted "the only absence he would tolerate without petulance or accusation." Instead of traveling to church on Sundays, Isabel leaves the house at the appointed hour and walks "the same path" each week for fifty minutes. "Unless it was raining," she explains, "in which case I would go to Milt's luncheonette and have a raisin bun."[38]

Isabel's loss of faith occurs because, as she says, "the Church ceased to be inevitable" and, when it did, it became "irrelevant." When Gordon aligns Joe Moore's stroke with Isabel's discovery that the Church also is impermanent, she introduces a comparison that runs throughout the novel: in *Final Payments* the Church of the late 1960s and early 1970s is a dying body. Almost everything that Joe Moore's life represented to the life of that other body, the Church, is passing away. The "parish" is aging and losing both its luster and its authority. What remains of its life is captured in a figure like the local priest and longtime friend of the Moore "family," Father Mulcahy, who in his dotage has become both weepy and prone to drink.

But it is important to remember that this is Isabel's story, not Joe Moore's, and that ultimately the future of the Church for her rests with whatever relation she might be able to establish between her own body and its institutional presence. While her father, that symbol of the hierarchical Church, was alive, "we were connected by the flesh."[39] With his death, however, she is "free." "I had borne the impress of his body all my life," Isabel says, and now that he is gone she is poised to enter the world.[40]

The question Gordon poses in *Final Payments* is whether Isabel, as a Catholic, can find a home in the world for her body. Gordon even creates a subplot, in order to make the question explicit, that involves Isabel's efforts to sell the house where she has lived all her life with her father. People "move from house to house," Isabel thinks, "losing, each time, a part of [their] lives."[41] Isabel's "homelessness" extends well beyond her lack of an address; it encompasses all aspects of her life: her spiritual, emotional, and psychological selves. Despite the extent of its effects, however, this lack of a "home" has its most profound consequences for the physical dimension of Isabel's existence. The novel makes it clear: what matters most is the fact that Isabel's body is homeless.

As readers might expect, this last sense of homelessness leads Isabel to treat her own body as though it were an object, something wandering and foreign to the rest of her. As it searches for a home, Isabel's "flesh" becomes, at least by the standards she has grown up with, promiscuous. She sleeps with two married men. The first is John Ryan, husband of one of her best friends and an insensitive chauvinist whom Isabel does not really like at all. The second is a co-worker named Hugh Slade, whom she admires and falls deeply in love with. In their own ways, both men give Isabel the means to address her homelessness by offering her some "place" for her body. Her encounter with John Ryan is based exclusively on lust, first hers and then his, and it provides Isabel with an answer to the small voice inside her that insists: "You don't want to be alone. You don't want to be lonely." The second encounter with Hugh strikes a much more important chord. No less "physical," the affair nevertheless lends a level of meaning to the physical dimension. Isabel is attracted to Hugh in part because, "like my father," she thinks, "he had authority."[42]

It is important to understand the way Gordon frames the significance of this connection. Nowhere does she imply that Isabel seeks to sleep with her father or with any image of him. What she does tell us is that Isabel wants to locate her body in a "home," to put it with something or someone as familiar to her as her father's body was. If initially Hugh's air of "authority" reminded her of her father, in the end she realizes that what attracts her is "not an authority supported, like my father's, with the certainty of his rightness and the wrongness of everyone who was not like him" but rather the simple fact that he is at home with himself; "entirely himself," she notes, and as a result "a man of kindness and ability," two qualities her father sorely lacked.[43]

In *Final Payments* "homelessness" becomes a prominent symbol of a lost sense of unity or wholeness. Although there is in both religion and literature a long tradition of describing such union in spiritual terms, Gordon chooses instead to allow the placement of Isabel's body to define her experiences of separation or wholeness. Isabel cannot remain with either John or Hugh, for example, because after making her home as "a servant to bodies, my father's body and my own," she is not prepared to live explicitly within her physical self.[44] John Ryan's aggressive sexual advances produce neither outrage nor even fear. Rather, when he grabs her breast she admits that it was "as if it had no connection to my body," as if "I felt myself fly away from myself." Sex with John becomes something that happens to Isabel, an event she notices "with a certain detached interest."[45]

Although she loves Hugh, their relationship fails in large measure because Isabel's persistent sense of self-detachment contrasts so sharply with Hugh's confidence. In a scene Gordon later admits was based on an angry exchange she had with her ex-husband, the author has Hugh confront Isabel with a moldy coffee cup he finds in her apartment. Angry and looking for a reason to explode, he exclaims: "How could I even contemplate living with someone who could live in such filth?" The incident is telling because it reveals both how quickly Isabel's sense of detachment surfaces and how deeply it runs. "How deceived I had been," she contemplates, "thinking I could be like other people."

I had thought I could be the kind of woman I dreamed of being, but I was wrong. Always there would be some proof, undeniable as that cup, that I had failed, that I had missed out on some vital knowledge that ought to have been passed down to me by some woman, some knowledge that was crucially connected to sex. I felt as I stood near Hugh that I was not a woman. . . .[46]

Hugh's final blow to Isabel's fragile sense of self comes not when he chastises her for the fungus that grows inside the cup but, instead, when he calls attention to its location. "It was right on the windowsill," he shouts, "in the middle of your living room where you sit every day of your life." The ultimate insult occurs when Hugh identifies the filth of Isabel's cup with her home.

Final Payments goes on to develop this association of bodies with places. When John Ryan gives Isabel a job in his office as a county employee, she is assigned the task of reviewing a new program where the aged and infirm are cared for by people who are willing to take them in. The job sends her into numerous homes where she talks with caregivers and with those receiving care, and in each case Gordon refines the association between the needy body and the giving environment. Her first case, which involves a racist woman named Mrs. Kerner who cares for a bedridden black lady named Mrs. Johnson, begins with Isabel's direct assertion: "I hated the Kerners' house."

Isabel is not inclined to separate the identity of individuals from their environments; in fact, her job virtually insists that she cultivate the connection. As she visits another "case," Patricia Kelly and her dying mother in a home strewn with garbage and overrun with cats, she finds that the two of them are in full compliance with all the county rules. Part of that "compliance" is the fact that they are the very images of their home: dirty, dilapidated, and as detached from it all as the cats who roam the rooms (Patricia fiddles with a "sore under her right ear" as though she were a feline trying to groom herself).[47] In the most remarkable of her visits, Isabel comes to the home of a woman named Mrs. Rosenfeld, "the smallest woman I had ever seen," whose house mirrors her fragility. "Everything in the house looked light and temporary," she says. "I wondered if it had been made of ice cream sticks."[48] At the Rosenfeld home she meets with an eighty-seven-year-old gentleman named Mr. Spenser. Mrs. Rosenfeld, who is divorced, has taken in Mr. Spenser "because she was lonely"; Mr. Spenser, who also is lonely, does not return the old lady's interest because, despite his age, his libido is strong and he seeks a woman who can arouse him sexually.

With this visit, Isabel becomes more than a reviewer of the relationship between individuals and their home. She becomes part of the shared arrangement. When Mr. Spenser asks her boldly to "Let me see your breasts," Isabel reluctantly complies. The gesture, as he says, is one of pure giving: "You have given me what I wanted," he says, "not what you thought I wanted or what you wanted me to want." By answering his outrageous request, Isabel effectively inserts herself into the home environment. Taking advantage of what Mr. Spenser calls the "only good feature of this otherwise featureless room . . . its lock," Isabel secures the door and opens her blouse and bra, giving the old man, who reads daily the *Memoirs of Casanova*, a memory that transforms the space around him and enables him to continue his life confined within it. "I had given him what he wanted," she thinks, "and neither of us had suffered loss. That was rare." Although the sexual content of the gesture cannot be repeated, the implication is that such an exchange need not be isolated. The space around Mr. Spenser is now uniquely "his," and it will be up to him to invite Mrs. Rosenfeld into it so that neither loneliness nor fantasy is allowed to overwhelm their respective lives.[49]

Because Isabel Moore's childhood home is linked so completely to her experience of her father's body, it too implies a set of connections. Specifically, "home" was where the body of her father and the body of the Church came together. Before his stroke, Joe Moore's house had been an intellectual center for priests within the parish and beyond. "Our house had always been full of priests," Isabel recalls, "talking to my father, asking his advice, spending the night or the week."[50] They came there and "argued about baptism," she explains, about "the precise nature of transubstantiation." During these visits, Isabel served them and they fumbled for her name as she "freshened their drinks." Isabel listened, and in "their ardor" the priests drank, discussed, gestured, and knocked "dishes of pickles onto the carpet."[51]

When Isabel packs the contents of this house and prepares to move, it is an entire series of connections that she abandons—"All this . . . I thought as I sat in the middle of the floor, weeping." Her tears, interestingly, are not only for the house but also for her own ambivalent feelings, her apparent lack of remorse. "I wept for my failure to love the house that had kept me since childhood." The long series of connections that the structure connotes includes memories that are both fond and terrible. When she tells the eventual buyer that "I'm starting a new life now," Gordon's readers see that the break is liberating but also painful. Not only is the house that place where

Isabel cared for her father's body, it also is the spot where Joe Moore had his stroke. Most potently for Isabel, it is where he collapsed from his illness just one week after he had caught her in bed with his graduate assistant and in the act of losing her virginity.

It would be trite—were it not so true—to say that *Final Payments* is, in many important ways, a novel about a character's search for a home during an acute sense of "Catholic guilt." Isabel is convinced, for example, that her father's discovery of her affair led to his collapse: "the failure of his own body [was] a result of the pleasure of mine." For this reason the years she spent caring for him constituted, to her mind, amends necessary for her sin. These years were her "penance," payment against a debt she incurred when she "fell" and could no longer be said "to remain intact."[52]

But as Gordon's title suggests, the years of caring for her father were not Isabel's final payment. A debt remains to the person whom Isabel robbed of her father's body when she was only thirteen years old: Margaret Casey. The former housekeeper from her childhood home looms large as the novel draws to a close. In the last chapters Isabel goes to her, prepared to "devote myself to the person I was least capable of loving." She intends to care for Margaret as she did for her father, and in doing so to perform "a pure act, like the choice of a martyr's death which, we had been told in school, is the only inviolable guarantee of salvation."[53] She travels to Margaret, and agrees to rent a bedroom from her. She shops for her, cooks for her, cleans for her, sleeps and grows fat. She begins what her friend Father Mulcahy—who appears one evening for a visit—correctly calls a "slow death."[54]

When her love affair with Hugh begins to unravel, Isabel's sudden change of heart toward Margaret is one result of the more comprehensive transformation she undergoes. Confronted by Hugh's wife, Isabel cracks. "Something slipped in me then," she thinks, "some solid bone dislodged." A nervous breakdown follows, and initially it sends her deep into herself. "I was swimming in pain," she says, and "would have to dive down lower still." What she seeks in the depths of her being is some confirmation that she is still "a good person." But as she approaches the sanctuary of her inner self, who is there to offer her consolation? "Priests in rooms," she thinks, "and my father, and strangers."[55] The only sanctuary she can find is the memories of her home, which she has left behind.

In the midst of this breakdown, Isabel collapses "through a hole in my own body" and, she admits, cries "like an animal."[56] The "terror" that follows turns on the one final realization she allows herself: "knowing in my body that my father was dead," that, as she repeats, "I would never see him again."[57] It is this sudden and profound awareness of an otherwise repressed fact that sends Isabel beyond herself to Margaret. The former housekeeper, whose own body signifies to Isabel both the acquisition of her father's frame and its loss, functions as a limit to Isabel's "flesh." "My sex was infecting," Isabel insists, "my sex was a disease." Margaret halts its spread, and henceforth Isabel will attempt to live as Margaret has: within the irony of her own physical existence, smothering her sexuality while watching her flesh grow and grow. The decision is the remedy she adopts to "make up for" her metaphoric infection.[58]

Of course, Isabel cannot live like Margaret, and eventually she must leave. Before she does, however, she makes what appears to be her final payment. "You ought to have some kind of pension from . . . my father and me," she says. "You worked for eleven years for us. You deserve something for that." She presents Margaret with a check for $20,000, "all the money I had in the world," and climbs into a car with her two friends, Liz and Eleanor. With this payment, she has redefined herself within the limits of her own body. Margaret no longer establishes the horizon within which Isabel can exist. She no longer owes Margaret for her father's body or, for that matter, her own; now the ugliness of Margaret's home no longer determines Isabel's beauty. As she watches Margaret's house "grow smaller and more thwarted" through the rear window, Isabel sits "up straight" between her friends and thinks that it is a "great pleasure simply to be near" their bodies. In the chill of this "first dawn," she thinks: "How I loved them for their solidity, for their real and possible existences, nonetheless a miracle."[59]

Gordon would like this to be Isabel's last payment. She desires it so strongly, in fact, that she aligns Isabel's stay at Margaret's home with the forty days of Lent. When Isabel finally gives Margaret her check, it is Good Friday; when she climbs into the car with Liz and Eleanor, it is three o'clock on Saturday morning. Like Christ, Isabel has paid, and all that remains for both is the final triumph of Easter, when not just spirit but flesh as well will be resurrected, when even the sound of laughter will feel "solid," stirring the air and hanging "like rings of bone that shivered in the cold, gradual morning."[60]

Isabel's payment to Margaret Casey offers only the illusion of closure in Gordon's first novel. The fact that the author begins almost immediately to rewrite that tale in her next book, *The Company of Women*, is a powerful indication of how inconclusive the original narrative really was. *Final Payments* ends with the solidity of bodies and bones; *The Company of Women*

concludes with the dreamy vision of the child, Linda, imagining herself running to her mother and grandmother and reaching only the most fragile
assertion about their common identity and home: "We are," she notes simply, "not dying."

The movement toward the more "open-ended" narrative structure that
begins with *The Company of Women* is significant for Gordon, for it places
her more firmly within the context of other authors writing about the
Church after Vatican II.[61] As Anita Gandolfo says, the "tendency toward
closure" in certain writers after the Council amounts to little more than a
"vestige of the preconciliar paradigm." Didactic fiction, so popular with the
Index prior to the Council, depends upon such a definitive sense of closure
(so do more popular, sentimentalized stories, as Gandolfo points out). By
contrast, a contemporary Catholic literature that "avoids premature closure
is not only closer to the ideal of the modern spirit, it most reliably registers
the transformational processes in contemporary Catholicism."[62]

But genuine ambiguity resists the single-minded preference of one topic,
theme, or narrative approach for another. In Gordon's *corpus*, the move to
more open narratives and the call for a transformational process introduce a
third element that, in the end, serves only to heighten her deep-seated ambiguity about the institutional Church of either era, pre- or post-Council.
That element is language. "I owed to my father," Isabel says in a manner
that Gordon will repeat seventeen years later in her autobiographical text
The Shadow Man, "the effort to find the proper word for things."[63] She will
hold not only herself and her characters to that charge; she will demand it
of the Church as well. And when Catholicism neither before nor after the
Council can provide the right words—when, as Isabel laments during her
participation in Reconciliation at Margaret's parish, what the Church asks
her to utter is "not the language of the sacrament"—then Gordon is left
with only her pursuit of the right vocabulary.[64] Her vocation becomes the
search for words worthy of her topic.

Loving a Shadow Man

There are two reasons that Isabel identifies the obligation she feels toward
her father to find "the right words" with a similar sense of duty toward
the language of the Church. On the one hand, she has spent her entire life
associating her father with Catholicism. To her mind, in fact, the two are
virtually synonymous. Thus the respect earned by one is grounded in beliefs
held by the other, just as the judgment of one is based almost exclusively on

convictions advanced by the other. Although Joe Moore would insist that his actions and his faith are founded upon Catholic doctrine, Isabel's experience inverts this otherwise straightforward claim. For Isabel, the Church possesses its authority largely because her father validated its assertions.

In one sense, therefore, these two realities generate their own connections for Isabel. In another, however, she actually joins them through the words she chooses or, more accurately, through the stories she tells herself about both. The reason she owes her father the "right words," for example, is because she has been raised a Catholic and, as she points out, "It is one of the marvels of a Catholic education that the impulse of a few words can bring whole narratives to light with an immediacy and a clarity that are utterly absorbing."[65] When the priest at Margaret's parish, St. Stanislaus, insists that Isabel recite the unfamiliar words of a now unfamiliar sacrament, the entire experience becomes "insubstantial" without any "sense of seriousness . . . [or] of inevitability." In a similar manner, when she finds an essay by her father in a magazine entitled, significantly, *The Catholic Word*, it alerts her to the full range of Joe Moore's thought, beginning with its most "exhausting occupation": "constantly supporting the [Catholic] hierarchy from the bottom."[66]

The conclusion of *Final Payments*, which gives Isabel a new voice to accompany her conviction that "There was a great deal I wanted to say," bespeaks a sense of confidence in the ability of storytellers to craft new narratives out of the fragments of various tales. Although Gordon's later work *The Shadow Man* proceeds toward an ending that easily could offer readers a similar sense of confidence in the possibilities afforded by a serious, existential transformation, Gordon refuses to finish it in that manner. *Final Payments* was a novel that turned the most remarkable features of Gordon's life—the death of her father, her sense of homelessness as she lived with her mother in the houses of various relatives, the awakening of her body, her struggle with faith after Vatican II—into subplots and symbols around which to construct a narrative. The story is occasioned by the death of Joe Moore and ends with a traditional climax, Isabel's final payment to Margaret and her subsequent freedom. *The Shadow Man* is conceived in ways that would allow Gordon to replicate this traditional pattern. Once again we read about a daughter who searches for words about her father and her faith, and for a second time we see how those words connect the man to very specific interpretations of belief and practice. If this time the man is not Joe Moore but Gordon's real father, David Gordon, and the "protagonist" is not the fictional Isabel but the figure of Mary, nevertheless, the ingredients remain almost identical. This could easily be the same tale, told once as a novel and again as a memoir.

Why, then, do they end so differently? One answer rests with their dissimilar use of bodies. In the opening pages of *Final Payments,* Isabel asserts that "After they lowered [my father's] body I would have to invent an existence for myself." Her invention is the first-person narrative that follows, and all aspects of it relate in some way to the fact that her father's body is now gone. The plot she follows depends upon that fact, as does her development as a character. From her sexual promiscuity to her nervous breakdown to the final payment she provides Margaret, all of Isabel's actions and emotions refer back to the growing awareness that the body she has spent eleven years tending is buried. Her final transformation, which includes not only a renewed sense of confidence but also radical changes to the weight and look of her own body, occurs within the context of mourning her father's loss.

Final Payments opens with the lowering of Joe Moore's body into the ground, but *The Shadow Man* ends with Gordon's effort to exhume her real father. And just as the first act occasions Isabel's story, the second controls Gordon's memoir and offers insights into why it is so distinctive. If the critic Frank Kermode is correct to assert that the stories we tell tend to evolve under "the shadow of an end," then David Gordon is in every respect "the shadow man."[67] Dead for more than thirty-five years when Gordon begins her memoir, he casts his image across every page. The final scene of her book not only highlights his role, it defines it in ways that help readers understand both this text and Gordon's development as a postconciliar Catholic writer.

David Gordon was buried in a Long Island cemetery when Mary was seven years old. Borrowing a term from *Final Payments,* one could say that this is his "home." More precisely, it is what his only child has known as his home for most of her life. It is not a place from which he might be exiled, left to wander like Gordon's fictional counterpart, Isabel. But it is a location fraught with problems, and by the end of her story Mary is blunt about the compulsion she feels to remove the body and rebury him: "It's obsessive: I won't give up; no obstacle stops me."[68]

At the conclusion of *Final Payments,* a personal, existential despair drives Isabel, first to end her life and then to save it. To this sense of obsession *The Shadow Man* adds a second dimension. The personal reasons for Gordon's commitment to exhume her father and rebury him are directly related to the demands she has created for herself in her narrative. As she explains, first come the passionate longings of a daughter for her father: "I wish to lie with my beloved for all eternity. Then," she goes on to say, "there is the problem of the writing, the bodying-forth of the form." By the end of her memoir, these two motives are virtually indistinguishable. "Do I believe that if I can get him into words properly, he can live again?" Gordon wonders. "Or is it that by getting him properly into words, I can finally allow him to be dead?"[69] The answers to her questions are both personal and textual. In *Final Payments*, Isabel's impulse to find the "right words" about her father was part of a highly personal response to his death; Gordon leads readers to believe that, with her character's final payment and self-transformation, the right words will come. By contrast, in *The Shadow Man* Gordon's search for words that will allow her either to resurrect or bury her father leads her and her readers to an intersection of personal impulses and narrative requirements. Exhuming her father's body makes him physically "present" in a way that is important to Gordon, but of course it does not bring him back to life. What it does provide, however, is an opportunity to change the way his "life story" ends, thereby redefining the purpose of that life. It is as close to resurrection as she can come.

Gordon's compulsion to change the end of her father's narrative is so strong because the conclusion of his life story, for lack of a better phrase, is so poorly written. For thirty-seven years David Gordon's body has been buried among his in-laws and under a stone that, as Gordon says, "bears not his name but that of my mother's family: Gagliano." This fact introduces the first complication that Mary must resolve in her quest to end David Gordon's story: he is unwelcome in this place. Gordon's father never felt he was part of his wife's family. At best they "tolerated or patronized him," Gordon explains; "at worst despised him." The history of their dislike includes the story of Gordon's grandfather refusing to attend his daughter's wedding. Buried now as a Catholic among Italian Americans, David Gordon remains there as an interloper.

This leads to another problem with the end of David's story. Not only is he not Italian, his ethnic background is far more "suspect" than he ever led others to believe. David Gordon is *The Shadow Man* to his daughter not only because of his influence upon the story she tells (the "shadow" he casts) but also because of the mystery of his identity. He spent his adult life telling people that he was born to Jewish parents in Lorain, Ohio, and that he later converted to Catholicism. During her research for the memoir, Gordon discovers that, in fact, her father was born in the Eastern European town of

Vilna, part of what is now the Czech Republic. And although he did convert to Catholicism, he never told his wife, Gordon's mother, that he had been married before (this means, among other things, that although he insisted they be married in the most traditional Catholic manner, he never bothered to receive the necessary dispensation or annulment). He also neglected to inform either his wife or child that he had a sister, a fact that emerges when, just before his funeral, the woman calls and asks to have his body transferred to Cleveland so that David can be buried in a Jewish cemetery "with his people." The discovery of his sibling creates yet another obstacle for the end of this story. David Gordon, it turns out, is not even David Gordon. He was born "Israel," with a last name that now is lost and probably forgotten.

All of these discoveries leave Gordon to conclude that her father was placed in the ground as a person who, it turns out, never existed. His burial was the end to someone else's story, not his. That point is crucial to Mary, who has fashioned her life as his legacy. David Gordon was a writer who wrote obsessively about Catholic themes. Careful to take only the most orthodox, preconciliar positions on topics as hotly charged as modernism and the rise of communism, his politics were radically different from those positions his daughter grew to adopt. Nevertheless, his vocation influenced hers, and one finds Gordon referring to him when she reflects on her own career. She is attuned to his style and connects it directly to what she knew of his background. "My father went to Harvard in 1917," she writes, thinking about her own education. After he graduated, he studied abroad, traveling "to Paris and England for a while in the twenties."[70]

The fact that Gordon published such comments about her father links her to him in multiple ways: he is her father, but he also is a formative influence on her as a young writer. In this particular case he is yet one more thing: a subject whose story lends credibility to her own words about authorship. What she discovers during her research for *The Shadow Man* threatens every one of those connections. David Gordon never graduated from Harvard; he never even attended college. He never journeyed to Paris or England. He was a clerk for the Baltimore and Ohio Railroad, "an autodidact," writes Gordon, who stole time from his office job to look "in the public library for what he thinks are the important names, beginning with *A*, reading through to *Z*." The discovery shocks her as a daughter but also as a writer. "His writing makes sense in a wholly new way," she realizes. The style is entirely superficial. "The name-dropping. The incoherence. The dream of the great, exalted, culturally embossed world."[71] The fact that he would go on to use his self-taught abilities to publish a series of journals and magazines, including a "girlie" weekly called *Hot Dog*, only throws into deeper relief the problem of Gordon's role as the published "legacy" of her parent.

Gordon's discoveries have such tremendous impact upon her because she is a writer, someone who is disposed to fashion stories from otherwise isolated incidents and unconnected details. If the elements of David Gordon's writing had at one time led Mary to imagine stories of him "in the classrooms of George Lyman Kittridge, of Irving Babbitt, of Alfred North Whitehead," now they suggest to her an entirely different tale. "If my father's an autodidact," she laments, "he's at best an admirable freak, at worst pathetic." The relationship between individual facts or incidents and the larger plot is essential. "We still feel a need," Frank Kermode insists, "to experience that concordance of beginning, middle, and end" in the stories we tell. Gordon obviously has lost control over the aspects that belong to the middle of her father's story; the best she can do is change the end.

Her compulsion to rebury him, therefore, is especially poignant because she is a certain kind of writer—one who takes her Catholic faith seriously. "There is madness in what I want to do," she admits, and it arises from what she identifies as "a confusion of the symbolic and the actual." This sense of confusion may not be Catholic, but her choice among ways to resolve it is. Gordon would repair the narrative of her father's life by producing his body. The logic that motivates this decision is far more complicated than a refusal to allow "David Gordon" to remain buried as one of the "personas" he adopted. It involves an attitude toward stories and the words that constitute them that is nothing less than sacramental.

At one point in *Final Payments* Isabel asks: "What did it mean to represent?" She answers with these words.

> It meant you were not yourself but something larger. Only you were not the thing itself; you were the parts of you that were like the thing you represented. It meant being connected to something so strongly that people could not think of you without thinking of that thing.[72]

Isabel's claim that representation involves participation in "something larger" resonates with Gordon's earlier assertion that being Catholic "is to feel a certain access to a world wider than the vision allowed by the lens of one's own birth." Her use of a terminology that cites "the parts of you that were like the thing you represented" even sounds echoes of St. Thomas on analogy. Ultimately, however, her insights about representation rest on a keen sense that the link between a word and its reference is sacramental; that one not only symbolizes the other but calls it into full, actual being.

This remarkable assertion receives its most powerful treatment in a chapter of *The Shadow Man* entitled "Telling Stories to My Father." The reason for the chapter is Gordon's exhausted state of mind during her search. "I have done things to my father," she remarks. "I have remembered him, researched him, investigated him, exposed him, invented him. Perhaps now," she says, "I can do something for, rather than to, him."[73] Each story she decides to tell him turns out to be about representation. "They are all called," she says, " 'This Is What It Is Like' "—short vignettes (almost parables) about the relationship between objects and their meanings. The first is the story of an archeologist who cannot reconstruct the history of a city by excavating it. The second is about a woman who searches a vault for treasure but finds only empty boxes. The third describes a daughter who keeps unwrapping packages, hoping to complete the puzzle of her father's biography only to find an incoherent jumble of pieces. One cannot discount the sheer frustration in each tale. But neither can readers forget that the purpose of the stories is Gordon's conviction that they enable her to address her father. More than that, they will do what all the research and investigation failed to accomplish: they will redefine the relationship she shares with her father and, with that new definition, introduce the possibility of a common identity. "I will tell you stories, my father, that will allow each of us to know who we are."[74]

At this point it is no longer clear if the source of "David Gordon's" identity is his life or the stories his daughter tells to and about him. The two feed one another in so many ways that a point of origin is lost. In the end, Mary will exhume his body because such a physical presence will provide the new ending that might in fact alter the rest of the story. But without a narrative already in mind, his body and all it represents would have no meaning. "This man owes me his life," Gordon writes, "and he will live forever."[75] How will he live? As "The figure behind every story" she tells, as the one who is, she insists, like "The stranger on the road." The allusion to Luke 24 in Gordon's remark is clear, and just like the apostles who traveled the road to Emmaus and brought Jesus to their eyes in the breaking of bread, Gordon resurrects her father with stories that will, in turn, change their shape under his gaze.

Is it fair to say, therefore, that at the end of *The Shadow Man* art resurrects David Gordon? "I don't believe in the religion of art," Gordon says, "though I do believe in the vocation of the artist—altogether a more slogging enterprise."[76] Perhaps the act of writing itself, with the demands it places upon an author to construct worlds and characters who "live" with conviction and inspiration, perhaps that act "raises" Gordon's father. But if writers "enliven" their narratives in different ways, Gordon bodies this one forth out of her deep intuition of the Catholic tradition. Although she never could craft her stories exclusively from the vocabulary of a preconciliar Church, Gordon continues to be shaped even by that institution. She is quite clear on this point, insisting that the Church of her childhood bequeathed to her the most basic quality an author must possess: a passion for language. The Tridentine Mass she attended daily as a child was "an excellent training ground . . . for an aspiring novelist." It exposed her, she points out, to "levels of language and types of literature": "scriptural invocation, reflective prayer, the poetry of the Psalms, the Old Testament and Gospel narratives, and the repetitions: the Sanctus, the *Agnus Dei*, the *Domini non sum dignus*, repeated three times. . . ."[77] The Mass, she claims, "bred in me a strong love for rhythmic prose" and encouraged her to experience the "ecstasy of words as words":[78]

> words white-flat and crafted: "monstrance," "chasuble"; words shaped to fit into each other like spoons, words that overlap and do not overlap, words that mark a way of life that has a word for every mode, a category for each situation: "gifts of the Holy Ghost," "corporeal works of mercy," "capital sins," "cardinal virtues."[79]

Gordon still believes in these words. They comprise a strong and vibrant lexicon, but what they represent is a principle of sacramentality that is not limited to or restricted by their individual definitions. They represent the connection between the tangible and the intangible, the profane and the sacred, the temporal and the eternal. Their power is to interact with the physical world in ways that reshape reality. That is why it matters so much, as Gordon claims in the final paragraph of *The Shadow Man*, that, in reburying her father, "there was something to touch, to be lowered, to put flowers on, and dirt, and a few stones." What "made a great difference" was the sacramental quality of this physical reality. The presence of David Gordon's body alters his daughter's world forever. The change begins simply but profoundly: "What I have taken from the cemetery," she explains, "is a sentence that keeps running through my mind like music: Love is stronger than death." This sentence is the end of Gordon's quest, the final statement of David Gordon's life, and the conclusion of the memoir his daughter has composed. As she speaks it to her husband over their eggs and toast the next morning, he adds the one piece of advice that, for Gordon, makes it real: "you should write that down before you forget it."

3.   Preserving the Body: Annie Dillard and Tradition

> **tradition:** The action of handing over (something material) to another; delivery, transfer. . . . 1601 W. Watson *Sparing Discov* 13. In that a Priest is made by tradition of the Chalice, Patten, and Host into his hands.
>
> —*The Oxford English Dictionary*, second edition

In an essay entitled "Expedition to the Pole," first published in *The Yale Literary Magazine* in 1982 and republished as part of the collection *Teaching a Stone to Talk*, Annie Dillard describes the experience of "attending Catholic Mass." She has been going, she states, "for about a year." Before that, she says, "the handiest Church was Congregational."[1]

It is a hallmark of Dillard's writing that one cannot summarize much more than such a brief portion before breaking off to provide background, establish a working chronology, or simply fill the gaps. For example: although she maintains that "I knew in my twenties I was going to be Catholic," in 1982, at age 37, Dillard was somewhere between the Presbyterianism that she grew up in, the Episcopalian preference of her college years, and the Roman Catholicism that would not become her faith for another ten years.[2] Therefore, although she will go on to say in "Expedition to the Pole" that she looks to the Mass for "mumbling in Latin" and "superstitious rituals," she likely never knew anything but a post–Vatican II liturgy.

That fact proves to be important because, as Dillard emphasizes, it is by no means the new liturgy that will attract her to Catholicism. "I have overcome a fiercely anti-Catholic upbringing," she writes, "in order to attend Mass simply and solely to escape Protestant guitars."[3] This particular Sunday in 1982 she is chagrined to find a singing group calling itself "Wildflowers" strumming the Mass and beating away at a tambourine. Subject to the "lagging emptiness and dilution of the liturgy," the Mass Dillard attends suffers from "terrible singing," "fatigued Bible readings," and "the horrifying vacuity of the sermon."[4]

Yet, as she is careful to tell readers, on this visit it is "the Second Sunday of Advent." If the service is enveloped in a "fog of dreary senselessness," it nevertheless remains a part of something larger than itself. Her reference to the Church calendar alludes to a sense of context that is extremely important to Dillard and her writing. On this particular Sunday of Advent, she notes its significance by emphasizing the way the calendar influences human behavior. The shortcomings of the Mass are many, but they are overshadowed by the relentless quality of the ongoing tradition, by "the wonder of the fact that we came; we returned; we showed up; week after week we went through with it."[5]

On this Sunday Dillard returns to the church with a keen sense not only of the liturgical year, but also of the sequential movement within the Mass itself. Recognizing the way in which this Catholic ritual emplots time—the manner in which action builds through the confession of sins, the acknowledgement that "we have become the people broken," and the "reluctant assent to the priest's proclamation of God's mercy"—Dillard arrives at what she considers to be the climax of rite: "the solemn saying of those few hushed phrases known as the Sanctus."

> Holy, holy, holy Lord,
> God of power and might,
> Heaven and earth are full of your glory . . .

"It is here," she reflects, "that one loses oneself at sea. Here, one's eyes roll up, and the sun rolls overhead, and the floe rolls underfoot." In an essay that weaves reflections about the Mass into several accounts (as the title suggests) of expeditions to the Arctic Circle, this moment calls to mind the movement of the Northern Ocean as it "rolls over the planet's pole and over the world's rim wide and unseen."[6]

In the reciting of the *Sanctus* during this Second Sunday of Advent, Dillard is caught up in one of her two great themes: the relentless flow of time. Among the many descriptions of the Arctic that Dillard threads into her account of the Mass are those that call attention to the strange experience of time at the Pole. It is, for example, a place where one can trace temporal movement with remarkable clarity. "The film from . . . [a] camera located precisely at the Pole will show the night's revolving stars as perfectly circular concentric rings," she notes. One finds similar descriptions of time elsewhere among the essays that constitute *Teaching a Stone to Talk*. Stand along a riverbank in July, for example, and you may smell time moving on "a ripple of wind," Dillard says, as it carries the "cool scent of tundra" and warns of "*another* fall."[7] Back at the Arctic Pole, the sky of endless nights reveals a perfect circle of stars; but so does the sky of endless days, for in those months "the sun never set, but neither did it appear."

In thinking about this sense of temporal continuity, what the historian of religions Mircea Eliade labeled nature's "eternal return," Dillard takes her readers back to the Second Sunday of Advent and the Mass that occasioned her reflections. Even when accompanied by the Wildflowers' guitar and tambourine, the singing of the Sanctus causes Dillard to experience a "low shudder or shock." It is as if the ground beneath her has moved, and suddenly she can imagine herself standing both in church and on an ice floe. "Split from the pack," she says, the congregation has "crossed the Arctic Circle" and is caught in time's movement. "The current," she insists, "has us."[8]

Before Dillard's readers can speculate on where the flow will carry this band of Catholics, they must recognize that with a return to the *Sanctus* has come a second set of issues. "Now, just as we are dissolved into our privacy and about to utter the words," Dillard writes, "the singer from the Wildflowers bursts onstage from the wings." The timing, of course, could not be worse. "Pumping his guitar's neck up and down," the singer "hits a chord with the flat of his hand" and Dillard realizes that "Alas, alack, oh brother, we are going to have to *sing* the Sanctus."

"Must I join this song?" she asks. With this question, we realize that the moment has occasioned not only Dillard's acquiescence to the temporal context for the Mass but also the introduction of her second great theme, "being" in all its plurality and "catholicity." The song cannot be private. It will be sung by the "tall, square jawed," teenage lead singer, by his girlfriend "who, to shorten herself, carries her neck like a horse," by the middle-aged woman with orange hair who accompanies the lead, and by the large Chinese man who holds the tambourine "as if it had stuck by some defect to his fingers."[9] Dillard will have to join them, no matter how comical the result.

As it turns out, it is most comical. The voices combine and drift heavenward, and Dillard imagines herself traveling with them. When she looks down, she discovers that she is wearing "the uniform of a Keystone Kop." The image gives her imagination further license to roam, and suddenly she sees herself not in the distant sky but somewhere again in the Arctic Circle—at the Pole—skating barefoot upon imaginary ice, bumping into people and saying, "I beg your pardon woops there!" When she tumbles into the water, one of the singers, "the Chinese man, extends a hand to pull me out, but alas, he slips and I drag him in." There they remain, "treading water, singing, and collecting a bit of a crowd" until "a troop of circus clowns" appears to pull them out.[10]

The imaginary flight is more than just comic relief; it is a moment when the movement along time's river intersects with a strange collection of "beings" performing a physical comedy. The clowns who come to Dillard's rescue begin the "wonderfully funny sight" of trying to build a human pyramid with "the four smallest clowns on the bottom, and the biggest, fattest clown . . . trying to climb to the top." When they fall "their crucifixes fly from their ruffled necks as they flip, and hit them on their bald heads as they land." All this happens while Dillard is busy imagining that another one of the singers, the middle-aged woman with the orange hair, is "fending off some of the larger bergs with a broom" and Dillard herself is playing games sliding on the ice, trying to "skid long distances like pucks." This bizarre example of beings adrift on an ice floe in time's current leads Dillard to imagine bodies doing things—not freezing or worrying about their plight, but performing the standard routines of slapstick comedy.

It is a vaudeville and, as such, a rather "low" form of art. But it is art, and that fact indicates another way in which Dillard tends to respond to the intersection of her two primary themes, time and being. She discovers in their connection the opportunity to create. The opportunity may present itself in vaudeville images or it may come as Dillard grows more serious, recalling in the Mass her own trip to the Arctic years earlier, when she stood at the Beaufort Sea and compared what she saw to paintings by the great American artist James McNeill Whistler. As she notes several pages after the clown scene, Whistler, in his later years, "used to walk down to the Atlantic shore carrying a few thin planks and his paints." What he painted were scenes that remind Dillard of the Arctic landscape: "broad, blurred washes representing sky, water, and shore."

To be more precise, they remind her of her experience *watching* that landscape. The distinction is important, because it suggests one of the leading features of Dillard's reflections on art: like the vaudeville she imagined, these ruminations on Whistler involve Dillard in the artistic moment. Of these "late Whistlers," she says, "I thought of them, for I seemed to be standing in one of them." Allowing her mind to travel from "the gravel at my feet" to the "chaos of ice at the shore" to the "blurry, light-filled stripes" of Whistler's scene, Dillard collapses the boundaries between the physical and artistic worlds. She conceives of herself as a physical presence in the work of art. It is, she announces, as if the "world was a color-filled painting wrapped around me at an unknown distance. . . ."[11]

The logic that carries Dillard's readers from reflections on time and being to the physical comedy of the Keystone Kops and the delicate watercolors of James McNeill Whistler depends upon the theological significance of the one moment that initiated the entire sequence: the singing of the *Sanctus*.[12] For Dillard, that moment gives rise to all of the connections that follow, and more. As one might expect, the nexus of relationships Dillard describes is unexpected and begins with a most unconventional claim, namely, that "In two thousand years we have not worked out the kinks" in our ritual prayer to God. In fact, Dillard goes on to assert as she breaks into song with the Wildflowers, "We positively glorify" these kinks, and "Week after week we witness the same miracle: that God is so mighty he can stifle his own laughter." Part of the wonder of the Mass is that God allows us to continue it despite the fact that its artistry is no more polished than "a high school play." "Week after week we witness the same miracle," she continues, "that God, for reasons unfathomable, refrains from blowing our dancing bear act to smithereens." Of course it is vaudeville, and it is that way because, evidently, we need it to be. The Mass will "work on you," Dillard points out, "not on [God]."[13] That point makes the final "miracle" Dillard witnesses this Second Sunday of Advent and every Sunday the most amazing of all: that in the midst of the poor reading, weak sermon, flat liturgy, and terrible singing, "Christ washes the disciples' dirty feet, handles their very toes, and repeats, It is all right—believe it or not—to be people."[14]

Within a general style of writing that otherwise resists conventional standards of chronology and plot, this scene at Mass provides Dillard's readers with a pattern. For all her reluctance to adhere to the customs of a given genre (in this case the personal essay), Dillard does tend to explore a consistent set of topics and to do so according to a recognizable order. For example, her intense interest in the natural world—broadly conceived as the realm of matter—repeatedly raises themes of temporal continuity and the plurality of "being." The intersection of these two themes in turn leads Dillard to respond as she did when writing about the Sanctus: with imaginative flights or musings that reveal her sense of artistry. Finally, because that sense of artistry remains intimately linked to her own identity, Dillard uses it to turn our attention back to the world of matter, but this time she insists that we consider the complicated roles our bodies play in both promoting a potential unity with the world and in establishing a distance from it.

Consider the way the pattern works in a second essay, the one that gives its title to the collection *Teaching a Stone to Talk*. In this piece, Dillard recalls two trips she has made to the Galapagos Islands, an environment that, through its physical terrain and legendary association with Charles Darwin, is almost the opposite of the Arctic Circle described in "An Expedition to the Pole." Despite these crucial differences, however, Dillard interprets the significance of all three journeys according to the same pattern or rubric. The intersection of time and being in the most recent journey is captured beautifully in the following metaphor.

> In the interval my attachment to them had shifted and my memories . . . had altered, the way memories do, like particolored pebbles rolled back and forth over a grating, so that after a time those hard bright ones, the ones you thought you would never lose, have vanished, passed through the grating, and only a few, big, unexpected ones remain, no longer unnoticed but now selected out for some meaning, large and unknown.[15]

The memory that remains with the greatest potency turns out to be the memory of scrubby, brush-like ground cover called "*palo santo* trees." Unlike her fellow travelers, who return to the island to see once again its collection of animals—lizards and birds and sea lions—Dillard returns to see the *palo santo* trees that distinguish themselves for her by their almost inherent artistry. Their appearance along the rough, red shoreline reminds her of the negative to a "black and white photograph." Their bark resembles a painter's pallet with "lichens pink and orange, lavender, yellow, and green." Standing together against the gray sky, they seem "as transparent as line drawings."[16]

From her descriptions of the trees as works of art, Dillard follows her pattern and leads readers to consider the connection between the *palo santos* and the human body. She imagines herself as one of these trees. "If I came back to life in the sunlight where everything changes," she writes, "I would like to come back as a *palo santo* tree on the weather side of an island. . . ." For Dillard, however, this vision of a reincarnated self is distinguished not by the way attributes of the tree supplant a sense of herself as a "body," but rather by the way her dedication to the language of the body controls her vision of herself as a *palo santo* tree. On the Galapagos shore, Dillard finds that, in her reincarnated state, she "could be, myself, a perfect witness, and look, mute, and wave my arms."[17]

This final piece of the pattern introduces a point that completes its shape. The compulsion Dillard feels to bear witness on the Galapagos shore is the same urge she discerned as she bore witness during the comical singing of the Sanctus. Rooted deeply in the material world of flesh and bark, Dillard discovers in both instances "the alpha and the omega" of the heavenly circle she witnessed in the night sky at the Arctic Pole: "It is God's brooding over the face of the waters," she writes, "the blended note of the ten thousand things, the white of wings." In the face of this great brooding presence, it matters little what part of creation you occupy, whether God handles your "meager deciduous leaves here and there" or washes your dirty toes. "Distinctions blur," Dillard insists, and we are called simply to witness the presence of the Lord. Our instructions come to our "bodies" as directly as the closing words of Dillard's essay: "Quit your tents. Pray without ceasing."[18]

For the Time Being

The narrative pattern that Dillard employs receives an extended and complex treatment in one of her most recent works, *For the Time Being*. Given the strange juxtaposition of topics in the book, the pattern is indeed welcome. In a 1996 interview, published three years before the book was released, Dillard admits that the topic of her manuscript is "impossible to describe." She does, however, go on to try.

> It's a personal narration about God and the problem of pain. It has a lot of Jewish theology in it, a lot of Catholic theology, and scenes from hospitals and births, birth defects, and a lot of geology of sand. It's about the birth and death of the generations.

Despite its eclectic quality, this early and brief synopsis of the book is surprisingly accurate. It is also consistent with Dillard's two main themes. As the diversity of topics indicates, the plurality of being is an obvious element in the text. But it will be the relationship of such plurality to time that will give rise to patterns within the narrative and eventually to specific religious ideals. When Dillard embeds her tales of the infinite variety of birth experiences, for example, into a genealogy of the earth itself, *For the Time Being* begins to imply a series of creative connections between the body and a sense of tradition that is deeply informed by the author's Catholic convictions.

The most obvious evidence of an ongoing relationship between the themes of being and time appears first in the title of *For the Time Being* and second in its structural arrangement. Each chapter of the book opens with a reflection on the concept of "being" in the form of a birth story; each one ends with a reference to the passage of time that appears under a series of headings that Dillard, for purposes of contrast between past, present, and future, labels "now." In addition to this organization within each chapter, Dillard uses the same arrangement to bracket her entire text. The first word of *For the Time Being*, for example, is "birth," and the concluding section of the book offers a protracted discussion of a series of images centered around time: the sight of the Baal Shem Tov walking the walls of Jerusalem, a family in New York City pacing in front of a hospital, Dietrich Bonhoeffer writing in his prison cell, an archeologist sorting bones in the desert sand. Such scrupulous attention to structural detail indicates Dillard's interest in establishing the importance of these themes for her entire text.

Careful organization of the themes does not, however, result in their straightforward usage. Birth stories offer excellent illustrations of an abstract concept like "being," but in Dillard's text these stories both clarify and obscure the concept. "Some writers," Dillard advances, "have given describing being a shot."[19] And so she wonders, with fellow author Ralph Harper, "Why should one not try to imagine one's arms around Being?"[20] To this end she quotes Muslim theologian Hisham ibn Hakim, whose descriptions of the source of being, Allah, amount for him to an illustration of the concept itself: "Allah has a body, defined, broad, high and long, of equal dimensions, radiating with light. . . ." But Dillard no sooner completes this quotation for her readers than she turns immediately to a second great religious tradition and asks: "What does 'Buddha-nature' look like?"[21] The implication would seem to be clear: such an abstract concept resists concrete descriptions. Who can put their arms around being?

But who among us, Dillard suggests, can witness a birth and not perceive something essential about our ontological status—about being itself? Dillard, who prepared to write her text by visiting the birthing centers of hospitals, describes the experience of locking eyes with one particular newborn and glimpsing the "other," our place of origin. The sight seems proof to her of what E. M. Forster recognized when he claimed, "We move between two darknesses."[22] In the eyes of this particularly curious child, Dillard sees into the essence of being itself, and she confesses that

> I want to walk around this aware baby in circles, as if she were the silver star's hole on the cave floor, or the Kaaba stone in Mecca, the wellspring of mystery itself, the black mute stone that requires men to ask, Why is there something here, instead of nothing?[23]

The red bodies of infants like this one (each child begins, Dillard reminds us, as "a ball of blood that Allah wetted and into which he blew") serve to reintroduce us to that principle of life which substantiates our existence.²⁴ To further this point, Dillard tells the story of a Cape Breton doctor who assisted in the delivery of a transverse-presenting baby. This infant was not breathing when she was born. "I didn't time how long I was using mouth-to-mouth," the doctor recalled, "but I remember thinking during the last several minutes that it was hopeless." Then "being" happened: "Anna McRae of Middle River, Victoria County, came to life." The account leaves a deep impression upon Dillard, for it describes a moment when someone did indeed "hold" being in his arms. "How many centuries would you have to live before this," she wonders, "and thousands of incidents like it everyday, ceased to astound you?"²⁵

But for all such stories in which we witness the advent of being in either the familiar drama of labor or the more suspenseful drama of a newborn rescue, there are other tales where we are forced to see it in the shocking fact of birth defects. *For the Time Being* begins with Dillard holding "in my hands the standard manual of human birth defects." The book, *Smith's Recognizable Patterns of Human Malformation,* by Kenneth Lyons Jones, depicts "in vivid photographs" what Dillard calls "variations in our human array." Not only are they various, but each variation has its own complexities. Thus there is a picture of a two-year-old girl in a polka-dot dress who has no nose, only two holes, one under each eye, and another of a girl with long hair on her cheeks and no jaw, and a third of a "three-fingered boy whose lower eyelids look as though he is pulling them down to scare someone." Each case, Dillard notes, prompts a confusing range of responses. "You pray that this grotesque-looking child is mentally deficient," Dillard writes of one image, and are crushed to discover the words "Normal intelligence" in the caption underneath. Of another you at first are relieved to learn that they will never live past early childhood having to function with an average IQ of 50, but your emotions are left unsettled when you read in the caption "These patients are usually placid . . . and often loveable."²⁶

Such an incredible "human array," according to Dillard, constitutes more than a difficult but unavoidable dimension of being. When this array of birth stories is paired with a similar array in our experiences of death, we discover that plurality determines much of what we can know about being itself. To emphasize this point, Dillard uses the same phrase to describe both sets of experiences. "The dying generations," she writes, "Yeats called the human array, the very large array."²⁷ To a great extent, our lives assume meaning from the perspectives we adopt toward such variation. "There's nothing makes us feel so much alive," Dillard writes, quoting the character

Ralph Touchett from Henry James' novel *The Portrait of a Lady*, "as to see others die." The "sensation of life," she goes on to note while developing the quote, is the sense that, in the face of such varied experiences of death, "we remain."[28]

Ralph Touchett's description of temporal continuity in the face of change puts before Dillard's readers her two main themes and recalls the pattern that so frequently emerges in her writings when the two intersect. Once again, insights into being and time call for an artistic response, in this case from one of the world's great novelists, Henry James. Reluctant to allow that artistry to move too far from the physical world of bodily experience, however, Dillard reminds readers that the "sense" of remaining alive entails more than the mere perception of watching death. "Do the dead rumble underneath everything," she wonders, "and will we ourselves churn underfoot or pound?"[29] The question implies what Dillard repeatedly insists: that when we truly experience these otherwise abstract categories of being and time, we cannot maintain a disinterested distance. "If you walk a graveyard in the heat of summer," she asserts, "you can sometimes hear— right through coffins—bloated bellies pop."[30] The "very large array" of being loses none of its physical specificity in its encounter with time. "The early Amish in this country used to roll their community's dead bodies in wraps of sod before they buried them," Dillard notes. "We are food," she claims, "like rolled sandwiches, for the Greek god Chronos, time, who eats his children."[31]

The brutal imagery of the Greek myth notwithstanding, Dillard's reference to Chronos calls attention to one of the most profound ironies associated with the effects of time on being. When Chronos consumes his children, he thinks he has eliminated them. He hasn't. True to the prophecy that even he cannot avoid, he actually winds up preserving them. Thus, as the story goes, after he is duped by Rhea into eating a stone he thinks is a child, the titan regurgitates all five of his offspring and falls victim to their rebellion under the leadership of the sixth, Zeus, who had been hidden from him since infancy. According to this tale, the effect of time on being is far more complicated than we think, for in its attempt to destroy, it may be that time inadvertently preserves.

Dillard offers a far less brutal but no less powerful scene in the opening pages of *For the Time Being*. The first children we meet in the initial section of her book are two "bird-headed dwarfs." They are three and six years old and, Dillard admits, at first glance into the photograph from *Smith's Recognizable Patterns*, they look their age. But upon closer inspection one notices in the picture the hand of the doctor. It appears from outside the frame like the very hand of time and props up the back of the six-year-old. The entire back of the child is no longer than the doctor's hand, its width "only slightly wider than a deck of cards." The image of this supportive hand foreshadows one of Dillard's conclusions: "If you gave birth to two bird-headed dwarfs . . . you could carry them both everywhere." They would be preserved "all their lives," she writes, "in your arms or in a basket, and they would never leave you, not even to go to college."[32]

But why preserve them? What has been ordained in time for these "variations" in the "human array"? Such questions lead to Dillard's second conclusion, which ultimately transforms the irony of the Chronos myth into a fundamental principle of Catholic theology and practice. "The bird-headed dwarfs and all the babies in Smith's manual have souls, and they all can—and do—receive love and give love." Despite such remarkable variation within being, no portion of it lacks dignity. It is all worthy of preservation. Any infant, she claims, "is a pucker on the earth's thin skin, and," she adds as a reminder, "so are we."[33]

Dillard's interest in the ability of time to preserve being leads her to explore the science that offers the most acute physical examples of that interaction, namely, archeology. From her pre-publication interview for the book in which she referred to one of its proposed topics as the "geology of sand," to her description of the text in the published "Author's Note" where she speaks of "scenes from a paleontologist's explorations," *For the Time Being* dedicates a great deal of space to discussions of archeological digs and findings. Its most consistent "character" (after, that is, the narrator herself, who we assume is Dillard), is the remarkable Jesuit scholar and scientist Pierre Teilhard de Chardin, who spent most of his adult life participating in archeological excavations throughout China. A paleontologist by training, de Chardin was credited in 1923 with the discovery of the famous fossil that became known as "Peking man," a skull that placed the presence of a pre-Neanderthal creature in China centuries before his Neanderthal counterpart showed up in Europe. The discovery revolutionized our scientific understanding of prehistoric life and its migration patterns.

Dillard's fascination with archeology grows out of the narrative pattern she uses to structure her work. As a science that literally "unearths" relationships between beings and time, archeology provides Dillard with a wealth of metaphors that resist the tendency toward abstraction. Metaphors of excavation, decay, and survival in fact return readers time and again to the alpha and omega of physical, bodily existence: the realization that we are dust and unto dust we shall return. Obviously, these metaphors are not without spiritual meaning, and Teilhard's role in *For the Time Being* is to bear witness in the desert as Dillard herself did on the Galapagos Islands. Teilhard's lengthy bibliography includes not only scientific studies but also numerous volumes that search for ways to connect science and faith and fashion what fellow Jesuit Avery Dulles called Teilhard's "lifelong meditation on Christ's relationship to the cosmos."[34] By referring to him and to his writings, Dillard can assert a link between spirit and the most obvious examples of matter—"people, landscapes, stones." The Jesuit is especially well-suited for this role in her text because, according to Dillard, the "realm of loose spirit never interested Teilhard." As a paleontologist at excavations throughout China, "He never bought the view that the world was illusion and spirit alone was real." In fact, Dillard points out that Teilhard "had written in his notebooks from a folding stool in the desert of the Ordos" thoughts that confirmed her own thematic interests, among them the simple and direct assertion that "There are only beings, everywhere."

One particular encounter between this array of beings and the natural history of the earth captures Dillard's attention for the way it epitomizes her recurring narrative pattern. The encounter appears first in Chapter 1 as Dillard recalls her own trip to China in 1982. There with a contingent of American authors, Dillard remembers a trip all of them take into the open countryside, where field corn, cotton, cauliflower, and wheat grow in the rich loess soil. This fine, yellowish loam is the product of accumulation across the centuries. It is both an archeologist's dream and nightmare, covering the past quickly and securely but packing exceptionally tight and hard to make digging difficult. On this trip, Dillard and her colleagues are traveling to an archeological site where excavation is currently taking place. "Some emperor's tomb," she muses, unimpressed; "the one with the clay soldiers."[35]

The tomb belongs to China's early emperor, Qin, and when she finally sees it she is anything but unimpressed. Reached by passing through a small museum and then climbing a flight of stairs to an open-air platform, the site elicits from Dillard a range of responses. Her first is to the environment that provides a context for the dig. It is as wide as the horizon, "acres and miles of open land, an arc of the planet, curving off and lighted in the distance under the morning sky." The context, it turns out, is necessary, for only a horizon this expansive could contain what Dillard sees at her feet, "stretching off into the middle distance."

I saw what looked like human bodies coming out of the earth. Straight
trenches cut the bare soil into deep corridors or long pits. From the trench
walls emerged an elbow here, a leg and foot there, a head and neck. Everything was the same color, the terra-cotta earth and the people: the color of
plant pots.[36]

When he died, Emperor Qin broke with custom and chose not to have his
army buried alive with him. This was a risk, for the Emperor would have
to travel into the afterlife "unarmed," as it were. Instead of taking his soldiers with him, Qin "interred their full-bodied portraits," somewhere between seven and ten thousand life-size figures, all with detailed facial and
bodily expressions and complete with armor, weapons, and horses. Buried
for centuries in the loess, these figures now were being excavated by an
archeological team that, as Dillard stands upon the observation platform, is
"mysteriously absent." All alone, Dillard watches as the earth yields the
bodies of these soldiers, erupting them forth, pressing them out.[37]

The moment compresses into a single scene every aspect of the defining
pattern in Dillard's text. For example, the encounter between the vast array
of beings in this army and the sands of time produces an artistry that is intensely focused on the body. As Dillard points out, this focus involves far
more than the realistic detail of the statuary. She reminds us that, to the men
who posed for them, these statues represented more than a simple likeness:
"The Chinese soldiers who breathed air posing for their seven thousand
individual clay portraits must have thought it a wonderful difference," Dillard points out, "that workers buried only their simulacra then, so their sons
could bury their flesh a bit later."[38] In representing these men, the statues
actually give the soldiers' back their bodies, even as their gain comes at a
moment when the emperor has lost his physical self.

But the artistry being uncovered at this dig is not limited to the "bodies"
that have been interred; it also relates to Dillard's own body. On one level,
the proposed relationship entails Dillard's emotional response to the sight:
"Who would not weep from shock?" she asks as the tears roll down her
checks. But on another level, the bond includes the actual "position" of
Dillard's body with respect to the site. For example, she makes repeated
references to the fact that, whether she remains on the platform above the
dig or leaves it to walk between the trenches that contain the emerging statues, she continues to look down upon the figures. "My feet," she notes,
"were far above the tops of their heads." "What were we doing," she wonders, "our generation, up so high?"

Her response to this scene at Emperor Qin's tomb intimates references to Teilhard, whose own experiences at excavation sites led him to talk of people as "children of the earth" with lives recorded in a "layer of time thick enough for characteristics and properties to appear."[39] At this particular moment in its narrative, however, *For the Time Being* alludes to a specific connection to Teilhard's writings, an allusion that will become evident later in Chapter 4 when Dillard recommends specific works by the Jesuit, among them his masterpiece published first in French in 1957 and later in a 1965 English translation, *The Divine Milieu*. In the introduction to that book, Teilhard asks his readers to "Place yourself here, where I am, and look from this privileged position." For Teilhard, the position is an imagined "platform built by two thousand years of Christian experience." It affords viewers a perspective that is "above" the world yet intimately related to it, a position where you can "focus your soul's eyes so as to perceive . . . magnificence."[40]

Standing now upon a platform above the dig at Emperor Qin's tomb, Dillard allows this passage from Teilhard to structure her response to the army of clay soldiers before her. As Teilhard says, what he offers to those who stand with him upon the platform is "a practical attitude—or, more exactly perhaps, a way . . . to see." Looking out at the scene before her, Dillard claims to "see our lives from the aspect of eternity," and in her surprise and confusion, Teilhard helps her to make sense of the experience. As though he is describing Dillard's eyes as they roam across the clay figures, Teilhard writes: "Under your gaze" the true God will "invade the universe . . . which so frightened you by its alarming size or its pagan beauty." With "the help of the great layers of creation," he goes on to say, God will "penetrate" the universe "as a ray of light does a crystal." In this way, God will become "universally perceptible and active."[41]

The words do not specify what Dillard sees but describe, instead, the way she chooses to look. Her relation to this particular scene bears evidence of God's presence. It is in the "sloshed rubble" around the figure of a man who looks as though he has "drowned" in the dirt around him. It is in the detail of "the many clay moustache hairs" that belong to the face of one soldier who is just beginning to emerge from the surrounding loess. It is in the soil itself, which "appeared to have contracted itself to form . . . [a] horse in a miracle, and was now expelling it."[42] In every instance, the artistry of these carved bodies demands that Dillard bear witness to God's presence. The demand is made even clearer when, in her parting glance, Dillard notices Chinese farmers in the fields beyond the dig and recalls the witness she hoped to bear one day on the Galapagos Islands. In the distance, she notes, the farmers "looked like twigs," their branches working the soil like the swinging arms of *palo santos* trees.

Because this scene at Emperor Qin's burial ground retains the full pattern of Dillard's narrative structure, she returns to it six times in the course of the book, including the last page. In that final example, she reminds readers of the two themes that coalesced to introduce the original, the remarkable conjunction of being and time. With a look back to "that morning by the emperor's tomb" when "I stood elevated over the loess plain," Dillard recalls the figures emerging from the dirt. But she also remembers the distant stick figures, recalling two in particular, the first harnessed to a plow and "breaking ground in perfect silence," the second walking "slowly with a spade" and turning "the green ground under." The first appears to the south, the second to the north, and in front of her Dillard sees a third movement. "I saw the earth itself walking," she says, "walking dark and aerated as it always does in every season, peeling the light back." She then describes why it walks: "The earth was plowing the men under, and the spade, and the plow."[43]

In this final memory of her visit to the tomb, Dillard indicates why the experience is such an outstanding synopsis of her larger narrative. It is not static. Men plow the earth, but the earth plows back and, as she says, "generations churn." The shame of it all is that "no one sees us go under." That is why the original experience at Qin's tomb was so remarkable: because the scene revealed the figures literally "crawling from the walls" of dirt. At that moment Dillard glimpsed something unique to her age, "for it is in our lifetimes alone that people can witness the unearthing of the deep-dwelling army of Emperor Qin." "Future generations," she goes on to lament, "will miss the crucial sight of ourselves as rammed earth."[44]

To value the sight of the earth turning us under, and the corresponding vision of our lives emerging from the dirt, is to refuse to rest satisfied with process alone. Dillard, for example, makes it clear that she cannot advance the ideas of a theology or philosophy of "process." She does not, for example, agree with "Whitehead's school" that we can "rescue the old deductive ideas of God by asserting that God possesses all good qualities to an absolute degree," making God, as she says, "absolutely vulnerable." The claim, she points out, simply makes "God sound like a sensitive, new-age guy," and nothing, she insists, could be further from our experience.[45]

The most accurate way to describe the value Dillard finds in "process" is to consider the way of looking at the world she strives to develop with the help of Teilhard's writings. Typically, Dillard's use of Teilhard begins with her interest in the images he employs. Just as her gaze from the platform at Emperor Qin's tomb was shaped by Teilhard's description of standing upon his own "solid platform" of Christian experience, so her efforts to convey the value of process is facilitated by Teilhard's frequent images of a world in flux. "Once upon a time," Teilhard writes in an address to God, "men took into your temple the first fruits of their harvests, the flower of their flocks." But now, he insists, "the offering you really want is nothing less than the growth of the world borne ever onwards in the stream of universal becoming."[46] The cause of that desire in God rests in the nature of divinity itself. "We are constantly forgetting," Teilhard insists, "that the supernatural is a ferment, a soul, and not a complete and finished organism. Its role is to 'transform' nature."[47]

The quotation from Teilhard that Dillard uses to introduce the image of the earth both burying and birthing us suggests that she remains particularly interested in the "Catholic" understanding of process and its value as proffered by the French Jesuit. "In our hands, the hands of all of us," Dillard writes, quoting Teilhard, "the world and life are placed like a Host, ready to be charged with divine influence."[48] The use of this insight in the final pages of *For the Time Being* is strategic, for it reminds Dillard's readers that Teilhard's view of reality, and the way of looking at the world that he has inspired in Dillard herself, cannot be understood apart from references to Catholicism. As Teilhard insisted in the introduction to *The Divine Milieu*, the "way of teaching how to see" that he proposes "does no more than recapitulate the eternal lesson of the Church. . . ."[49] It is crucial to realize that, for both Teilhard and Dillard, the changes associated with a notion of "process" occur against the backdrop of teachings that are constant, unchanging, "eternal."

But their consistency does not eliminate their essential mystery. Rather, the endurance of these teachings serves to call attention to their mysterious quality, for they persist in a world otherwise dominated by the fact of evolution and the experience of transformation. In a lengthy description of continental drift that surely influenced Dillard's imaginative flight upon her ice floe during Mass, Teilhard speaks of how "everything in the universe has begun to slide under our feet." The world, which once "seemed solid and fixed," has now become the realm of process and change, "no longer the cosmos," writes Teilhard, "but cosmogenesis." We stand upon a ground that, despite our efforts to enforce consistency, "breaks up under our eyes into a heap of frozen and disjointed planes."[50]

Like Dillard's careful placement of her ice floe images within the framework of the Catholic liturgy, Teilhard deliberately provides us with images
of "pulsation and drift" so that he can highlight their context. To all of our
"individual movements" there is, he insists, a "base or background" that
appears "to be formed of a vast and homogenous immobility." It is "as if a
certain number of rapid changes . . . were drawn and ran on the surface of
some immovable platform."[51] *The Divine Milieu* develops this notion of a
foundational platform or substance but, as its title indicates, chooses a metaphor that suggests greater flexibility, namely, "a sort of unique milieu, unchanging beneath the diversity and number of the tasks which, as men and
women, we have to do. . . ."[52] "If we want a full and vivid understanding
of the teachings of the Church," Teilhard insists, then we must search for
terminology that can account for "an incontrovertible natural fact—which
is that our spiritual being is continually nourished by the countless energies
of the perceptible world."[53] Metaphors of "fixity" and "foundations" are
too limited, he suggests; what are needed are terms that describe the "urgency contained in the most powerful interconnections revealed to us in
every order of the physical and human world."[54]

Teilhard's deliberate reference to Church teachings raises a topic that few
associate with his name: tradition.[55] Of the relationship between the plurality of individual movements and the consistency of an imagined base or
background, Teilhard notes that "We will continue to call it by the name
that has always been used [by the Church]: *mystical* union." According to
Teilhard, the richness of that name implies "the existence of links between
us and the Incarnate Word." More specifically, the name introduces a remarkable comparison: the "prodigious identification of the Son of Man and
the divine milieu" itself.[56] That comparison, Teilhard argues, involves four
steps that culminate with a goal that Dillard both shares and will develop.
"A first step," Teilhard writes, "is to see the divine omnipotence . . . as *an
omnipotence of action*. God enfolds us and penetrates us by creating and preserving us." In a second step, we perceive that God preserves us through
our desire, specifically, "under the form of an essential aspiration toward
him." Thirdly, we realize that such preservation results in a union "in which
the substantial *one* and the created *many* fuse without confusion in a whole
which, without adding anything essential to God, will nevertheless be a sort
of triumph and generalization of being." The fourth step takes us to "the
active centre." Union occurs in and through the one whom St. Paul pro-
claimed "with all his resounding voice": "Christ dead and risen *qui replet
omnia, in quo omnia constant*."[57]

The comparison culminates in the body preserved, "dead and risen." As the entire narrative of *For the Time Being* has maintained, the body, like all matter, is preserved because it is valuable in and of itself. Again, Dillard takes her cue from Teilhard when she quotes his words: "The souls of men form, in some manner, the incandescent surface of matter plunged in God." Nothing, Dillard claims, could be more Catholic than a notion of God "blazing from within" the created world. And nothing brings the power of that concept home more convincingly than the realization that, for us, such a blaze permeates the matter that is our bodies. To make this very point in the closing pages of *For the Time Being*, Dillard recounts the sermon of one Brother Carl Porter, an Evangelical Holiness minister from Georgia, who preached the following words to a responsive crowd in Scottsboro, Alabama.

> "God ain't no white-bearded old man up in the sky somewhere. He's a spirit." *Amen. Thank God.* "He's a spirit. He ain't got no body." *Amen. Thank God.* "The only body he's got is us." *Amen. Thank God.*

"The only body he's got is us": Dillard considers the minister's sermon and concludes that it comprises "a fine piece of modern theology. That it bollixes the doctrines of God's omnipotence and completeness-in-himself," she muses, "apparently bothers few believers. . . ."[58]

Although such a theological claim may not bother Brother Porter's congregation, it troubles Dillard immensely, "for ours is a planet sown in beings," she insists. Deeply appreciative of the mystical dimension of our relationship with God, Dillard nevertheless maintains throughout her text that part of what makes this mystery genuinely mysterious is the fact that it involves our entire selves, spirit and flesh. All of our lives, not just our spirit or soul, are present at the intersection of her two great themes, being and time. In the struggle to find concepts and words that can express this relationship, Dillard repeatedly finds herself confronted with a claim that she discovers in Teilhard's letters, namely, that "the Catholic Church"—for all its administrative hierarchy, its self-aggrandizement, its paranoia about "publishing, lecturing"—"is still our best hope for an arch to God."[59]

Using Teilhard's images, language, and argument to support her own thesis, Dillard makes it clear that, for her, the "arch" is sacramental. She insists, however, that although "sacrament" is defined for her by Catholic theology, it is not limited to conventional Catholic practices. To illustrate her position, she tells the story, in Chapter 5, of Teilhard's role in World War I as a medic. One day, camped with his regiment in a forest in the Oise, the priest finds himself with "neither bread nor wine to offer at Mass." He has an idea, however, and five years later he commits it to paper one evening while he sits beside a dig outside Peking. "He reworked his old wartime idea on paper," Dillard explains. Without bread or wine, "what God's priests, if empty-handed, might consecrate at sunrise each day is that one day's development: all that the evolving world will gain and produce, and all it will lose in exhaustion and suffering. These," Dillard explains, "the priest could raise and offer."[60]

Dillard is deeply moved by this sacramental moment because it formulates the desired "arch" to God while also spanning her two most prominent themes, being and time. As Teilhard goes on to elaborate in *The Divine Milieu*, "the sacramental Species are formed by the totality of the world, and the duration of creation is the time needed for its consecration."[61] The proposition is both infinitely broad and tightly focused, for it takes all of creation and concentrates it on one instance of material reality, the Eucharist. To grasp "the formidable implications of this elementary truth," Teilhard asserts, one needs to understand that "the Incarnation, realized in each individual, through the Eucharist," makes of "all communions of men, present, past and future . . . one communion."[62]

This claim by Teilhard for the Eucharist constitutes what Dillard, in her earlier essay "An Expedition to the Pole," called the "Absolute." In that account, Dillard wove together descriptions of travel to the Arctic Circle with her experience at the Eucharistic liturgy for the Second Sunday of Advent and, as she did, she was able to demonstrate two points. First, "the Pole" is not just a physical location but also a spiritual state: that "point of spirit farthest from every accessible point of spirit in all directions." Rife with metaphors, this "pole" refers to a "place" that is defined in part by the difficulty of the journey it takes to get there. In this manner, it is "Absolute" because it is "the pole of great price."[63] Of its value, Dillard writes:

> I am searching, and have been searching, in the mountains and along the seacoasts for years. The aim of this expedition is, as Pope Gregory put it in his time, "To attain to somewhat of the unencompassed light, by stealth, and scantily." How often have I mounted this same expedition, has my absurd barque set out half-caulked for the Pole?[64]

As other portions of Dillard's essay make exceedingly clear, however, the Pole is also an actual area on the globe, and if it truly is "like" the Eucharist, as the two elements seem to be given their close narrative proximity, then it is so because both are much more than spiritual entities. They are matter, and this is Dillard's second point. As those who have traveled to the Arctic know, its environment is real: the elements of its landscape will kill you. In the same way, Dillard points out, the material of the Eucharist constitutes a "power" we all too "blithely invoke." "It is madness," Dillard warns, "to wear ladies' straw hats and velvet hats to church; we should all be wearing crash helmets." In the presence of God, we are like children, she says, playing on the floor with chemistry sets and unaware that we are "mixing up a batch of TNT to kill a Sunday morning." We pray, but what would we do if God really answered? The "sleeping god may awake someday and take offense," she writes, or worse: "the waking god may draw us out to where we can never return."[65]

According to Dillard, God has charged matter with a potent energy. Those who see sacramentally recognize the power and embrace the one entity that most effectively preserves its source, that valuable "well-spring" in the desert that Vatican II called a "deposit" of faith: tradition.[66] By no means does Dillard's embrace suggest that she is willing to "entrust" her own faith uncritically to this tradition. Her compulsion to explore it through art—both serious and humorous—is ample evidence of her readiness to perceive tradition "by stealth, and scantily." Nevertheless, she does advance a hope that "someone is minding the ship, correcting the course, avoiding icebergs and shoals, fueling the engines, watching the radar screen, noting weather reports from shore. No one," she observes, "would dream of asking the tourists to do these things," for to do so would be to endanger, not just the souls of God's believers, but their physical selves as well.[67] At the intersection, therefore, of what Teilhard called "the totality of the world and the duration of creation" and what Dillard, in her expanding metaphor, now imagines as "throngs" aboard the "broad stern" of her ship, tradition appears to preserve our bodies from the dangers all around us, including ourselves, "cheerful, brainless tourists on a packaged tour of the Absolute."[68]

"Barque of Peter" or ship of state, in bearing us across generations and toward the Absolute, tradition maintains and imparts meaning according to a particular model or paradigm. The process of traveling to the Pole or, to change the metaphor, the act of watching bodies fold into and emerge from the earth, acquires meaning when it works "like" the Absolute, which remains a combined spiritual ideal and physical reality that, ultimately, is captured for Dillard in the body and blood of the Eucharistic liturgy. To her question—"is there no link at the base of things, some kernel or air deep in the matrix of matter from which the universe furls like a ribbon twined into time?"—she answers with her most direct image of an Absolute encased in tradition: "Here is a bottle of wine with a label," she writes. "Christ with a cork."[69]

Holy the Firm

That last quote appears in a work Dillard published in book form in 1977, more than twenty years before *For the Time Being*. Even though *Holy the Firm* precedes by a decade what is supposed to be the time of Dillard's "conversion" to Catholicism, many consider it to be her most representative "Catholic" work. It is, for example, the one work that appears for discussion in the recent *Encyclopedia of Catholic Literature*. In an entry that gives Dillard's oeuvre a rather "cool" reception, Vincent Casaregola notes that, despite its slim size, *Holy the Firm* "contains perhaps the highest concentration of poetic and conceptual energy that can be discovered in any of Dillard's writing."[70]

Holy the Firm is a prose poem in three parts. Deeply reflective and often intense, the poem opens with a section entitled "Newborn and Salted." "Every day is a god," Dillard proclaims in the opening line, "each day is a god, and holiness holds forth in time." From this initial insight on new beginnings, we find Dillard awakening in her bed. She is teaching creative writing and living in a small house that overlooks Puget Sound in Washington State. She relishes her surroundings and, as she salts her breakfast eggs, she exclaims "all day long I feel created."[71]

But all is not well in her life, and from the details she provides, we discover early in these pages that Dillard is living a somewhat fragile existence along the rugged Washington coastline. The first sign of a problem is indicated by the symbolism attached to her pet cat, significantly named "Small" and recently the victim of surgery (an operation that probably left it neutered, though we never know for certain). A more telling indicator emerges when she recounts an outburst she recently has had in her college classroom. Lecturing her students about their need for greater commitment if they wish to become writers, she insists: "you can't be anything else." To those who would persevere, she asserts: "You must go at your life with a broadax." The response is negligible, and Dillard wonders if the students simply think she is "raving again" as she sits before them "trembling from coffee, or cigarettes, or the closeness of all the faces around me."[72]

The most remarkable example of Dillard's troubled state of mind comes early in this first section, just before she speaks about her experience in her writing class. She is fascinated by a spider in her bathroom "with whom I keep a sort of company" because everything about the creature seems to suggest her own frailty, beginning with the delicacy of its web, which works somehow "to keep her alive." The spider and its web offer a note of encouragement to Dillard, who repeatedly gazes at her own surroundings, hoping to discover a similar source of strength. Foreshadowing events that will follow in section two, the narrative describes the area around the web as scattered with "corpses"—the bodies of other insects who have traveled too close and been caught. Among those remains, however, are "two moth bodies, wingless and huge and empty." Their insubstantial torsos should bother Dillard, but instead she notes that, with reverence, "I drop to my knees to see."[73]

The religious overtones of her gesture are deliberate, for the sight of these dainty moths occasions a memory in Dillard that operates at multiple levels, but none deeper than the religious. "Two summers ago I was camping alone in the Blue Ridge Mountains in Virginia," she recalls. She had traveled to the campsite to "read, among other things, James Ramsey Ullman's *The Day on Fire*, a novel about Rimbaud that had made me want to be a writer when I was sixteen." When she adds, "I was hoping it would do it again," we suddenly realize the significance of this particular memory. Positioned between accounts of her isolated existence on Puget Sound and her classroom tirade, the memory announces a topic that is crucial to *Holy the Firm*: Dillard's struggle to recover her vocation as a writer. "Which of you want to give your lives and be writers?" she asks her class about their passion to write. As she awaits their answer, she cannot be dispassionate. "Why," she wonders, "do I want them to mean it?"[74]

Kneeling before the moth "husks" in her Puget Sound bathroom, Dillard recalls one particular incident that occurred while she was camping. In her account of that trip, she details one evening while she read Ullman's book by candlelight. "I looked up when I saw a shadow cross my page," she says, "A golden female moth, a biggish one with a two-inch wingspan, flapped into the fire, dropped her abdomen into the wet wax, stuck, flamed, frazzled and fried in a second." In an instant, Dillard writes, its features disappeared into the flame: wings, head, clawing legs are all gone. "And then this moth-essence," she says, "this spectacular skeleton, began to act as a wick."

> The wax rose in the moth's body from her soaking abdomen to her thorax to the jagged hole where her head should be, and widened into flame, a

saffron-yellow flame that robed her to the ground like any immolating monk. That candle had two wicks, two flames of identical height, side by side. The moth's head was fire. She burned for two hours, until I blew her out.[75]

Faced with a crisis in her "vocation," Dillard experiences in this incident nothing less than a moment of grace. She is able to go on and fulfill her role as a writer. The most remarkable feature of this affirmation, however, is the way it happens or, perhaps more precisely, the way Dillard sees it happening. As her description demonstrates, for the struggling writer this manifestation of God's grace comes to her as a sacrament, understood precisely according to the definition advanced by the Catholic tradition. If sacraments operate as the Catholic tradition holds, that is, as "effective symbols" designed to cause or "confer the grace they signify," then this scene dramatizes sacramentality in virtually every detail. The moment is an intense Pentecost. The fire does more than come to rest upon the head of the moth, it subsumes it. The result, however, is not an outpouring of the spirit for its own sake; it is not a "Pentacostalism." On the contrary, in this context the moth reveals the presence of the spirit, represented by the flame, through its ability to "communicate" the spirit outward to the world.

In this way, although the experience is deeply spiritual, indeed mystical, it is not intangible. This fact is central to the Catholic concept of sacrament that Dillard is trying to explore and grasp. According to Catholic tradition, sacraments require matter: water, oil, bread, wine, the laying on of hands. Even the "largest" sacrament, the Church itself—born at Pentecost—needs the physical world to convey its character.[76] So the moth, without its body, communicates no flame. That flame is no mere symbol, Dillard insists, it is real with consequences that "confer grace" by transforming the world around it. Just as a sacrament confers the grace it signifies, so the flame enlarges the circle of light, "creating of the darkness the sudden blue sleeves of my sweater, the green leaves of jewelweed by my side, the ragged red trunk of a pine." Like a sacrament to Dillard, who searches for her call "while Rimbaud in Paris burned out his brains in a thousand poems," the body of the moth gives to her the light of the candle. And night is left to pool "wetly" at her feet.[77]

In this scene, Dillard begins to attain what Teilhard's writings will encourage her to pursue in earnest twenty years later as she prepares *For the Time Being*. She begins to see the world sacramentally. In *Holy the Firm*, this scene operates much like her account of the visit to Emperor Qin's tomb in her later work. It is both an episode in the narrative flow and a summary of all that precedes and follows it. It serves, in other words, as an "Absolute" and provides a model or paradigm for understanding all that surrounds it.

The scene is crucial as readers move into the second part of Dillard's narrative, titled "God's Tooth." This second section challenges those who would accept uncritically the wonder and beauty of the moth's sacramental body, for there is another in *Holy the Firm* whose head is aflame. This time, however, the one who burns is not an insect but a young girl, real enough but symbolically named "Julie Norwich" after the great fourteenth-century mystic. Young Julie is the victim of a plane crash that Dillard, tucked away in her Puget Sound cabin, actually hears. "I heard it go," Dillard writes. "The cat looked up. There was no reason: the plane's engine simply stalled after takeoff."[78] As terrible as the crash of the small plane is, the remarkable news is that both passengers, Julie and her father, Jesse, survive. In fact, Jesse is "hauling her off" from the wreckage when it happens: "the fuel blew" and a "gob of flung, ignited vapor hit her face, or something flaming from the plane of the fir tree hit her face. No one else was burned or hurt in any way."[79]

The impact of the crash on Dillard is devastating. "I sit at the window, chewing the bones in my wrist," she writes. The accident strikes at the very center of the web she has been spinning so carefully to support her life and her vocation. Indeed, the impact of the crash is made even more intimate by the fact that, she says, "we *looked* a bit alike," both "pointy-chinned, yellow bangs and braids," both attracted to Small, the cat, whom Julie dresses up to look like a nun.[80] In her window seat, Dillard thinks: "Her face is slaughtered now, and I don't remember mine."[81]

"Everything I see" after the accident, she says—"the water, the log-wrecked beach, the farm on the hill, the bluff, the white church in the trees," all of it—"looks brittle and unreal."[82] For Dillard, this no longer seems to be a world lit by the moth's light, and the challenge the text poses as we enter its third section, also entitled "Holy the Firm," is to see if Julie's tortured face casts any light. Is it also sacramental? "Has God a hand in this?" Has he, she asks, "a hand at all?"[83]

In her final section, the sacramental model obtains, but only because Dillard understands that it too has its source in a tradition that begins with the bald realization that "we are created, *created*, sojourners in a land we did not make."[84] It is as such a sojourner that Dillard sets out one Saturday to buy "communion wine" for the small church she attends.[85] There is no word from the hospital about Julie Norwich's condition, and as she walks to town for the wine, Dillard is alone with her thoughts about burn patients, including what she has learned about the high suicide rate they experience when they discover what they "had not realized, before they were burned," namely, that "life could include such suffering," that they would "be permitted such pain."[86]

With the wine purchased at the local store, Dillard strikes out "on the road again walking." In her pack she carries nothing less than "a backload of God," bottles of wine that weigh her down as she starts up a hill. Although she totes the wine for the small church in town and its "Congregationalist" minister, its significance depends upon her growing inclination to view the world through the experience of Catholic sacramentality. Unconsecrated, the wine nevertheless rests against her back as though it were "Christ with a cork," and it reveals to her God's presence in a manner that can only be grasped according to the Absolute established by a Catholic sacramental theology. Acting like the flame that engulfed the moth and literally created the colors all around it, the wine also begins to change "the world" for Dillard. First, the "landscape begins to respond as a current upswells." Then Dillard herself begins to alter.

> Through all my clothing, through the pack on my back and through the bottles of glass I began to feel the wine. Walking faster and faster, weightless, I feel the wine. It sheds light in slats through my rib cage, and fills the buttressed vaults of my ribs with light pooled and buoyant. I am moth; I am light. I am prayer and I can hardly see.[87]

Illuminated as though she were a Gothic cathedral, she sees a vision of Christ being baptized and standing before her as the source and summit of a tradition intended to "gather God's scattered children together" sacramentally.[88] In the final pages, Christ, the Absolute, stands before her as a body. Upon that body are the traces of Dillard's two great themes, for Christ stands "wet in the water" dripping with beads that contain their own worlds, "light and alive and apparent in the drop." Dillard gazes into these drops and sees "all there ever could be, moving at once, past and future, and all the people." "I deepen into a drop and see all that time contains." She marvels at "all the faces and deeps of the worlds and all the earth's contents. . . ."[89]

In this moment "there is not speech nor language; there is nothing, no one thing, nor motion, nor time. There is only this everything. There is only this, and its bright and multiple noise."[90] At this instant Dillard submits to the physical, erotic image of Christ, and her actions result not only in a union with the savior but also in a sense of solidarity with the entire world that he allows to slide slowly across his chest. The kinship she feels with Julie Norwich deepens profoundly, and at that moment she imagines herself speaking with the burned child in her hospital bed. Just as quickly, however, she realizes that she actually is talking to herself. When she advises Julie's scarred body that "You might as well be a nun. You might as well be God's chaste bride," the instructions fall only upon her ears. But that is Julie's sacramental role: Dillard's sense of self becomes the world illuminated by Julie Norwich. Thus the final words of the book, spoken by Dillard out of her experience of God through the life of the young girl: "I'll be the nun for you. I am now."

With this final image of herself as a nun, Dillard lays claim to a tradition that preserves her body by linking it to the sacramental presence of the one God who preserves all bodies. Julie Norwich "is preserved like a salted fillet from all evil, baptized at birth into time and now into eternity."[91] She has been, Dillard writes, "salted with fire," and this metaphoric salt preserves her not only because it imitates the enduring qualities of our physical reality but also because it implicates the essence that provides a foundation for the physical world. There is, Dillard imagines, something "underneath salts," a substance that transcends all substances by being "in touch with the Absolute at base." Dillard calls it "Holy the Firm" and conceives of it as that which binds all reality together. "What would happen," she wonders, if we were to "hold hands and crack the whip?" We would "yank the Absolute out of there and into the light." From beneath the Puget Sound salts and even the sandy loess outside Peking would come "God pale and astounded, spraying a spiral of salts and earth, God footloose and flung."[92]

Something like this imagined entity, Holy the Firm, must exist, Dillard asserts, if we are going to follow Teilhard's argument that

> All the communions of a life-time are one communion. All the communions of all men now living are one communion. All the communions of all men, present, past and future, are one communion.[93]

Holy the Firm is positioned at the intersection of "Lines, lines, and their infinite points."[94] But tradition has made certain that it is not just the sum total of all such points. Speaking from within that tradition, Teilhard identifies the Absolute point of convergence: "a single event," he writes, "has been developing in the world: the Incarnation, realized, in each individual, through the Eucharist."[95] By preserving the Eucharist, tradition preserves sacramentally an Absolute that, in turn, makes genuine life possible.

Dillard's dependence on literary language to communicate this concept troubles critics like Vincent Casaregola a great deal. According to Casaregola, Dillard's repeated use of metaphors and their many connotations blur distinctions that otherwise should define her text: for example, the categorical differences between "an inspiring prose poem" and "a theological treatise." In the end, Dillard's prose "seems poetically compelling," writes Casaregola, "but theologically awkward." "We may expect to be engaged, entertained, and enlightened by the sacramental union of artist with art form" but, unfortunately for Dillard and other contemporary writers, that union "is the only theology they really know."[96]

Although Casaregola raises an important point, it does not necessarily follow, as he claims, that Dillard's "theological perspective lacks much connection with a Catholic Christology."[97] In fact, it is difficult to see how Casaregola can maintain that Dillard's detailed use of metaphor and image fails to "acknowledge the complex paradoxes inherent in the Catholic understanding of God's nature." The only way to sustain such an argument, it seems, is to insist upon a very narrow sense of Catholic "tradition," one that excludes the literary structures and languages that Dillard employs. But even the Second Vatican Council was pressed into such language as it sought to describe the very concept that Casaregola would restrict. "This sacred Tradition, then, and the sacred Scripture of both Testaments," the Council concludes in *Dei Verbum*, "are like a mirror, in which the Church, during its pilgrim journey here on earth, contemplates God, from whom she receives everything, until such time as she is brought to see him face to face as he really is."[98]

As Dillard seeks to convey the significance of God's sacramental presence in Julie Norwich, she too chooses the image of a mirror. "Wait till they hand you a mirror," she says to Julie in a reverie that, of course, is addressed to herself (she who has forgotten the appearance of her own face). The reflection occasions an opportunity to contemplate God, but such contemplation is not limited either to the language of abstract idealism or the details of physical reality. The reflection in the mirror includes both the ideal and the real by revealing a new way of being in time that is, in one moment, both ancient and modern. The mirror reveals a new way of living in the world that is also an ancient way, for it transforms that "black shroud of flesh on your skull" into a "veil." The image in the mirror reveals to Julie and to Dillard that, "by the long and waking day—Sext, None, Vespers," we are able to find ourselves "holding the altar rail" and feeling the "smash of the holy once more," a presence that is not anonymous outside the limited realm of individual experience, but one that actually has been "signed by its name." The image shows us cloaked in the habit of tradition and "Held fast by love in the world like the moth in wax." In this image, "your life is a wick, your head on fire with prayer, held utterly, outside and in you sleep alone, if you call that alone. . . ." For Dillard, the power of God has been named for centuries, described in the characters Jesus traced while "writing on the ground," and as long as we rest upon those sands, we never sleep alone.[99]

4. Clothing Bodies/Making Priests: The Sacramental Vision of J. F. Powers, Alfred Alcorn, and Louise Erdrich

There is a scene in J. F. Powers' 1988 novel, *Wheat That Springeth Green*, in which the protagonist, Father Joe Hackett, is watching television in one of his favorite positions: reclined in a Barcalounger with drink in hand. His attention is evenly divided between what he sees on the screen and what he is hearing from his new curate, Father Bill Schmidt, who is trying to hold a conversation with him about fundraising. When the sudden appearance of a commercial for breakfast cereal captures Father Hackett's eye, he sits up and studies the action in the ad. He then remarks to his curate: "sack race."

Father Schmidt turns to notice the action on the screen and answers, "Yeah, I can see," perturbed that his pastor is more interested in the figures jumping around trying to sell cereal than in the conversation they are supposed to be having.

> "Not a hundred yard dash. Not a mile run," Father Hackett continues.
> "Joe, I don't know what *you're* talking about."
> "It's a sack race, Bill," Father Hackett announces. "The priesthood."[1]

The importance of this scene for the novel is noted by Powers' daughter, Katherine A. Powers, in her introduction to the 2000 paperback edition. "The original title given by my father to [the book] . . . was *The Sack Race*." It was, she says, the title that appeared on the original contract with Knopf and on twenty-five years' worth of correspondence between J. F. Powers and his editor, Robert Gottlieb. Her father, Katherine Powers says, kept those letters neatly clipped together in his desk drawer "as a scourge" to remind him of the book he promised to write, a text that, she adds, seemed forever mired in "tinkering and procrastination."[2]

Undoubtedly the title held an attraction for Powers as time passed and the challenge of finishing the book became itself something like a sack race. Katherine Powers' introduction even makes reference to Ecclesiastes 9:11, suggesting that, after twenty-five years, the race to write certainly was not won by the swift. But the metaphor of the sack race held a much deeper significance for Powers than any allusion it might have made to his own mounting struggles with an incomplete manuscript. In fact, the metaphor provides an extremely good description of Father Joe Hackett's career in this novel. As a priest, Father Hackett is neither a sprinter nor a distance runner. His movements are too clumsy, too awkward. Like someone running a sack race, Powers' protagonist falls down, gets up, and only with much effort manages to bounce toward the finish line. There is hardly a better description of Joe Hackett's trajectory throughout the plot.

We meet Joe Hackett as a child growing up innocent in the less-than-innocent world of the 1920s. As a Catholic schoolboy, he worries about committing a "sin against the Holy Ghost," and his earliest impressions of the priesthood come from the nuns who are his teachers and who tell him in no uncertain terms that "Priests were in a class by themselves. To them alone," the nuns insist, "had Our Lord given the power to turn water and wine into his body and blood, and to forgive sins."[3]

From the innocence of childhood, Joe encounters the "sins" of adolescence: he moves from telling the older girl next door about "the power of the priesthood" to having sex with both her and her friend and, eventually, to catching the clap from one or both. He enters the seminary as one of the more "worldly" candidates but gradually becomes ostracized for being zealous in his faith—wearing a hair shirt and spending all of his spare time praying in the chapel. He takes this extremely devout attitude with him into his first assignment at Holy Faith Parish, where he is pulled more deeply into the affairs of those around him. By the time the Archbishop transfers him to the position of Assistant Director of Catholic Charities, Father Joe has become not only less reclusive but also quite outgoing, and with his newfound gregariousness he is showing the early signs of the disease that will dog him for the rest of the novel: alcoholism. When he gains his first pastorate at Saints Francis and Clare, he is drinking heavily.

The reference to the priesthood as a "sack race" is therefore an accurate assessment of the outward course of Joe Hackett's vocation. But it also describes an inner movement. Joe's comment about the race to his curate stems from a memory, one that Powers does not allude to directly but is nevertheless an important incident in Joe's past. It occurs sometime in his childhood, the late 1920s. Prohibition is in effect, and Joe's Uncle Bobby has "borrowed" the company truck from the coal business Joe's father operates. Trouble follows when Bobby is caught by police transporting liquor with the truck. The arrest makes it to the front pages of the local paper, with a large photo of the vehicle, complete with the company logo, and the crime immediately casts a long shadow over the integrity of the Hackett name.

The photo runs the very day of a festival sponsored by the neighborhood parish. Confused about whether or not he should attend and risk embarrassment, Joe decides to go so that he can redeem himself and his family by winning a scheduled foot race competition. By all accounts, Joe is the fastest student in his class, perhaps even the school, and he feels confident that he can finish first. His efforts, however, are thwarted by the pastor, who tags him to help two nuns watch an ice cream booth while he retreats into the rectory. When the priest learns Joe has missed the scheduled dash, he hauls him off to the track to participate in the only event that remains, a sack race. Joe does not want to run but does, and as he passes the last of his competitors—"a big eighth-grade guy who smoked Wings (ten cents a pack) in the boys' washroom during recess"—it happens: he falls. At that point the cheers he was sure he heard while he was ahead turn into catcalls: "His old man's a bootlegger!" someone shouts.

The freshness of the memory, with its confusion and guilt, is surprisingly relevant to Father Joe and the clerical world of the late 1960s that he inhabits throughout most of the novel. As an event that describes both his uneven actions and his inner turmoil, the sack race defines an essential quality about Joe's life as a priest. Joe had been a "natural" runner, recruited in school by the priests who coached both track and football. Nicknamed "Speed," he was, as the Irish parish priest Father Day intoned, "vairrree fleeht of fooht." Naturally, he should win the race. But this is a race unlike any other; it is unnatural, a sack race, characterized by the fact that the "runner" must restrict himself, manage or "contain" his gifts in such as way that they cannot be used to their greatest effect.

Yet, as Joe Hackett's life goes on to demonstrate, such containment does not preclude success. In fact, this particular obstacle helps to determine his triumph. Joe falls, and his memory of the event stops at that point. To a great extent, therefore, the narrative of his life becomes the story of his prolonged and repeated efforts to regain his feet and finish the race. He must discover a way to live with the fall he has taken and, in so doing, respond to it differently than he does as a child (after the race Joe runs home and retreats to the "little tower that bulged out of the attic" and cries).[4] He must surmount this inclination.

Joe acknowledges this challenge years later when he asserts to his curate, Father Bill, that the image of a sack race on TV captures the essence of priestly life. In fact, his assertion elevates the incident to the status of a paradigm. The elements of the race and their corresponding meanings describe the leading qualities of priesthood for all who enter it. Moreover, as a paradigm, the image of the race (and the subsequent tale of Joe's response to it) is prescriptive: those who would enter the priesthood should interpret their experience as a sack race and "run" accordingly. As Joe holds, its paradigmatic quality is not related to the race as a test of speed or endurance but, more accurately, as a measure of endurance within strict limitations. The problem, Joe understands, is the sack. The actual bag, he recalls, was "dusty, which he didn't mind so much, but damp on the bottom, which he did, and said BIG BOY POTATOES on it." On the day of the race, when Joe sees his classmate Delbert Freeman standing on the sidelines of the race—a big kid who nevertheless wets his pants in school—Joe figures he knows the source of the dampness and remarks under his breath, "*Piss Pants!*"

Powers' description of the literal sack connotes more figurative meanings. For example, his account of the contest supplements his daughter's reference to the scriptural "race" in Ecclesiastes 9:11 with another from Joel 1:13: "put on sackcloth and lament, you priests . . . come, pass the night in sackcloth, you ministers of my God." Furthermore, in the specific context of a priestly paradigm, his description also resonates with a larger principle of Catholic sacramentality, especially as it applies to the sacrament of Holy Orders. All Catholic sacraments operate in a manner that is similar to Father Joe's "sack": all bring something to the body and its senses from the outside. All "cover" recipients physically and symbolically by applying elements of the physical world—water, oil, salt, bread, touch—to areas of the body that "hold" the senses—eyes, ears, mouth, etc. Only Holy Orders, however, literally "cloaks" the body. Upon ordination, the priest receives a chasuble, which he drapes over his head and shoulders in such a way that it appears to be the direct counterpart of the sack young Joe steps into and wears on his bottom half (interestingly, the original "chasubles" were simple peasant garments worn to protect against sun and rain; in cut and fit, they looked a good deal like sacks).

In addition to donning the chasuble, priests from Joe Hackett's ordination class would have undergone a second ritual during Holy Orders. After anointing the palms of each candidate, the bishop would have used a roll of cloth to bind their hands together. The resulting image would have suggested in each candidate a posture of prayer, but the most immediate consequence would have been a sense of restricted movement. The action parallels what Joe experiences when he places his feet into the sack (including the sensation of dampness, which, in this case, comes from a very different source). The actions are parallel in another way: both seem to be strikingly inappropriate given their contexts. In one case, the runner hears: "we have bound your feet, now run a race"; in the other, he is told, "we have tied your hands, now serve as a priest."

In Powers' narrative, however, it is precisely this incongruity of actions that becomes paradigmatic. One of the most distinguishing features of the priesthood for Joe Hackett is that it follows the logic of so many religious experiences, rooted as they are in irony and paradox. Just as St. Paul would "free" Christians by making them "slaves" to Christ, so the Church would bring its ministers closer to God through a "hierarchy" that nevertheless defines them as "servants."[5] To accept this logic—which indeed is liberating for so many who enter the priesthood, including, by the end of *Wheat That Springeth Green*, Joe Hackett—to accept it demands that one acquiesce to the authority of the single body that maintains this mysterious confluence of opposites, the Church. "No one can bestow grace on himself," the authors of the most recent *Catholic Catechism* assert; "it must be given and offered."[6] It must, in other words, come from outside the individual and engage body and soul.

During ordination the Church drapes the mantle of grace upon its priests and leaves evidence of its actions. By "reason of the sacerdotal consecration which he has received," the ministerial priest, Thomas Aquinas writes, "is truly made like the high priest and possesses the authority to act in the power and place of the person of Christ himself." There is a "character imprinted by ordination" that is, as the *Catechism* states, "for ever." For the priest, "the vocation and mission received on the day of his ordination mark him permanently."[7]

Offered in love, these marks nevertheless conjure strict, even violent images of "indelible" traces or "imprints."[8] Intended as "gifts" of the Holy Spirit that "can make us free collaborators in his work in the Church," the marks are more naturally tied to metaphors of constraint. They are traced upon the flesh by an Episcopal officer whose role, as the *Catechism* again reminds us, involves the "binding and loosing" not only of sins but, as we have seen, also our appendages—hands and feet.[9] Therefore, when Father Joe tells his new curate, Father Bill, to change out of his T-shirt and jeans and into a cassock, he makes his request in the name of the Church, "literally," he says, "for Christ's sake." The request contains not only a reference to the authority of the institution but also an implied note of violence, for the T-shirt the pastor insists his curate remove reads: "Thou Shalt Not Kill, Bend, Fold, or Mutilate." It is not clear from Powers' narrative that the indelible mark of the priestly uniform truly supplants this message with another that is so direct or convincing.

Because Powers grounds his metaphor of the priesthood as a sack race upon traditional notions of Catholic sacramentality, the image that results applies to realities beyond the world created in *Wheat That Springeth Green*. The essential components of the metaphor—the ironic comparison of a liberating vocation to the experience of being physically bound—shape the narratives of two other novels. *Vestments*, by Alfred Alcorn, tells the story of Sebastian "Bass" Taggart, a writer and editorialist for a Boston television station who initially becomes attracted to the priesthood when he thinks his interest will win him an inheritance from his aunt. In the end, he accepts his vocation because he realizes how empty life is without it. *The Last Report on the Miracles at Little No Horse* by Louise Erdrich narrates a more complex tale of Father Damien Modeste, longtime priest on a northern Native American reservation called Little No Horse. Like Sebastian Taggart, Father Modeste also comes to the priesthood later in life, specifically after losing almost everything: worldly possessions, a lover, even a sense of identity. In what could be read as extended reflections on the sack-race metaphor, both of these novels describe the growing awareness of religious vocations with references to the same formative event: the act of stepping into priestly attire. In this way, both insist that, to complete the race that follows from sacramental ordination, one must learn to live with certain paradoxical restrictions represented by the garments of the office.

Vestments

Alfred Alcorn's novel, his second, was published in 1988, the same year as Powers' second effort. It introduces "Bass" Taggart, a self-absorbed bachelor who lives with his girlfriend, Clara, and reads editorials for WLMN on the nightly news. He also writes the editorial copy but, as he points out, he does so utterly without conviction. Between assignments, he runs a marketing promotion at the station that seeks to discover "The Smile of Boston." That particular task requires that he evaluate and rank thousands of pictures sent to the station by city hopefuls looking to win anything from $100,000 to a Hawaiian vacation. The superficiality of it all leaves him jaded and cynical.

In response to growing dissatisfaction with his life, Sebastian does two things: he drinks heavily and he awaits the death of his aunt, Esther O'Donnell D'Arcy, who rescued him from a British orphanage after his parents' death and raised him in Boston. She is wealthy, and it is the promise of an inheritance that keeps him both attached to her and confident that better days lie ahead. "The fact is I'm going to be quite wealthy after she goes," he tells Clara, "I'm going to be rich and free." When Clara presses him to explain just what he thinks he will be free of, he responds quite simply, "everything," and although he goes on to detail a litany of intolerable situations at work, his final response to her question is the most accurate. "Free of myself," he mutters.[10]

Ultimately, this freedom does come to Sebastian, but not in the form of a temporal inheritance. When he decides at the end of the novel to enter the priesthood, Alcorn's point is clear: Bass's inheritance will be spiritual. That decision, however, is anti-climactic compared to the process Sebastian follows to reach it. The first chapter of the novel establishes the predicament that advances the plot of the novel. The book opens with Sebastian venturing out one evening after several drinks to the Mother of Mercy Home for Aged Women, the Catholic nursing home where his aunt lies in semi-consciousness for her final months. He is greeted by the director of the home and Mother Superior of the order that runs it, Sister Vincia. She whisks him into her office with its "frightfully neat desk" and tells him that his aunt is suffering from "moments when she has certain delusions." The delusions, she explains, are quite specific, and they involve Sebastian directly. "She seems to think," Sister Vincia tells him, "that you have been to the seminary and are a priest."[11]

The humor of his aunt's delusion is not lost on Sebastian, but neither is the opportunity it presents. When his aunt questions him—"Father Taggart, where is your collar?"—he hits upon the scheme that becomes the true subject of the novel: he pulls on a black suit and turtleneck, adds a piece of white tape, and begins to visit his aunt as though he indeed were a priest. With the eventual purchase of a clerical shirt and collar from a religious goods store, he then begins to travel about the city dressed this way, visiting restaurants, museums, and even the red light district, where he gathers a range of reactions that, for Sebastian, are oddly reassuring.

These reactions comfort him because they seem to promise the very freedom he initially sought with his aunt's finances. What Bass feels, Alcorn tells us, is much more than a vague sense of gratification at being treated with deference by clerks and old women. The experience is nothing short of transformative for him. Wearing his shirt and collar, he visits his aunt and sees not his inheritance but "the most real thing in the world, which is another person." Slowly he begins to understand death "as radical, as mysterious, as miraculous, as life itself."[12] When his aunt receives her final sacrament, the Anointing of the Sick, he changes into his work clothes and finds that he must answer the priest for her. He is surprised to discover that he performs the task with genuine conviction and with a growing feeling of belief in the ultimate "transformation, a return to spirit as well as to dust."[13]

Coming while he is still uncertain of his future, this transformation does not coincide with Bass's "reception" of grace; it does not occur symbolically at the moment of ordination, nor does it happen when he finally decides to enter the seminary. Rather, it arrives according to the manner Joe Hackett describes when he identifies his paradigm—in strange and awkward leaps of discovery, in falling down, and in wearing garments that initially function in ways that oppose their intended effects. Bass's renewed appreciation of life and death, his awareness of life as both dust and spirit, suggests that he is searching for a sense of completion or wholeness. He seeks the very quality his coworker, Leah, perceives the first time she catches a glimpse of him masquerading as a priest. "That collar," she says to him, "you look amazingly authentic in it."[14]

But for Bass, as for Joe Hackett, authenticity requires an extended journey through the inauthentic. In *Wheat That Springeth Green*, Joe Hackett's natural abilities as a priest are revealed through his foray into what turns out to be the unnatural setting of parish ministry, much like the runner who discovers his genuine gifts only after applying the disingenuous restrictions of the sack. In a similar manner, Bass's sense of authenticity or wholeness follows from his prolonged duplicity. It begins from the moment he dons "the suit" and stands before the bedroom mirror. He again experiences transformation, but this time the result is far more confusing. He "found himself," Alcorn writes, "so transformed as to be a stranger, another self." " 'Father Taggart,' he [says] tentatively, one self speaking to the other, a kind of introduction." For Bass, Alcorn explains, the suit has become a "kind of presence."[15]

Sebastian Taggart experiences that presence as something "other" than himself, and as such he develops a "preternatural sense that he was quite literally watching another, strange, distinct self emerging."[16] The process, he readily admits, "raised questions about his essential identity. Who am I," he asks at one point, "that I should be doing this?" The question is especially

vexing because Bass considers himself "a thoroughly lapsed Catholic, a passive agnostic who scarcely thought consciously about the existence of God,
not to mention the whole elaborate system of Catholic belief." He is challenged by this presence: it comes to him from without and seems to be
beyond his control as it encourages him to become "something other than
what I am."[17]

In this situation, *Vestments* dramatizes the encounter between "self" and
the "other," a topic and theme that is central to a good deal of postmodern
thinking. But the context for this encounter is specifically the Catholic understanding of sacrament and sacramentality, the same context that lends
theological significance to Joe Hackett's paradigm. Because Catholic sacraments always are mediated by physical reality, the one entity that links self
and other in this encounter becomes extremely important: namely, Sebastian Taggart's body. Although he may experience it as "other" during this
encounter, that body is, as he discovers about life generally, "both alien and
intimate."[18]

This is a condition familiar to Catholic anthropology at least since
Thomas Aquinas. On the one hand, Thomas points out, we act, and "an
acting thing as such is actual."[19] On the other hand, we are beings with
potential; "in bodies," writes Thomas, "there is always potentiality."[20] We
live, as it were, between these two poles, a fact demonstrated best by the
very process that Thomas himself valued so deeply, that of "understanding."
The human soul, he writes, "has an imperfect understanding; both because
it does not understand everything and because, in those things which it does
understand, it passes from potentiality to act."[21] This condition, Thomas
explains, helps to distinguish us from God. In his famous argument from
causation for the existence of God, he maintains that humans have this "potential of division" while God, by contrast, "contains not potentiality but is
sheer actuality."[22] For this reason (among others), Thomas concludes,
"God, therefore, cannot be a body."[23]

God may not have flesh as we do but, as the corpulent Thomas well
knew, God cannot escape the problems associated with our bodies, especially the divisions they "contain." Although that fact helps to expand the
distance between ourselves and the ultimate "other," God, it also indicates
an important basis for interaction between the two. According to the philosopher Paul Ricouer, we too often mistakenly conceive of the self as a
single entity. Ricouer argues that in fact we exhibit a "polysemy of selfhood." According to this argument, human selves are much more open to
and receptive of "the other" than this fundamental distinction suggests.[24] To

see the self as plural is actually to help reveal "the work of otherness at the heart of selfhood."[25] Ricouer illustrates the rudiments of this interaction both philosophically and metaphorically, proposing to "root" being in "a ground at once actual and in potentiality."[26] "The main virtue of such a dialectic," he explains, "is that it keeps the self from occupying the place of foundation" and returns us to a balanced understanding of the self as neither "exalted" nor "humiliated."[27]

What Ricouer (and Aquinas before him) seeks to promote through philosophical and theological discourse, Alcorn dramatizes in his narrative. In *Vestments*, Sebastian's own body becomes the ground of a selfhood that is both act and potency. When Sebastian puts on the priestly suit, looks in the mirror, and addresses himself as "Father Taggart," he acknowledges the very distinction Aquinas (and, even before him, Aristotle) insisted upon. In that scene, Sebastian's physical self appears to be double: the Sebastian who is "actually" present before the mirror addresses his counterpart, the one who is "potentially" present within that same glass. Slowly, Alcorn's novel unfolds as an extended study of the interaction between these two identities. Exposed by a sacramental reality that begins its work long before Sebastian decides to accept Holy Orders, the quality of "otherness" attached to this potential self gradually transforms life and becomes, in effect, the "substance" of his actual existence.

The key to the successful transformation, however, is the same thing that prevents it from occurring in a manner entirely consistent with the categories of either Aristotelian or Scholastic logic. The potential priest within Sebastian's sense of identity can only become his actual self by "convincing," as it were, his body, and the body complicates the transition in ways that are both extremely difficult and wonderfully creative. Alcorn's narrative alludes to the connection the first time the idea of priesthood is mentioned to Bass. "'A priest?' It was like sex being mentioned in delicate company," he muses. As references to priesthood and the body continue throughout the novel, Sebastian admits, for instance, that he dresses like a priest because it "makes me feel good," and although part of that feeling involves a vague sense that he becomes "a benign force in the world," another part includes the fact that priesthood promises to satisfy very physical urges. Sex may be on Sebastian's mind a great deal, but the novel makes it clear that, in the end, it leaves him unfulfilled. In bed with Clara, Bass finds that "lately he had begun to slip at the critical moment." Unable to maintain an erection, he suffers from a nagging doubt that there must be more to his life than all of the material details that surround his passionate moments: a "beautiful woman, a tasteful room, good liquor, pleasant music, the setting sun."[28]

But the potential presence of the priesthood in his life does not simply offer an alternative to his physical desires; it changes his bodily response to those desires. For example, when he makes a trip into Boston's red light district dressed as "Father" Taggart, he attracts the attentions of a young prostitute who offers him, among others pleasures, "the best butt fuck in town." Bass clearly wants her; "his mind," Alcorn writes, is nothing less than "a monkey house of sex, his blood aflame." But in the end he is forced to admit to himself that, since beginning his masquerade, an encounter like this one has become "more than ordinary temptation." Now "it was," Bass says, "as if he really were a priest with a vow of celibacy to keep." The profound sense of "otherness" he experienced in the early stages of his charade has become part of his identity; his potential self has impinged upon the realm of actual, lived experience.[29]

Bass walks away from the young prostitute and jokes to himself that, "in the future," he would have to be more careful "as to where he conducted his ministry." Given what is happening to him, the "joke" is more ironic than funny. When the spurned girl shouts after him, "Faggot!" we are instantly aware of how the "No" he speaks "through his teeth" comes from an identity that is both consistent with the person Bass is at that moment and very different from the person he has been in the past. It is the voice of "otherness" within the self, and its medium is Sebastian's body. The act of putting on priestly garb begins to lead toward an intangible but nevertheless objective call toward a vocation. As Alcorn's story will point out, eventually Bass "no longer needed to commit the sacrilege of dressing like a priest to have an aura of priestliness come over him."[30] In the end, to assume that identity will not require that Bass live "disguised from his true self."[31]

The struggle to reach that end, however, is intense, for the more Bass sees the priesthood in his "reflection," the more aware he becomes of difficulties associated with all bodies, not just his own. For example, there is the old man who stares through a restaurant window at Bass while he eats his breakfast, finally pushing through the door and to the table. Though Bass continues reading his paper, he smells the "feculent stench" that comes off the old man "in solid wafts," and when he finally looks up he is surprised to find not "the begging eyes of a wino" but a "steady" gaze that will not be averted. The reader understands that the stench of the body has lead Sebastian to look into eyes that belong both to the old man and to Bass himself, and we wonder if the experience indicates a more sacred appeal. But as we approach the climax of Alcorn's novel, the answer appears to be "no." By that point in the story, Sebastian's aunt has died and he has inherited his money—a much smaller sum than he had expected. He has moved into an apartment by himself in an effort to discern if indeed he does have a "call" to the priesthood, but the ensuing loneliness only leads him deeper into the alcoholism that has bedeviled him from the outset of the book. He volunteers at a homeless shelter, but succeeds in having himself thrown out when he arrives one day drunk and almost starts a fire in the kitchen. Every "feeble attempt to prop up some worthier version of himself before his own eyes" fails, and by the time we reach the final chapters his bitter, self-effacing laughter leaves Sebastian "talking to himself, one of the living dead."[33]

Faced with the irrepressible and maddening otherness of his very self, Sebastian struggles to keep what is left of his body alive. He admits that he feels "as though he were already dead" and, to a great extent, he is. Which is to say that he simply is not who he was when the novel began. Frightened by the change, the only recourse that remains is to dispose of his own body, to shed that which has betrayed him so thoroughly. With suicide on his mind, he plans to break into the grounds of a nearby factory, climb an enormous smokestack, and pitch headlong into "a dark and private death." In this way, he believes, "He would disappear."[34] Drunk one night, he begins his journey by climbing the factory fence. When he cuts himself severely on the barbed wire, he stumbles back to his apartment to obtain a pair of cutters and to fortify himself with whiskey.

Alcorn writes that Sebastian returns and accomplishes his task. Still drunk, he ventures up and down a few rungs of the smokestack ladder before he decides finally to make the climb. As he approaches the top of the chimney where "the rungs were loose and the bricks rotten," the city "beneath him . . . spreads in dazzling splendor." He need only act upon his intentions, which, we believe, he does. "He let go and fell in a bright shock, falling and turning in a voiceless scream to death, feeling himself at the last second hit the ground face first with a sickening thud."[35]

When Sebastian awakens on the floor next to his couch with a bloody nose, we realize that the death has been a hoax. He has dreamed the fall and tumbled no further than the distance from the cushions to the floor. From a narrative perspective, the surprise is problematic; Alcorn's decision to mislead readers by turning the apparent suicide into a dream simply is not convincing. Thematically, however, the decision is consistent with ideas he has introduced and maintained within the story. Sebastian in fact does "die," only to find himself "reborn" in the very manner that Christianity conveys when it structures life from baptism to the resurrection. Alcorn has prepared readers for this moment through his persistent attention to Sebastian's body as a site of interaction between a self that is fully present and another whose potentiality is transformative and even dangerous. In one sense, *Vestments* narrates the victory of potency over act; thus the novel leaves Sebastian with a heightened awareness that "life suddenly seemed to brim with possibilities."[36]

But to interpret the character of Sebastian as nothing more than the passive recipient of influences from outside himself would be wrong. The changes he experiences begin from the outside when he dons the suit and all that it signifies. But that is only the beginning. Sebastian also acts upon himself. The difference is that, over time, he stops acting for himself. When he wakes up beside the couch, heart pumping and convinced he must be dead, what begins to unfold within him is love, "not of self," Alcorn insists, "but of being." Sebastian recognizes the source of his feeling to be the otherness that has come upon him and transformed him both from without and within: "the redemptive power of God's love as personified by Christ." As he staggers to his feet, his hand bandaged from the barbed wire like the priest's at ordination, he discovers a new context for his fall, one that Joe Hackett would describe simply as part and parcel of the sack race he now finds himself running.

The ambiguity associated with the source and meaning of dreams like Sebastian's has long made them ideal literary symbols. Most often, that ambiguity involves uncertainties about whether the dream is a manifestation of inner turmoil or whether it has somehow been "sent" from without; whether, in other words, it truly constitutes a communication from the other to the self. For all its faults, the conclusion of *Vestments* wisely retains this sense of ambiguity. Sebastian, Alcorn writes, "confounded dream with memory and memory with dream" as he pondered the sensations of his imaginary suicide with the physical reality of his mangled hand. In the end, Alcorn's strong suggestion that the dream indeed was a product of the "other" verifies for Sebastian that its source is "a God he did not have to imagine to know he existed." That conviction enables Bass to name the "feeling of peace and purpose" he experiences as "grace."[37]

When Alcorn decides at the climax of his story to identify grace with an objective reality so powerful that it not only changes Sebastian's emotional state but also bloodies his body, he links *Vestments* to the central preoccupations of Catholic literature since Vatican II. That identification alone, however, does not result in the only connection, for at this critical moment

Sebastian confounds not only his dream of suicide with the memory of climbing the fence and his experience of falling off the couch, he also joins his prayer "to a God he could not imagine" with the physical realities associated with the institutional Church. The climax of *Vestments* takes place between two sacraments, both of which are distinguished for Sebastian by their physical properties. The first is the Mass he attended the day before his dream takes place, an experience he remembers as being distinguished for the sensual "pleasure" it provided: "the incense drifting back, the priests in procession, the music." The second is the Sacrament of Reconciliation he intends to receive that very morning when he travels to church. He "would find a priest," he insists, "to hear his confession and give him communion." To that bodily representative of God and the Church, Sebastian would unburden himself: "Bless me Father, for I have sinned, and sinned, and sinned."[38] One could claim that the victory of otherness over selfhood for Sebastian occurs at the intersection of these two sacraments, a conjunction represented by "the cross he had hung between the windows," a crucifix supporting the body of Christ that Sebastian looks upon as his own rebirth and resurrection takes place. This is the body he witnesses when, "in that instant, he believed."[39]

The Last Report on the Miracles at Little No Horse

The correlation of an abstract sense of otherness with the tangible realities of an institutional Church—from clothing to crucifix—is a persistent feature of the third novel considered here, Louise Erdrich's *The Last Report on the Miracles at Little No Horse.*[40] Interestingly, it is another dream that introduces the comparison. When Erdrich's central character, a priest on a North Dakota Indian reservation called Little No Horse, dreams, worlds appear that clearly come from beyond the dreamer. All indications are that the dreams and the characters who populate them are sent to Father Damien Modeste, and the best evidence of this "objective" reality is the fact that others are able to participate in the realities they bring. This is how the priest's housekeeper, Mary Kashpaw, is able to follow the priest into a "series of dreams" that open up after the gloom of a deep psychological depression. The dreams are "tunnels of brilliance snaking into the low hill, then out, then further back—through unknown swamps," and Mary Kashpaw follows them until she is able "to guide [Father Damien] back."[41] Like the earlier vision of a devil who comes to the feverish priest in the form of a dog and actually sets its foot into a bowl of soup on the priest's dinner table, this and other manifestations of psychological and physical trauma in the novel cannot be limited exclusively to the inner realms of Erdrich's characters. The experiences are broader, and they leave their marks on the larger world outside the self (the uneaten soup, for instance, is poured back into a pot and served again, giving all of the nuns on the reservation who eat it terrible nightmares).

In Chapter 11, approximately halfway through the novel, Father Damien emerges with Mary Kashpaw from these dream travels and immediately begins another journey, this one through the woods that stand thick across most of the reservation. The motivation for this excursion is similar to the intended purpose of Sebastian Taggart's trip to the smokestack: Father Damien intends to commit suicide. But just as Sebastian's intentions change as he becomes aware of the sacramental context that embraces his life at this moment—the memory of the Mass from the previous day and the anticipation of Reconciliation—Father Damien's proposed reason for the trek changes when the priest enters a section of the narrative within Chapter 11, a portion of the novel entitled "The Sacrament."

Although the pattern of suicidal depression and sacramental redemption is similar for both characters, there is an important difference in how the two are rescued. Sebastian's decision to continue his life coincides with his capitulation to the recognized sacramental rites of the Church. In this way, Alcorn is able to dramatize how an expression of otherness from the institutional Church can influence and transform the life of his character. *Vestments* is both clear and consistent on this point: the "other" comes to the self sacramentally, which in this case means from the outside in a manner as tangible and obvious as a chasuble, a hand-wrapping, or a suit of clothes.

Father Damien's experience is analogous but different, and that difference is illustrated by the sacramental encounter that awaits the priest in the woods. When Damien's friend Nanapush coaxes the "satchel full of strychnine" from the cleric's hand, the priest lies down in the grass and falls into a "sudden and childlike sleep." Upon awaking, Nanapush announces: "We put up a sweat lodge for you." In this small enclosure, with its fire and darkness and sweet smoke, Father Damien's troubled soul finds rest. "This is our church," Nanapush says, and although Damien admits that, "according to Church doctrine, it was wrong for a priest to undertake God's worship in so alien a place," the ability to "feel suddenly at peace" proves too strong to deny. In the ritual of the sweat lodge, Damien discovers a set of symbolic elements that are so strikingly similar to the elements of the Catholic sacramental tradition that the priest is compelled to treat them with the reverence they command. At this moment in the process of recovery, Damien is confronted with the same sacramental elements that Sebastian Taggart recalled. Sebastian's mind had drifted back to the incense of the Mass, its priestly procession and music; here in the sweat lodge, Father Damien sits within the sacred smoke, witnesses the circle of participants, and listens to both their words and songs.[42]

The difference between Sebastian's experience and Father Damien's, therefore, is not that one involves Catholic sacraments and the other does not. The difference is that one culminates in a recognition of the power of sacraments and the other involves an interpretation of actions according to Catholic theology, specifically, the principle of sacramentality. This distinction calls attention to a distinguishing feature of Erdrich's novel. *Vestments* had dramatized the pull of the other upon and within the self, a power that resulted in that otherness asserting its dominion over the life of Sebastian Taggart. *The Last Report on the Miracles at Little No Horse* depicts a different phenomenon. In this novel, the lines of influence are neither direct nor clear; otherness must be interpreted to discover its meanings. Unlike the Catholicism of Alcorn's tale, which establishes itself like a paradigm "again and again, still faint, but persistent" over the world he represents, the dominant faith tradition in Erdrich's narrative is the product of encounter.[43] The world of *The Last Report* becomes Catholic; it is not necessarily given that way.

Yet, like both *Vestments* and *Wheat That Springeth Green*, *The Last Report* initiates this encounter with a specific reference to putting on a "garment." This story, which spans more than eighty years, begins in 1912 in eastern North Dakota when a massive flood by the unpredictable Red River wipes out all homes and businesses for miles. During the aftermath of the deluge, Erdrich's protagonist comes across a body hanging lifeless in a tree. It is familiar—the body of a priest who had introduced himself two days earlier as Father Damien Modeste, a missionary on his way to the Ojibwe reservation, Little No Horse. Now drowned and lifeless—like so much of the surrounding landscape—Father Modeste's body is draped across a branch, its wool cassock clinging to its flesh. Erdrich's protagonist, homeless and exhausted from a long, dangerous struggle with the river, slumps at the base of the tree and prays for "a sign—what to do?" The answer suddenly seems clear, and after being worked from its branch with a hooked stick, the body of Father Modeste is buried along with the clothes of Erdrich's protagonist. Munching a bit a cheese and a crust of wet bread, Erdrich's character begins the long walk north "into the land of the Ojibwe" wearing the priest's damp garment.[44]

Among the items that Erdrich's protagonist buries with the body of Father Damien Modeste are long strands of freshly cut hair. The body that changes place with the dead priest belongs to Agnes DeWitt, widow of a common-law marriage to a local farmer named Berndt Vogel. It is Agnes who meets the priest days before when he stops at her farm to offer her communion. She accepts. A former novitiate who spent time in a nearby convent under the name of Sister Cecelia, Agnes left the order and wandered the local countryside until she came upon Berndt Vogel's farm. The two never married, but instead lived together as husband and wife for two years. During that time Berndt worked the land and Agnes, an accomplished pianist, gave music lessons on the massive grand piano they had installed in their otherwise small home. The relationship ends when Berndt is murdered by a bank robber named Arnold Anderson, dubbed "the actor" because his thefts involve dressing in costumes and staging elaborate hold-ups for both himself and his accomplices. When he shoots Berndt, he has just robbed the local bank and taken Agnes hostage. Throughout this particular assault on the local bank, he had masqueraded as a priest.

The emotional devastation of Berndt's death has a counterpart in the physical destruction of the flood that follows. As a result of that catastrophe, Agnes loses her home, land, and, most tragically, her piano, which is swept deep under the raging waters with her clinging to it all the while. When she emerges from the current, she collapses on shore and awakes sometime later in a strange "bed, covered with a quilt and sheepskin," the air "heavy and warm with the smell of cooking venison." She does not recognize the cabin or the man who serves her soup in bed. They exchange no words as Agnes eats greedily. She then lies down beside him listening to his deep breathing, this "very tired man who smelled of resin from the wood he'd chopped, of metal from the tools he'd used, of hay, of sweat, of great and nameless things that she'd known as in a dream," what she had learned to call for two years "her husband's arms." Waking the next morning, she discovers that she is alone. Moreover, she is lying not in a "settler's cabin" but on the ground in a "long abandoned hovel," with swallows nesting above her head and "no sign of the man, no bowl, no track, no spoon, no sheepskin blanket."[45]

The initial suggestion is that Agnes has been "rescued," either imaginatively or literally, by the spirit of her deceased partner and lover, Berndt. She even refers to the figure as her spouse. But Agnes and Berndt never were married, and a closer look at the context for her reference indicates that the presence she experienced was more than human. To describe it, Agnes turns to the words she "remembers" from "every Mass, every confession I made." The source of her description is liturgical, coming specifically from that moment of consecration in the Catholic Mass when the priest lifts the body and blood and intones: "Through You, in You, with You." Agnes repeats those words now, insisting that only such "beautiful words" could do justice to the "sheer kindness" of the man who rescued and fed her.[46]

This experience of rescue dramatizes the presence of an otherness that is decidedly "real." By saving Agnes, this "other" not only preserves her life but also validates the direction it will take, namely, toward a remarkable union with the body of Father Damien Modeste. Agnes wanders only a short distance from the abandoned hovel before she finds the dead priest and changes both clothes and identities with him. Her decision extends the encounter she has had with the stranger in the cabin and it offers her a reason for the rescue. Donning the clerical garb and presenting herself as a priest becomes the natural outcome of a meeting with someone whose profound care and pungent odor remind her of the tangible presence of Christ, the carpenter.

That association continues as an exhausted and nervous Agnes arrives at Little No Horse as Father Damien. The season is difficult. Buried deep in snow and cold, the reservation seems lifeless and its people are starving. The nuns who live there have killed their only horse for meat, an act that allows them to survive the winter. Upon arriving, Agnes, as Father Damien, eats her/his first breakfast—coffee, stale bread, and a thimble full of raisins—only to realize suddenly that the food constitutes the last morsels in the entire convent. With a troubled conscience, the priest steps outside and trudges to a small chapel.

In that chapel, the new Father Damien says his first Mass as a priest. The congregation includes the band of starving sisters who live on the reservation plus one "parishioner," Pauline Puyat, a young woman whose own story develops into an important subplot within the novel. When Agnes enters the chapel for this first Mass, Pauline immediately sees through her disguise and fights back cackles of laughter. The other nuns merely sit frostbitten and broken, "death . . . poking through their very skins," and wait for this new "priest" to begin the service.[47]

"Let us pray," Agnes says as she kisses the altar. With "fourteen holy wafers and a thread of wine," she begins the Mass and carries the attention of the sisters, who are "slumped against the wood of the pews," up to the consecration.

"Quam oblationem, tu Deus, in omnibus quaesumus, benedictam . . ."
Father Damien intones. He crossed his breast five times, within those words,
and the next: "Qui pridie quam pateretur, accepit panem in sanctas ac vener-
abiles manus suas. . . ." And lifted his eyes and said the words "Hoc est enim
corpus meum," and the bread was flesh.

Lowering the ciborium, Father Damien continues: "'Hic est enim calyx
sanguinis mei novi et aeterni testamenti mysterium fedei. . . .' The wine was
blood."[48]

At this point Agnes brings the bread to her lips and is shocked to find
that what she tastes is "Real and rich. Heavy and good." While hunger roars
inside her, with every bite she discovers that the "consecrated Host" has
"turned into a thick mouthful of raw, tender, bloody, sweet-tasting meat."
She is shocked, and as she feeds the sisters and Pauline, she wonders if they
too taste what she does. "Had Christ's real presence entered them all?" she
asks. Or "was this something that happened, always, to priests?" Swallowing
the food, she discovers that her hunger is satisfied, and she queries again:
was it "just part of the ritual, or was it miraculous?"[49]

The answer to the last question, of course, is "both," and Agnes spends
the rest of her life as Father Damien learning how to live with a Catholic
sense of "sacramentality" that will lead her to this answer. Part of the challenge involves the irony of the situation: as Father Damien's physical self
starves, he is rejuvenated by food intended for his soul, the consecrated host.
But Erdrich's readers must understand that the irony of this Mass Father
Damien celebrates turns into a paradox: he is full afterward not because he
has been fed spiritually but because he has eaten meat. As a sacrament, the
Mass Father Damien says does not direct him to the intangible realm of
spiritual existence and well-being. Instead, by its mystery, it addresses an
immediate physical need, his hunger.

The mystery, however, requires interpretation even to be understood as
mystery. "I am reeling," Damien writes, "I have such questions." Like the
experience of God's presence in the figure from the cabin, an experience
Agnes comes to understand in terms of the Catholic Eucharist, the otherness
of this miraculous event must be interpreted as well. To begin the process,
Agnes (now Damien) searches for a way to interpret what has happened to
her. The inquiry leads her to write what will be the first of hundreds of
letters addressed to the institutional leaders of the Church, those Popes who
will reign throughout Damien's long priestly career: Pius X, Benedict XV,
Pius XI, Pius XII, John XXIII, Paul VI, John Paul I, and John Paul II. Like

so many of the letters that will follow, this first one tries to come to terms with the ways divinity becomes present within a physical reality. "Did the wafer turn into visible meat," Damien asks, "the wine into actual blood?" Not only is the question posed to the "Leader of the Faith," it presumes that the answer will come from within the complex nature of Catholic sacramentality.[50]

The Church, however, does not answer. No Pope responds to Damien's letters until after the priest has died. In a different way, though, Catholicism does reply, showing Damien a world that is so charged with God's presence that it is wholly sacaramental. Sebastian Taggart experienced something similar when he awoke from his suicidal dream and found that a "newfound elation encompassed the artifacts of a life forsaken—the books, the music, his journal."[51] Father Damien's experience upon exiting the sacramental setting of the sweat lodge is even more pronounced. The priest, Erdrich writes, grew to love in new ways "not only the people but the very thing-ness of the world." The range of images Erdrich chooses to demonstrate this love is wide, from the "squat little black stove" in Damien's room to his memory of the equally stocky old lady who fed him carrots and fresh warm bread as a child—the "crisp juice of carrots" and "the buttery interior whiteness of the bread," broken open in childhood hunger as "the bread of life." After the sacramental experience in the sweat lodge, Father Damien looks upon all these things with eyes that lead him to see in them nothing less than the "vast comfort of God."[52]

But, for Damien, to see is to interpret. "Life is crazy," he asserts. A fellow priest who is visiting Damien on the reservation, Father Jude Miller, responds to this statement with his own claim that "Our job is to make it less so." The response comes from the visiting priest's confident world-view and his certainty that "Black is black and white is white." As he says: "There are no gray areas in my philosophy." Father Damien claims that he sees things differently. "The mixture is gray," he says, and so when the craziness of life confronts him, he concludes simply: "Our job is to understand it."[53]

What happens, however, when the eyes that look upon the world for God's presence belong to a particular body? As Father Damien, Agnes De-Witt is constantly interpreting who she is now and who she is likely to become. Given that process, Erdrich's point is not that Agnes is more open-minded than Father Miller because "he" is a woman. Her point is that Agnes' decision to accept God's apparent "call" has made the process of interpretation paramount for her life. Moreover, Erdrich wants to point out that it should be no different for men who hear and heed a similar call. If

Catholic sacraments confer the grace they signify, then the men who receive Holy Orders are altered in ways that at least parallel Agnes' transformation. The difference seems to be that Agnes cannot escape what others simply take for granted. This situation implies that the acceptance of the sacrament from the outside "like a garment" entails an ongoing response to the mysterious sense of otherness that bestows the robe or, to continue our initial metaphor, bags the feet in a sack. Catholic sacramentality, epitomized in this novel by the example of Holy Orders, simply is not self-evident.

To explore the complicated relationship between sacramentality and the body more thoroughly, Erdrich introduces a sub-plot into her tale. Pauline Puyat is the unwanted offspring of a mother by the same name and a nineteenth-century Polish aristocrat who visited the "wilds of Canada . . . one dry northern summer."[54] The father returns to Poland, and mother and daughter remain behind, showing no love to one another. When the senior Pauline dies, the younger makes her way to Little No Horse and the convent that stands upon reservation land. Her bizarre behavior becomes attributed to her deep spirituality, and when she demonstrates a flair for fundraising, the nuns accept her into their community as Sister Leopolda.

If we find that Agnes' transformation into Father Damien describes a process that begins with her decision to drape the damp cassock across her shoulders, we could expect that Pauline's change into Sister Leopolda should also start with her adoption of the veil and habit. But there are two important differences between these examples. In the first place, Agnes' decision to put on the cassock is validated by a source of authority in the narrative that transcends her point of view yet remains intimate with her. When Agnes comes upon the dead body of Father Damien and prays for a sign, Erdrich indicates that it comes to her, but from within: Agnes, we are told, "already knew" what to do. The decision to pull the priest's body from the tree and change both clothes and identities with him therefore belongs to Agnes, but when she sets out on her journey to Little No Horse something outside her appears to confirm her decision by showing her the way. "The clear sky revealed its map," Erdrich writes, "star after star, until the world was again marked out for her."[55]

This kind of exchange between self and other distinguishes several events in Agnes' life. She has a vision of Christ in Mary Kashpaw's face as the two struggle through the snow to help others on the reservation who are dying of Spanish influenza during a raging epidemic. She prays for God to stop her menstrual flow so she can continue her ministry in disguise, and with that prayer she dries up. In a fit of "unbearable thirst," she drinks "deeply" of holy water and finds herself able to play her piano with fingers so limber that, "for an hour, two hours, almost three of her waning life" she lives "fully and intimately in a state of communion."[56] And in the final scene of the novel, as she lay dying of a stroke, she reaches her arms upward where they are met by a "work-toughened hand," the same hand that fed her soup years ago after the Red River flood. Now, in her last moments, its coarse skin extends out and, "with a yank," pulls her across the void that separates this world from the next.[57]

In all of these events we discover an ongoing interaction between Agnes and the presence of a God who is mediated to her by the tangible realities of this world, especially her own body. The interaction repeatedly suggests to Agnes that, as Father Damien, she "was part of something larger" and that "the design," moreover, is "uncanny." There are parallels to this interaction in the events of Pauline Puyat's life, but her role in the "design" is limited by her strong personal desires and her ferocious sense of self-interest. In Pauline's life, there is little room for the "other." She seems to will herself into the convent (she is allowed to join only after she proves adept at raising money for the sisters), and the fact of her self-induced "call" is symbolized by the clothes she wears.

Because *The Last Report* invites readers to pay particular attention to the role of clothing, it becomes significant that Pauline, as Sister Leopolda, "dressed in her own homemade habit" and not in one provided by the order.[58] To emphasize the qualitative difference between her vocation and Agnes', the novel frequently depicts Pauline's relationship to her garments in ways that are directly opposed to descriptions of the relationship Agnes maintains with her dress. As Father Damien, for example, Agnes continues to equate God's presence with the act of covering her body. Her first meeting with Nanapush, her closest friend and spiritual confidant, comes after she has "wrapped her blistered and frost-burned feet in several layers of the nun's dish towels for protection." Each time she says Mass, she dons vestments that are "like a shield, like armor" against "the devil." In death, the stillness of her body becomes equated directly with God's creation—"the immobility of the earth" itself—and thus is it protected by Mary Kashpaw, who wraps the old bones that are "like flower stalks" and the "skull fragile as a blown egg" in a blanket that serves as a shroud. To it she lashes stones before sinking the bundle into the deep water on the reservation, an act that guards the secret of the old priest's gender for eternity at the bottom of the lake.

Such examples stand in sharp contrast to Pauline's repeated efforts to shed her garments. When the nun begins to experience strange markings on her hands and weird contortions in her body, she is found "naked" in the church, "prostrate before the altar, covered with muck and raving." When she fasts, denying food to her inner self, she also refuses to wear anything upon her flesh. "She would not accept a single comfort, kicked off anything but one thin sheet," Erdrich writes, and slept "on the bare floor."[59] Unable to bear any covering on her own body, she attempts to strip the cassock from Father Damien with the "cold clutch" of her hands. At one point her claw-like fingers rake the air around Damien "reaching for her bound breasts" in an effort to expose Damien's "true" identity and change the priest's relationship to a sacramental God.

This particular contrast between Pauline and Agnes—between Sister Leopolda and Father Damien—leads to a second, more significant point of departure between the two characters. The process of transformation that causes Agnes to assert convincingly at one point "I am a priest," actually helps to promote and sustain her life. Agnes is reborn—"drowned in spirit but revived"—and through her rebirth she maintains the sacramental life originally given to her namesake, Father Damien Modeste.[60] Her journey into the forest to meet Nanapush for the first time results in her ability to help both the Indian and his adopted daughter obtain their first meal in weeks. The vestments she wears like armor at Mass link her not only to the miracle of transubstantiation she experiences when the bread turns to heavy meat in her mouth but also to one of her greatest accomplishments on the reservation, the building of a new church. And the garment of stones that sinks her body to the bottom of the lake both preserves the secret of her identity and permits her visitor, Father Jude Miller, to proceed with "a new project" he has adopted by the end of the novel: "the proposed blessedness and possible sainthood" of the old priest.

In contrast to all of these examples, Pauline's transformation into Sister Leopolda is filled with images of death. Hidden inside her homemade habit, she staggers about the reservation, "arms piled with buffalo skulls."[61] Her naked prostration before the altar and her subsequent fast is motivated by the fact that she has committed nothing less than murder, killing a fellow member of the reservation, Napoleon Morrissey, during one of his many sexual encounters with her. That encounter produces a child, whom she at first abandons and later abuses viciously. Even her effort to disrobe Father Damien stems from a desire to blackmail the priest; she believes that, if he fears being revealed, he will resist divulging what he knows of Pauline's crime.

The contrast between Agnes' life-giving transformation and Pauline's destructive change, and the relationship of both to the symbolic function of clothing in the novel, is drawn most decisively in the murder of Napoleon Morrissey. The crime, of course, is a sin that Father Damien could never commit. But Erdrich calls our attention not only to the outcome of this wickedness but also to the way it is enacted. Pauline strangles Napoleon with a rosary made of barbed wire while he is in the act of performing oral sex upon her. As his face rubs against her thighs, she loops the rosary around his neck and tightens her grip. The barbs sink into Napoleon's throat and cause thrashing so intense that, as Pauline confesses to Damien, "I went dizzy with the effort of holding him."[62] Found days later "in a child's play spot" in the woods, Napoleon's body lies sprawled in "poor nakedness" among tufts of goldenrod and beds of blue asters.[63]

Pauline's rosary was the last garment Napoleon wore. Placed over his head like the opening of a chasuble and wrapped tight like the swaths of cloth around the priest's hands, the rosary nevertheless is the gruesome counterpart of those symbolic elements bestowed upon priestly candidates during ordination. If Holy Orders offers candidates the ability to serve *in persona Christi Capitas*, Napoleon's fate leaves him in a state that is the antithesis: he is almost decapitated. But that difference produces only one of the many ironies associated with the murder. Pauline's actions after the crime become notorious, and in a manner that is completely unanticipated, her exploits work to promote in many a notion that she is blessed, perhaps even holy. When Father Jude Miller eventually arrives at the reservation years after the nun's death, he comes to investigate a collection of tales associated with the life of Sister Leopolda, who by 1996 has received much notoriety, including a book written about her by "a lay Catholic, a professor of sorts."[64] By interviewing Father Damien, Father Miller seeks to verify the "miracles" at Little No Horse associated with the dead nun, specifically with her body. As he explains to Damien, there are reports of cures associated with coming into contact with Leopolda's remains. To support his claims, he produces two letters, one from a farmer who was cured of piles and another from a doctor who witnessed the restoration of diseased membranes around a young girl's heart.

But as Father Miller emphasizes, these reported "healings" take their miraculous quality from the larger context of Leopolda's life, which begins to assume a "holy" quality shortly after Napoleon's murder. He notes that the nun exhibited marks on her hands that could be evidence of stigmata and that her body began to contort in strange ways, becoming inexplicably rigid and even folding up into "a kind of permanent V shape." At the time, these events suggested to many on the reservation that the young postulate "was lifting herself into the air, straining toward the sky world, arrowing her spirit toward the west."[65] People came in great numbers to the convent to pray outside on the grass and to petition the ailing nun for her help. Now—years later—Father Miller suspects that others may still be willing to make the pilgrimage.

As the novel points out, however, shortly after Napoleon's death Pauline's features alter in horrible ways. Her face becomes "ratlike, her teeth stood out, her nose was a severe bone centered like a keel."[66] Significantly, after the murder she is unable to open her mouth, and eventually a tube must be inserted to pass water and broth. No one recognizes it at the time, but years later Father Damien realizes that what the young nun was experiencing in the throes of her agony was the onset of tetanus, "lockjaw," the result of piercing her own flesh with the barbs on the murderous rosary. This of course explains the supposed "stigmata," as well as the fact that her vital signs show normal while her joints are bent and frozen.

The cures attributed to her scant physical remains speak more to the way the nun died than they do to the manner in which she lived. At the moment of death, her body is nearly obliterated. She is presumed to have been struck by lightening, and it is her ashes that people claim demonstrate curative powers. Some are blown into a nearby flowerbed, for example, where bees are supposed to have carried them back to their hive to produce a miraculous form of honey. But the conditions of her death would seem to associate any legitimate healing power with the simple fact that Leopolda is gone from the world of the reservation. Her burnt remains appear to form the shape of a cross, and believers interpret that sign as a mark validating Pauline's holy life. The evidence suggests, however, that the sign points to a more important miracle: God's decision to rid Little No Horse of this self-righteous imposter.

Despite Erdrich's willingness to craft her story around what one of her characters calls Agnes' "sacrilege," *The Last Report* nevertheless affirms the crucial role of the Church as a sacrament capable of mediating God's presence.[67] In the end, Father Miller repudiates Sister Leopolda and refuses to recommend that the inquiry into her possible beatification continue. Instead, he proposes that Father Damien, not Pauline, should be the object of such an inquiry. This decision signals an important shift in his understanding of holiness or "sainthood," and it is consistent with what Agnes herself discovers as she lives through the long process of transformation into Father Damien. As Agnes learns by the end of her long life, the wonders of stigmata and of miraculous cures pale in comparison to "daily habit." Of Leopolda, the old priest now asks Father Miller: "Did she lead an exemplary existence? Was she fair, was she honest? Did she give up her foodstuffs, her blankets, her comforts to the poor? Did she have any bad habits, tipple unblessed communion wine? Smoke?" The last question produces for Father Damien a particular sense of irony, for, as he muses, "if only she had smoked!" Leopolda might have found an outlet to soften her bizarre actions, a simpler sin to capture her need for forgiveness.[68]

Those who live with the trials that accompany daily habits do not run their lives as a race; at best, perhaps, they hop from problem to problem. In this condition, their lives seem to bind them or, to put it another way, to weigh them down. This realization is one of the last insights Agnes acquires as she prepares to die. It comes to her in the shape of a memory, triggered specifically by her body and the headache that "spiked her temples." "The pain probed open a door," writes Erdrich, and from the frame emerges one last memory of the robbery that took Berndt Vogel's life. In this memory, Agnes is gazing at the barrel of the gun that the bank robber, Arnold Anderson, boldly brandishes with the intent of killing her. She recalls telling "the Actor" of "an old belief of her mother's people that the soul of a murderer's victim passes into the killer at the moment of death." In this split second of tremendous tension, she asks her captor pointedly, "Are you prepared to bear the weight of my soul?" The question arrives "before the gun went off," and its impact so unnerves the shooter that the bullet goes wide of its mark. The question leaves Agnes with her soul, and the flood that follows gives her the weight of Father Damien's spirit to put on as well. As she prepares for her own death years later, she notes: "I've never realized the weight of myself until now." And when she tries to "lurch to her feet" she feels that weight in "the stifled warm report of a blood vessel bursting just above her left ear." Agnes' body "sank to earth" and she experiences the heat of a "leaping fire on her face" as she reaches up.[69] These two movements—down and then upward—constitute the last motions Agnes will experience. They mark the final progress of her own sack race, the last "hop," if you will, before Mary Kashpaw arrives to bury her corpse in the "feminine depth" of the dark reservation waters.[70]

Conclusion

When Agnes works the body of Father Damien Modeste free from the tree branch it hangs upon, Erdrich tells us that it falls to the ground "like a sand-filled sack."[71] As Father Joe Hackett might point out, it is this sack that Agnes dons to run her race. It is heavy, restrictive and, in many ways, a real burden. But as Powers' title would suggest to Agnes, it also is an essential means of producing "wheat that springeth green." In another novel written six years before Powers' book, Graham Greene employs a remarkably similar metaphor. *Monsignor Quixote* is a retelling of the classic Cervantes tale, complete with a protagonist who is the supposed descendant of the Hildalgo and a companion named Sancho. Like Joe Hackett, Sebastian Taggart, and Agnes DeWitt, Greene's characters also are on a journey that begins with the Monsignor's need for clothing, specifically the purple socks and *perchera* that comprise what Sancho jokingly calls the "uniform" of a monsignor.[72]

The journey they take becomes a race, one that the Monsignor appears to lose when his car (named, of course, Rosinante) crashes outside a monastery. But the loss is only apparent, for the gains he and Sancho can claim from their trip outweigh even the specter of death. One of those gains made along their route involves the Monsignor's first view of two people making love. It comes when he and Sancho attend a pornographic film entitled *A Maiden's Prayer*. The experience leaves a deep mark on Quixote, who realizes that his priestly ministry has been diminished, not just by his celibacy but also by his lack of any sexual desire for another. His response, however, is not just sorrow and frustration but also humor, which, in Greene's talented hands, becomes the more lasting impression. The Monsignor, Greene writes, is taken by the "lot of exercise they were all taking" in the film. "The actors," he comments to Sancho afterward, "must be quite exhausted." In his own life, he reflects, "he had seen a great deal of hopping," but "he had not experienced this lively love."[73]

Perhaps Powers had Greene's tale in mind as he struggled to complete his long-awaited narrative; for, in the end, the two offer similar messages. Joe Hackett's analysis of the priesthood as a "sack race" seems to owe a debt to one of the final images Quixote conjures for his friend Sancho: "By this hopping," the Monsignor tells his traveling companion, "you can recognize love."[74] For Powers, Alcorn, and Erdrich, the purpose of a race as clumsy as the priesthood can be only that: love. Father Joe realizes it when he leaves his wealthy parish for the poverty of another that is named, appropriately, "Holy Cross." Bass Taggart knows it when he ends his long struggle for genuine identity by placing flowers on his aunt's tombstone. Agnes DeWitt knows it when she writes a note asking the one who finds her body to bury it anonymously. In these selfless acts, life not only finds its appropriate endings, it also discovers hope for fresh beginnings. As the hymn reminds us, "Love is come again, like wheat that springeth green."

5.   *The Body in Doubt: Catholic Literature,*
      Theology, and Sexual Abuse

On 20 June 2005, about fifty people gathered at the diocesan headquarters of the Catholic Church in America's heartland, Davenport, Iowa, to dedicate a monument to victims of clergy sexual abuse. During the ceremony they surrounded the "Millstone Marker," a large, rough-hewn millstone suspended on a hastily made wooden frame, and listened to Bishop William E. Franklin. Today visitors can find the monument in a garden on the grounds, sitting atop a polished granite slab that contains three inscriptions. The first two come from the Gospel of Matthew and the third is provided by the Archdiocese; it praises the resilience of abuse survivors and expresses a "commitment to their healing."

The diocesan inscription refers to the monument as a "symbol," and in his remarks Bishop Franklin wisely noted that, like all symbols, this one has multiple meanings. After all, as he pointed out, millstones can be used for good or ill; their value in the ancient practice of grinding wheat is well known, but the danger they pose to someone whose flesh is somehow struck with the weight of one is equally certain. The Bishop went on to draw an analogy between the stone and the priestly vocation: the stone is like the abusive priest who follows a vocation intended for good only to find himself inflicting pain.

His message drew support from Jesus' words in both Gospel passages etched upon the monument. The first passage from Matthew 18:6 calls each listener to account when Jesus says: "Whoever causes one of these little ones who believe in me to sin, it would be better for him to have a great millstone hung around his neck and to be drowned in the depths of the sea." The second offers comfort to individuals: "Come to me, all who labor and are burdened, and I will give you rest" (Mt. 11:28).

But good symbols are notoriously complex and seldom limited to one interpretation. As Paul Ricoeur notes, symbols "give rise to thought," and although certain interpretations are more effective than others, it is rare that one thought exhausts all symbolic meanings.[1] Considered in the light of the two Gospel passages the diocese chose to include with the stone, the symbolic quality of the Millstone Monument becomes far more complicated. Jesus' words challenge a much wider audience.

In the passage from which the monument takes its title and design, Jesus speaks not only to individuals but also to groups of people. As with so many statements by Jesus, the occasion for this remark is a discussion about that most remarkable of social phenomena, the kingdom of heaven. Matthew's Jesus gives harsh instructions to the bodies of those who experience sin yet seek to enter the kingdom: "If your hand or foot causes you to sin, cut it off and throw it away" (18:8). But he also refuses to associate sin with only individual actions: "Woe to the world because of the things that cause sin!" (18:7) The "millstone" passage occurs during one of Jesus' visits to Capernaum, a city where extensive forms of communal living must have prompted citizens to see individual actions as inextricably bound up with social arrangements. As if to emphasize further the close relationship of individual action to social context, Matthew embeds the millstone passage within a longer reflection on social interactions: the arrival in Capernaum begins with an exchange about taxes, ends with the parable of the ungrateful servant, and includes Jesus' much-quoted insistence that "where two or three are gathered together in my name, there am I in the midst of them" (18:20).

The Church in Chapter 18 is mentioned specifically as an arbiter of disputes, and it would seem to be the one social entity free of the call to sever limbs or put out eyes to avoid sin. But the symbolic status of the Davenport monument suggests that even the Church is not without challenges from Jesus. Seven chapters earlier, Matthew is even more emphatic about the possible social contexts of sin, including frameworks provided by institutional religion. Again, Jesus is in Capernaum and, again, children are the focus of his praise, for God is "revealed . . . to the childlike." But what is revealed to children is simultaneously "hidden . . . from the wise," and in Jesus' words there is no mistaking that the perceived seat of wisdom rests specifically with Jewish leadership. It is a "generation" of Jews who have read "all the prophets and the law" who should have recognized the Baptist but did not (Mt. 11:13). It is the Pharisees that Jesus must correct shortly after he leaves Capernaum when they criticize him and the disciples for picking grain on the Sabbath. It is the rules of the synagogue that Jesus violates early in Matthew 12 when he heals the man with the withered hand. It is the hierarchy he challenges when he recalls the tradition itself and points out that even David and his companions violated institutional rules when they entered the Temple and ate the bread offering that "only the priests could lawfully eat" (Mt. 12:4).

Certainly the term "priest" did not mean the same thing to first-century Jews that it means to twenty-first-century Roman Catholics; but neither does the term "sexual abuse." Again, it is the symbolic nature of the Davenport monument that invites the comparison. Even Bishop Franklin notes the connection. According to Matthew, Jesus resists giving listeners the opportunity to lay responsibility for sin at the feet of either the individual or the social group; they share responsibility. For that reason, the millstone is related not only to the individual vocation, which can be used for good or ill, but also to the institution that provides the context and legitimacy for the vocation. Clergy sexual abuse, the Davenport monument tells its viewers, pulls not only the body of the individual clergy into sin, it threatens to drown the Church itself—the body of Christ—"in the depths of the sea" (Mt. 18:6).[2]

Beyond Reasonable Doubt: The Body in/on Trial

In a cycle of poems that explores the consequences of clergy sexual abuse, Robert Cooperman tries to dramatize how the actions of individual abusers and victims occur within institutional frameworks. The controlling metaphor for the twenty-eight poems Cooperman has gathered for his collection is the experience of abuse as "trial." The title of his collection, *The Trial of Mary McCormick*, introduces both that metaphor and the main character of his work.[3]

When we meet Mary McCormick, she is a sixteen-year-old member of an unnamed Catholic parish presided over by three priests, Fathers Matthews, Kriek, and Connolly. She is the object of intense desire by all three men, a virgin (we discover after her first encounter with Father Kriek) whose appeal lies in the fact that she is no longer a girl but not yet a woman. Kriek describes her this way when he sees her "breasts strain / against her green sweater / like buds trying to break into bloom, / rising to the bee in a fury of completion." Before the cycle of poems is finished, Mary McCormick will have been sexually abused repeatedly by all three priests. She also will have given birth to a child who belongs to one of them and, finally, made wealthy by a court settlement. Throughout her ordeal she will have touched the lives and prompted the voices of no fewer than twenty other characters in the poems.

This nexus of lives and voices is the strength of Cooperman's work. The structure he creates reminds readers that the horror and scandal of such abuse cannot be contained within the heart and soul of either the victim or the criminal. In this case, the only victim we know of is Mary, and the criminals are three, Matthews, Kriek, and Connolly. But in addition to their voices, we have Mary's drunken father, her boyfriend, two additional priests who chastise her in the confessional, the local bishop, a newspaper reporter, parish housekeeper, and a parishioner. There also are several poems that give voice to people associated specifically with Mary's court appearances: the lawyers and judge, a prospective juror, even the court stenographer. Mary's charge of abuse is the occasion for all of these figures to speak, and their words comprise the content of separate poems in Cooperman's collection.

What binds all of the diverse voices and poems together, however, is the tightly focused notion that Mary's experience is, both publicly and privately, "a trial." If she is not the defendant in the actual court appearances, she is placed on the defensive and made to wear the symbolic millstone by many who reflect upon her situation: from the ignorance of the housekeeper, Mrs. Lynch, who blames Mary for "mooning / after the fathers like a kitten / wanting milk," to Mary's (ex) boyfriend Tommy O'Brien, who can see her as nothing but a "bitch, putting out for priests," to the reporter for the local paper, Simon Leftridge, who will "try" Mary in the media as someone "sixteen/not ten or twelve" who "waited" too long to report her abuse. Their attitude toward Mary is summed up by the planned strategy of the defense attorney for Matthews, Kriek, and Connolly:

> I'll get the polygraph dismissed,
> inadmissible evidence,
> and imply that she seduced them,
> whispering in the confessional's twilight,
> hopeless love for men approachable,
> austere as the Baptist—
> when three prince charmings appeared
> from the air of her fantasies,
> genies rubbed into being
> by her wet thighs.[4]

In the end, this strategy fails, and the court awards Mary a settlement large enough to leave her wealthy but still profoundly troubled. "I doubt if there's a priest in the world," she thinks,

Who'll hear my confession now.
"You're rich," they'll smile.
"What do you need salvation for?
Just remember, Christ waits to judge."

These lines, which open the final poem of Cooperman's cycle, emphasize the strength and weakness of his central metaphor. Because matters of power and authority dominate all facets of Mary McCormick's experience with the offending priests, the poems he creates need to remind readers how both issues come to define Mary's social existence. In fact, with these lines and those that follow, Cooperman even suggests how power and authority define Mary's relationship to her own identity: she is speaking here to herself when she wonders how the monetary settlement will affect her salvation. This insight is one of Cooperman's genuine accomplishments in his collection. In the image of the "trial," he has found a metaphor that is both pervasive and insidious. As this final poem goes on to show, the abuse Mary suffers has opened a rift within her that she may well negotiate forevermore by judging herself unworthy of goodness and love. Her final fantasy is for a man who will marry her and take her to "the Grand Canyon" and "never think my sin so deep / it could fill that hole in." Her ultimate fear, however, is that she will never be able to accept such love for, in her eyes, the sin not only fills the hole but makes "a mountain of the evil left over."

Cooperman's metaphor is intriguing for the same reasons that the Davenport monument is provocative: it suggests multiple interpretations. Unfortunately, just as Bishop Franklin could see the monument as significant only for the vocations of individual priests, Cooperman's limited abilities as a poet prevent him from developing the metaphor as both a positive and negative force within the poem.[5] For Cooperman, the notion of a trial suggests only success and failure, and with that connotation comes the corresponding voices or personalities: those who are innocent versus those who are guilty. Part of the problem may be his lack of familiarity with the workings of Catholicism and its traditions.[6] The poems ring false in certain areas. We never know the name of the parish Mary belongs to, a point that is both unthinkable for a Catholic and a missed opportunity for Cooperman. Regardless of the parish name, it would be rare that this church or any in the recent past would have the benefit of three clergy.[7] Finally, to send Mary to confession on a regular basis is by no means preposterous, but she would have to be a unique teenager to go that frequently (if at all).

This last point is particularly troubling, because it raises questions about how well Cooperman understands the concept of Catholic sacramentality, especially the kind of "reconciliation" that is intended by the confessional. *The Trial of Mary McCormick* extends its metaphor indiscriminately, equating what happens in the courtroom to what transpires in the confessional (which may or may not be arranged as Cooperman describes, that is, as the traditional "anonymous" black box). In Cooperman's hands, the sacrament becomes an occasion for judgment alone, as in his poem about Mary confessing her abuse to Father McClaughlin, a priest presumably outside her parish, who only "scalds" her with the words "You little bitch" and warns her of God's willingness to

> strike you so dead
> not even ashes will remain
> of your charred, miserable corpse,
> your soul flying straight to Hell
> the second it's snatched by Satan,
> your true father.[8]

In more deft hands, the metaphor of Mary's experience as a trial likely would turn back upon itself, exploring the ironies that arise when the judgment passed in the Sacrament of Reconciliation is compared with both a court of law and with God's decision to sacrifice the ancient Jewish figure called in both Testaments "the Beloved Son." In both cases there is justice involved, and it emerges from the authoritative status of the "law" and its representatives. But, as theologians across centuries have pointed out, the authority of the Kingdom of God and of the Church is love, and although that fact does not necessarily diminish the "trial" metaphor, it certainly complicates its meaning.[9]

Trials arise from a call for justice, but courts settle them only after they eliminate reasonable doubt. Cooperman employs the trial metaphor as a way to emphasize sources of authority for sacred and secular forms of justice. In his interconnected group of poems, a story builds that highlights the conflict between representatives of good and evil. According to *The Trial of Mary McCormick*, the case is solid: there is no doubt Fathers Matthews, Kriek, and Connolly are guilty as charged, and no doubt that Mary is innocent, a victim in the courtroom and wrongly accused by the institutional Church in the confessional. Justice has been served and we are relieved. Artistically and theologically, however, we are not necessarily satisfied. We cannot help feeling that Cooperman missed an opportunity to explore a much more complicated and troubling issue, that he rushed to pen his verdict long before he succeeded in creating interesting characters or conflicts.

Doubt

Satisfaction increases markedly with the next work. In 2005, the Pulitzer Prize for Drama went to *Doubt: A Parable*, which is a relatively short play by New York City playwright John Patrick Shanley, the author of a number of strong scripts, including the screenplay for the popular film *Moonstruck*. Shanley's characters frequently are Catholic, or at least knowledgeable about the tradition because they grew up within its parish structures. There are "John and Mary," two characters in the vignette "The Red Coat" who belong to the parish St. Nicholas of Tolentine. There are Denise Savage and Linda Rotunda from Saint Anthony's in *Savage in Limbo*. There are "Irish Catholics" in *Beggars in the House of Plenty* whose self-identities arise in part from the fact that they come from neighborhoods that aren't "Polish Catholic." In each case Shanley describes these urban, ethnic worlds from the inside, with a thorough sense of their Catholic beliefs and practices. These are places where people "utter Hail Marys and speak about the mystery of virginity"; where forgiveness is equated with the confessional; where you "offer it up" when you come home from work and your feet hurt.

In Shanley's entire corpus of plays, however, none is more Catholic than *Doubt*.[10] Set in 1964, *Doubt* has four characters who appear onstage amid references to many others. On stage are Father Flynn, a "working class" priest from "the Northeast" who is in his late thirties, two nuns from the order Sisters of Charity—Sister Aloysius Beauvier, in her late fifties or early sixties, and the much younger Sister James, who is in her twenties—and the mother of a boy we never meet, known only as Mrs. Muller. The immediate setting is a grade school and junior high at Saint Nicholas Parish in the Bronx, where Sister Aloysius is principal, Sister James a teacher, and Father Flynn the associate pastor.

The cause of "doubt" that gives the play its title involves Sister Aloysius' strong suspicion that Father Flynn is sexually abusing Mrs. Muller's son, Danny, a ninth-grade student probably fourteen or fifteen years old. Her suspicion is complicated by several factors. She has no definite "proof." She has observed strange behavior in the priest toward boys in the school, including one incident where another boy pulls away from the priest when he touches him on the arm. She knows that Flynn has taken Danny into the rectory for "special counseling" and that Danny has returned upset and smelling of alcohol. But the source of Danny's condition is reported to her only by Sister James, whose own youth and inexperience leaves her uncertain of what she has witnessed. Moreover, when Aloysius determines to question the boy's mother, she discovers that the mother thinks her son is gay and that any advances from the priest would be acceptable, since Danny's father responds to him only with beatings. "That's why his father beat him up," Mrs. Muller says. "He beat Donald for being what he is."[11] As if matters could not be any more complicated for a school principal in 1964, Shanley gives us a potential victim who not only might be gay but definitely is African American, the only "negro" in St. Nicholas school. Danny, we discover, has come to the school to escape harassment from peers at the public school. Graduation means that he might finally be able to enter a good high school.

Despite her resolve to protect Danny at all costs, and her firm assertions to the priest that she is certain he has "seduced" the boy, Sister Aloysius is wracked with doubt. Shanley gives her the last line of the play, and it is an emotional confession to Sister James that, "I have doubts! I have such doubts!" The words are powerful for a host of reasons, beginning with the fact that Shanley gives explicit instructions that they are to be uttered "bent with emotion" while Sister James "comforts" her superior. The explicit stage directions remind viewers that the central dilemma of the play belongs not only to Sister Aloysius but to her audience as well. Although incidents of clergy sexual abuse certainly occurred in 1964, when *Doubt* raises the issue it is the series of cases exposed by the *Boston Globe* in 2001–2002 that the audience has in mind. An early twenty-first-century generation of Catholics must come to grips with the "facts" of this case just as Sisters Aloysius and James must, but they must do so in ways that are responsible to life outside the theatre as well as inside the plot.

By deliberately giving viewers information that deepens the circumstantial quality of the case against Father Flynn, Shanley makes certain that his audience confronts the complexity of the challenge. We "see" the priest speaking to a group of boys from the basketball team (he is alone on stage addressing an imaginary team; we never witness reactions from the players). He responds to their laughter when he instructs them to "move your hips" when they prepare to shoot a foul shot. And he chastises them for having dirty fingernails. "I'm talking about cleanliness. See?" He may in fact be insisting upon cleanliness; after all, he goes on to tell a story of a childhood friend who died of meningitis because he couldn't keep his dirty fingers out of his nose and mouth. But the priest's presentation raises questions for the audience, especially when he insists on showing the students his own nails. "Look at my nails," he says. "They're long, I like them a little long, but look at how clean they are. That makes it okay."[12]

Long (clean) fingernails do not make a priest gay, and they certainly don't suggest that he might abuse his relationship with a student. But Shanley makes us wonder. Like Sisters Aloysius and James, we doubt, and the discomfort is deliberate. This is one reason for the subtitle of the play. Ever since Joachim Jeremias' 1947 book on the parables, Jesus' teachings have been examined and appreciated for the challenges they place before their listeners. When the last thing Aloysius says to Father Flynn is "cut your nails," the audience realizes that Shanley has made it possible for everyone—both characters and viewers—to draw conclusions about a man's guilt or innocence based in part on the length of his fingernails. That possibility is, of course, extremely disturbing. Like both of the nuns, we too have to conclude at the climactic moment that what troubles us most is our doubt.

In the preface to his play, Shanley argues that we are living in a period that is defined by doubt and that, by setting his play in 1964, he is able both to contrast that period with our own and to suggest that the changes happening then helped to foster the uncertainty we feel today. "I've set my story in 1964," he writes, "when not just me, but the whole world seemed to be going through some kind of vast puberty. The old ways," he goes on to explain, "were still dominant in behavior, dress, morality, world view, but what had been an organic expression had become a dead mask." The changes were perhaps particularly troubling for someone like Shanley, who was in a Catholic grade school in the Bronx. No Catholic needed to grasp the full significance of the papal decision to call the Second Vatican Council to know that change was coming. The world of Shanley's parish was seamless, a place where classmates, nuns, and priests were bound together by a faith. "It was," he writes, "a shared dream we called Reality. We didn't know it, but we had a deal, a social contract. We would all believe the same thing. We would all believe."[13] That world and the faith upon which it was built would change as puberty gave way to adulthood, and though Shanley admits "I still long for a shared certainty," he acknowledges that he "has been led by the bitter necessities of an interesting life to value that age-old practice of the wise: Doubt."[14]

Interestingly, one of the metaphors Shanley chooses to illustrate the contemporary sensibility is similar to Cooperman's central comparison: "We are living in a courtroom culture," Shanley writes. "We *were* living in a celebrity culture," he notes, but that has changed: "Now we're only interested in celebrities if they're in court." For Shanley, the metaphor helps to explain some of the consequences that arise from a loss of unity and certainty.

"Communication has become a contest of wills" that mirrors the most contested courtroom cases. And "public talking," which long has been an expression of legal training, "has become obnoxious and insincere."[15]

But legal terminology and rhetoric provides only one of the metaphors Shanley uses to explain the role of cultural doubt. The primary metaphor comes instead from positing a difference between two types of human experience, which could be labeled, respectively, as "superficial" and "deep." According to Shanley, certain questions we pose merely identify matters related to the surface of life: "What was your father like? Do you believe in God? Who's your best friend?" Your answers, he holds, comprise "your current topography, seemingly permanent, but deceptively so." Our challenge is to ask and answer different sorts of questions—ones that rest "below" the metaphorical "surface." He begins with literary examples: "What's under a play? What holds it up?" But he continues by pointing out that, once you start to ask these sorts of questions, others follow. "You might as well ask what's under me?" he concludes, and once you do, you begin to discover that both the dramas of this age and the individuals who populate them have second meanings. Under "that face of easy repose, there is another You. And this wordless Being moves just as the instant moves." During this particular "instant" in which we live—that one that reached "puberty" sometime around 1964—the nature of the second Being is defined by one overwhelming attribute: "Doubt."[16]

Unlike Robert Cooperman's rather strict dependence upon the juridical connotations of his central figure of speech, Shanley's treatment of surface and depth, and his use of the concept of "doubt" as the one term that ultimately links the two, is more supple and suggestive. For example, in Shanley's text, doubt is not necessarily a bad thing. After all, as he explains: "It is Doubt (so often experienced initially as weakness) that changes things. When a man feels unsteady, when he falters, when hard-won knowledge evaporates before his eyes, he's on the verge of growth." The fact that the "reconciliation of the outer person and the inner core" may be difficult is not uncommon. "Life happens when the tectonic power of your speechless soul breaks through the dead habits of the mind."[17] What is particularly troubling for contemporary viewers or readers is the possibility that what lies beneath the surface is uncertainty; that, as Shanley says, "There is no last word," only "silence under the chatter of our time."[18]

Sister Aloysius wants more, Sister James thinks she has found it, and Shanley has several reasons for discouraging any easy sense of confidence. In the first place, he maintains, confidence is inconsistent with the age in which we live; it is simply our attempt to defend a way of life that otherwise is "on the verge of exhausting." In the second place, it suggests a level of trust we no longer can afford. "When trust is the order of the day," Shanley points out, "predators are free to plunder."[19] Finally, he discourages this type of confidence because, in the end, it impoverishes the imagination, preventing it from reimagining the body in ways that might restore its honor.

This is the plea that Father Flynn makes to Sister Aloysius in their final scene together. Flynn has been persistent throughout the play in references to the imagination; he uses the word "imagine" five times. In this final scene, it is his own body that he asks the nun to imagine differently. "Please! Are we people? Am I a person flesh and blood like you?" If Flynn has committed a crime (and we don't know that he has), it likely stems in part from his own sense of confidence that the institutional Church supports his body in privileged ways. He makes this clear when he chastises Aloysius for her lack of "obedience," telling her emphatically that "You answer to us!" His first reference may be to his ordained status, but in the eyes of Sister Aloysius (and the audience), the "deeper" reference is clear: he is in charge because he is a man and, as Aloysius asserts when she speaks to Sister James, she is "helpless" in any investigation of Flynn because "The hierarchy of the Church does not permit my going to the bishop."[20]

But Flynn's reminder to Sister Aloysius of their respective gender identities in the penultimate scene of the play is legitimate. We are not, as Flynn declares, "just ideas and convictions," and Aloysius has come perilously close to reducing people around her to those abstractions.[21] She must allow doubt to reenter her thinking, perhaps even to serve as a foundation for her decisions. "Doubt," argues Shanley, "is nothing less than an opportunity to reenter the Present," and it is essential to the Catholic tradition that both Aloysius and Father Flynn recognize that any sense of a "present" include reference to the body.[22] Even if this sense is controlled by metaphors of trials and juries and the guilt or innocence they determine, the body is never absent. It is true that Father Flynn betrays a kind of clericalism that inflates confidence in the superiority of his male flesh, but in his most difficult moment with Sister Aloysius his plea is honest and to the point: "There are things I can't say," he tells her. "Even if you can't imagine the explanation, Sister, remember there are circumstances beyond your knowledge." This failure of imagination, Flynn reminds Aloysius, is a direct result of neglecting the body and the kind of doubt it can engender. "Even if you feel certainty," he tells her, "it is an emotion and not a fact."[23]

It is a remarkable feature of the Vatican II document dedicated to the training of priests, *Optatum Totius*, that it helps the Church account for this kind of doubt. Five times the document refers to the contingencies of time and place that influence both the intellectual and pastoral training of priestly candidates. "In every such program," the document insists, "the general regulations will be adapted to the circumstances of time and place."[24] Such accommodation speaks to a more general awareness by the Council that it was bringing the Church into a new age of pluralism. Certainty was not necessarily the ideal, a point further evidenced by multiple references in the document to priestly training that will "make full use of aids provided by modern psychological and sociological teaching."[25] The aim of the document is to guide the Church as it trains pastors, individuals who dedicate their lives not to doctrinal accuracy but to service. "Due qualification" is a mark of almost every guideline in *Optatum Totius*, for what is important is that the candidate "should form the habit of drawing close to [Christ] as friends in every detail of their lives."[26]

Ironically, this is precisely what Father Flynn has sought to do with Donald Muller. "That child needed a friend!" he exclaims to Sister Aloysius.[27] Clearly he is not mistaken to try to provide one, though Shanley's play insists that, if the priest has exceeded the boundaries of that friendship and perverted it, he is unequivocally wrong. But nowhere in *Doubt* does Shanley suggest that the motive to abuse Donald Muller would necessarily be a direct result of Flynn's possible homosexuality, any more than a criminal act by Sister James could be attributed to her obvious virginity or an evil action by Aloysius to her previous life as a married woman ("My husband died in the war against Adolf Hitler," she explains).[28] That is the point and, for many, the challenge of accepting doubt. As Shanley says in his preface, "Doubt requires more courage than conviction does, because conviction is a resting place and doubt is infinite—it is a passionate exercise."[29]

Optatum Totius alludes to that passion when it speaks of seminarians striving to live in "intimate union" with God. When the document asserts that those interested in the priesthood should "offer a complete surrender of body and soul" and "hold fast to their Lord with that undivided love which is profoundly in harmony with the New Covenant," it asserts that candidates should be formed in all aspects of their lives if they are "to take on the likeness of Christ the priest." Those aspects include "spiritual, moral and intellectual . . . physical and mental" dimensions of their selves.[30] To integrate these aspects into a vision of the priesthood that values "sincerity, a

constant love of justice, fidelity to one's promises, courtesy in deed, mod-
esty and charity in speech" is one of two central messages of *Optatum Totius*.
The other is the related claim that such integration occurs in various and
surprising ways but always, in the end, according to "the Mystery of the
Church."[31]

One of the most recent documents written explicitly "in continuity"
with *Optatum Totius* is the 2005 instruction "Concerning the Criteria for
Discernment of Vocations," by the Congregation for Catholic Education.
That text opens not only with mention of the earlier Vatican II work but
also with a nod to its comprehensive approach to priestly training, acknowledging that, ultimately, "the Holy Spirit configures the candidate to Jesus
Christ." "There are two inseparable elements in every priestly vocation,"
the instruction states, "the free gift of God and the responsible freedom of
man."[32] According to this formula, the mix between the two is both contingent on the individual involved and quite mysterious. The Church would
appear to be the body that negotiates and nurtures this relationship in all its
particularities.

But despite claims of fidelity to the earlier Vatican II text, the Congregation's departure from this model is obvious. What was an open and contingent, historical and cultural context for the conciliar document has been
closed. The "free gift " of God and the "responsible freedom" of the individual have both been put in the service of the Church, which is now prepared to make explicit what the Council had left mysterious and implicit,
to articulate certainty where the Council had left room for doubt. This 2005
criterion for discerning vocations claims to "bring to completion the doctrine of the Council" and it proposes "precise norms" for what God gives
freely.[33]

No place is this instruction more explicit than in the area of the priestly
body, especially its sexual orientation. Here the Congregation for Catholic
Education evinces no doubt whatsoever: "the Church, while profoundly
respecting the persons in question, cannot admit to the seminary or to holy
orders those who practice homosexuality, present deep-seated homosexual
tendencies or support the so-called 'gay culture.'" The restriction is remarkable for its attempt to eliminate any trace of doubt that may be associated with a prospective candidate. Such men can show no outward signs of
homosexual behavior, nor can they possess any such inclinations or desires.
As if to emphasize this remarkable position of certainty, the Congregation
further asserts that its instruction will help the Church address the urgency
of its "current situation," namely, the sexual abuse of minors by members of

the clergy. To borrow one of Shanley's metaphors, it is as if in this document "doubt" has been moved from the depths of human experience and made manageable by locating it closer to the surface. With no sense of doubt about his own position, a bishop, for example, may prevent ordination of a gay man or of any man who heeds the call of "due qualification" in *Optatum Totius* and supports a (so-called) "gay culture." The millstone now becomes a symbol of sacrifice, not punishment.

According to the 2005 instruction, "serious doubt" finds a balance in "moral certainty," which appears to be a product of neither experience nor intellect but of obedience to the hierarchy, specifically to a bishop who holds "personal responsibility" for the formation of a candidate. As many commentators have noted, this recent instruction echoes attitudes of an earlier, pre–Vatican II Church. Shanley makes just that point when he has Father Flynn chastise Sister Aloysius by reminding her: "You have taken vows, obedience being one!"[34] The irony, of course, is that many Catholics—in the world of Shanley's play and in the postconciliar era—are being asked to obey with a "spirit of truth, loyalty, and openness" that the episcopacy itself has failed to demonstrate. In a tradition as vast as Catholicism, obedience has a long history indeed, although it has not always been a successful response to the experience of doubt.

Changing Paradigms

It is one thing to use metaphors of surface and depth to call attention to the bases upon which faith rests and then to argue for the importance of "doubt." It is another to allow this hermeneutic of suspicion to turn into a "faulty foundation" of "free-floating rage." Yet that is precisely what Peter Steinfels, the journalist and observer of contemporary Catholicism, fears has happened during this scandal of sexual abuse.[35] The reaction is understandable. "More than once," Steinfels observes, "in reading accounts of predatory priests and their unavailing superiors, I felt it myself." Yet rage, according to Steinfels, does not allow concerned Catholics "either an understanding of the sex abuse story or an adequate remedy for what it revealed." If the goal is to rebuild the Church, such blind emotion leaves builders with neither the requisite history nor the necessary information to begin the process.

It would be convenient to develop this metaphor with reference to Matthew 7:26 and compare this "faulty foundation" to the proverb about the man who attempted to construct his house on sand. The problem is that the subsequent images are misleading. Steinfels' point is not that rage offers a loose foundation that is apt to dissolve; rather, he insists that the emotional impact of this scandal polarizes the Church around images that are too fixed and rigid to accommodate any serious attempt at reconstruction. The history of this scandal does not begin with exposés by the *Boston Globe* in 2002 but almost a decade earlier, with stories by writers like Steinfels himself in the *New York Times* and *National Catholic Reporter*. By 2002, Steinfels reports, "I was not seeing a new wave of post-1993 sexual abusers. I was seeing the same wave—risen, as it were, from the grave." The distinction is important because, as Steinfels goes on to point out, it helps the Church recognize that its adoption of "new policies" after the revelations of 1993 meant little without a corresponding set of "mechanisms for public oversight." In this case, a better understanding of the history of the scandal between 1993 and 2002 could lead the Church to better information about its successes and failures.[36]

Such understanding cannot occur under conditions that generate only stereotypes. "Not only did the bombshells convince one to believe the worst about the stories that were hard to understand," Steinfels argues, "but most people, even journalists, appear to have made sense of this torrent of reports by taking one or two outstanding examples of predator priests or uncomprehending, even complicit bishops—a Geoghan, a Birmingham, a Law—as the paradigms for all."[37] It is the fixity of these paradigms that inhibit or even preclude the conversations so desperately needed to foster change and promote justice. Steinfels makes clear that, for him, such rigid models are found on both sides. Some Catholics saw the Church in the shadow cast by figures embroiled in the scandal; others, like Honduran Cardinal Oscar Rodrigues Maridiaga, chose a different paradigm, but one no less fixed. For Maridiaga, the Church was innocent, the victim of U.S. media coverage that was as severe in its persecutions of the faith as were Hitler and Stalin.[38]

According to Steinfels, these paradigms merely supported preconceived analyses of the contemporary Church and its problems. Both liberal and conservative Catholics, he argues, "found the sex abuse scandal proof of their preexisting diagnoses of what ails the church, namely, competing ideals about the body, especially the clerical body. For liberals," Steinfels points out, "that meant celibacy, a flawed attitude toward sexuality, the refusal to ordain women, and the lack of a real voice for laypeople in church governance. For the conservatives," he continues, "that meant theological dissent, a breakdown in clerical obedience and sexual discipline, and the toleration of homosexuals in the ranks of the clergy, if not even among the hierarchy. The polarization of leading Catholics," Steinfels concludes, "was blatant."[39]

If the attitudes of the Church toward the body constitute a problem for both liberals and conservatives, one of the lessons Catholicism can learn from contemporary writers and thinkers is that the body is also a source of hope. But this hope springs from complexity and complication, not from the promise of singular, well-defined paradigms. Nowhere is this lesson taught more clearly than in the first encyclical letter by Pope Benedict XVI, *Deus Caritas Est*.[40] To the claim that one concept of the body can account for myriad experiences of vocation—ordained or otherwise—Benedict seems to answer that it is not that simple. His primary point, however, is not that God is more complicated than that but, rather, that human beings are.

As Benedict's title indicates, the source of this complexity is also its purpose or end: love. We express genuine love, the pontiff claims, at the intersection of two experiences, both captured in Greek language by the terms "*eros*" and "*agape*." Interestingly, Benedict begins to make this point by dispelling misconceptions about Christian attitudes toward both experiences that are the product of grand claims and rigid misperceptions. It is Nietzsche, he maintains, who effectively "poisoned" the impression modern thinkers had of the Church and its teachings. Nietzsche, Benedict claims, raised all the wrong questions about the attitude of the Church toward the body. "Doesn't the Church, with all her commandments and prohibitions, turn to bitterness the most precious thing in life?" Nietzsche seemed to ask. "Doesn't she blow the whistle just when the joy which is the Creator's gift offers us a happiness which is itself a certain foretaste of the Divine?"[41]

The Pope's answer to both questions, of course, is "No," and his reasoning depends upon a specific claim, namely, that Christianity never diminished the body but only recognized it for what it is: a combination of impulses and motives that sometimes cooperate, sometimes compete. When we love in ways that restrict our attention to our own needs and desires, we experience the worst that "*eros*" has to offer. By contrast, when we extend ourselves into the world beyond our selfish concerns—and toward "the other"—we begin to grasp what New Testament Greek names "*agape*." Benedict's claim is that we do both; that, as creatures "made up of body and soul," doing both actually defines our humanity. "The challenge of *eros*," the Pope points out, involves reducing the body to "a commodity, a mere thing to be bought and sold." This exclusive emphasis upon the flesh neglects *agape* entirely and thereby diminishes the "authentic grandeur" that is human life. In a similar manner, should a human being "aspire to be pure spirit and to reject the flesh as pertaining to his animal nature alone, then spirit and body would both lose their dignity."[42]

According to Benedict, "Christian faith . . . has always considered man a unity in duality." To describe how such union emerges from difference, the Pope turns to metaphors of movement. *Eros* is described as "ascending love" and *agape* as "descending love," suggesting different but related motions. The first point to note is that both metaphors reverse our usual understandings of these terms. Because *eros* is "worldly love," we tend to imagine it as "descending" into the physical realm. By contrast *agape*, which is "love grounded in and shaped by faith," should ascend to its source, God. Benedict's letter presents us with opposite images, and his use of the two metaphors leads us to reinterpret their relationship.

In *Deus Caritas Est*, unity emerges when Christians recognize the "erotic" qualities of *agape* and the "agapic" nature of *eros*. By definition, *eros*, which leads to ecstasy, takes us out of ourselves in ways that we typically find erotic or sensual. But *eros* can be both secular and sacred, it can pursue the profane, Benedict reminds us, even as it seeks to "rise 'in ecstasy' towards the Divine." Both movements "lead us beyond ourselves" and "involve a real discovery of the other." The ascent of *eros* toward that other can become the descent of *agape* into a world that offers joy not only in sensual development but also in "renunciation, purification and healing."[43] At that point, love "becomes concern and care for the other." "No longer is it self-seeking, a sinking in the intoxication of happiness; instead it seeks the good of the beloved: it becomes renunciation and it is ready, and even willing, for sacrifice."[44]

This remarkable intersection of movements depicts the body as anything but an irreducible paradigm. In part, that surprising flexibility results from the One in whose image we are created. God's love, argues Benedict, is "passionate." The *Logos* may demonstrate a "primordial reason" that fixes philosophical principles but, he insists, it "is at the same time a lover with all the passion of a true love." According to this combination, "*Eros* is thus supremely ennobled, yet at the same time it is so purified as to become one with *agape*."[45] Neither conservative nor liberal, God nevertheless conserves and liberates his creation. And the Church, as the body of the divine, "is an expression of a love that seeks the integral good of man," both *eros* and *agape*. The combination, Benedict says, has long had consequences for the stories Christians tell: for the "evangelization" of such love "through Word and Sacrament," he notes, constitutes "an undertaking that is often *heroic* in the way it is acted out in history."[46]

Benedict's description of the body experiencing or expressing love challenges the confidence of those who presume to answer with certainty problems in the contemporary Church—even problems as egregious as clergy sexual abuse. If the authority of the Church is love, we find in *Deus Caritas Est* descriptions of a source for authority that is as complicated as the most troubling voices of the Christian tradition. Benedict's willingness to contend with Job when he admits "God has made my heart faint; the Almighty has terrified me" (23:15–16); his acknowledgment of Jesus' cry of dereliction from the cross, "My God, my God, why have you forsaken me?" (Mt.27:46); his reference to Augustine as the one who gives answer to faith's sufferings with the claim "*Si comprehendis, non est Deus*"—"if you understand him, he is not God"—all of these quotes affirm for Catholics what the tradition has long asserted but often forgotten: that "the earthly and heavenly city penetrate one another" and that the interaction constitutes the greatest "mystery of human history."[47]

"Mystery" is not "plan." God's "silence remains incomprehensible," Benedict writes, and therefore the "site" of interaction between the cities of man and of God is also a space for doubt. Benedict concludes his encyclical with reference to the faith Christianity asserts in the face of such uncertainty. "Faith tells us that God has given his Son for our sakes and gives us the victorious certainty that it is really true: God is love!" But faith is effective, the pontiff concludes, because of its power to change us, to "transform our impatience and our doubts." The fruit of such change introduces the one term that seems to motivate contemporary Catholics who have listened to the "silence" described here by Benedict; to the "silence beneath the chatter of our time," as John Patrick Shanley has called it. To the "familiar backdraft of doubt," the poet Mary Karr tries to "prove that hope may not be so foolish."[48] In a world without certain paradigms, faith is a hard remedy for doubt. The persistence of love, however, leaves room for hope.

Sinners Welcome

In a voice as hard and direct as the life she chronicles, Mary Karr tells her story in two volumes of autobiography. The first is a 1995 bestseller entitled *The Liars' Club* that, as she admits, saved her from obscurity as a struggling single mother and poet. The second, published five years later, thoroughly removes any question that the difficult, sad, and often bizarre circumstances of her childhood helped to fashion her into an adolescent with all those same qualities. Despite the stark quality of life described in both volumes, however, there is an abiding sense in this ongoing narrative that Mary Karr is meant for more. In both books, that excess is associated with literary art and is signaled by the quotes that begin each major division of her story. There are passages from the works of writers like Ezra Pound, Cormac McCarthy, Jorge Luis Borges, and Michael Herr. A decade later, in an essay originally written for *Poetry* magazine and then reprinted as an afterward to her collection of poems entitled *Sinners Welcome*, she would describe her early life this way: "In the Texas oil town where I grew up, I was an unfashionably bookish kid whose brain wattage was sapped by a consuming inner life others just didn't seem to bear the burden of."[49]

For Karr, the poetic "more" that is meant for her arrives as part of an "inner life" requiring religious terminology. "Poets were my first priests," she writes, "and poetry itself my first altar." In that same afterward, which she titled "Facing Altars: Poetry and Prayer," Karr goes on to describe how this nagging inner life eventually led her to prayer, then to organized "religion," and ultimately to the Catholic faith. It was a destination she by no means sought. In some ways, her "unlikely Catholicism" seems to extend her adolescent rebellion into adulthood. Contemporary poetry and religion are not supposed to mix, especially if the religion is Roman Catholicism. To confess such a faith, as Karr did in the pages of *Poetry*, threatened to put her outside the mainstream. In hyperbole meant to remind her readers that she can still be "a gloomy and serotonin-challenged bitch," she claims the confession made her feel as though she was committing "an act of perversion kinkier than any dildo-wielding dominatrix could manage on HBO's *Real Sex Extra*."[50] The guilt was not made any easier by the fact that she was "not victim but volunteer," a convert to Catholicism after a "lifetime of undiluted agnosticism."[51]

What kind of Catholic is Mary Karr? Given that many would dismiss her Catholicism out of hand for its supposed lack of orthodoxy, this is a rather important question. In the broadest and best sense, she is tolerant: "I took the blessing and ate the broken bread" of the newly initiated member, she admits, and "I continue to take the sacraments despite my fervent aversion to certain doctrines." She would not be John Paul II's "favorite Catholic" she admits; "nor he," she continues, "my favorite Pope." To use a current pejorative phrase, she is a self-styled "cafeteria Catholic, if you like." However, as she is quick to add: "Who isn't?"

But in another sense, Mary Karr is deeply committed to what has animated the Catholic tradition ever since it made its way into the "pagan" world. "There is a *body* on the cross in my church," Karr explains. To describe her Catholicism as "incarnational" is perhaps too abstract. For Karr, it matters most that "the very word incarnation derives from the Latin *in carne*: in meat," for the pleasure she takes from her faith is sensual, not just spiritual. "For me," she writes, "joy arrives in the body." In the direct, concise language of the poet, Karr makes concrete the preferred terminology of Benedict XVI; Catholicism satisfies because it is grounded in *eros* as well as *agape*.

Given life prior to her conversion, this admission is both profound and hopeful. According to her autobiography, Karr was sexually abused twice as a child. The first time, she was just seven years old when a boy in his early teens penetrated her in a neighborhood garage. The second time occurred a year later when an adult male babysitter, who was hired to watch Mary because she was too sick to attend school, made her perform oral sex. That scene, which Karr describes with the same dispassion she undoubtedly has forced herself to feel all the years she carried the memory, ends when the man ejaculates into her infected throat.

Although she was not sexually abused by a member of the ordained, Catholic clergy, Mary Karr is a Catholic poet who was raped as a child by figures she understood to be in positions of authority. As literature associated with the scandals and horrors of clergy sexual abuse have sought to establish, this is fundamental to the experience of all victims. In *Our Fathers: The Secret Life of the Catholic Church in an Age of Scandal*, David France details the studies of Michel Dorais and Michael De Bellis.[52] Dorais, a Canadian psychologist, has identified a variety of common symptoms among male victims of abuse. He traces those symptoms, which often manifest themselves in feelings and acts of self-loathing, to a sense of violation made significantly stronger by the discrepancies of power between the abuser and the abused. De Bellis's neurological research is even more troubling. Using MRI brain scans of both male and female victims of childhood rape, De Bellis has discovered physiological differences in both sexes. France summarizes the findings this way: "Most suffered from post-traumatic stress and all showed abnormal brain development, including smaller inter-cranial volumes overall and specific structural anomalies associated with major depression, anger management problems, anxiety, and difficulty managing interpersonal relationships."[53] When adults abuse their authority and violate children, the damage on a variety of levels appears to be permanent. Additional problems arise when the relationship between abuser and abused has a religious dimension, but part of what makes these examples of abuse so troubling is that they are so much like other cases; that, in other words, ordained ministers who rape are no different from other rapists.

Mary Karr was never sexually abused by a priest. She is, rather, a victim of rape who chose to become a Catholic. But she is also a poet who takes her own bodily experiences as one of the principal sources of her writing and who frequently turns to Catholic Christianity as a way of instilling those experiences with meaning. In the Catholic tradition she appears to have found a faith capable of addressing the reality of a body that has known both terrible violence and remarkable joy. A "strong bone in the crypt of flesh," Karr writes openly of her varied and mixed relationships. On the one hand, she will admit that:

> For years I chose the man to suit the instant,
>   from good guy to goat boy,
> dreadlocked to crewcut. Not one could bridal me.
>   In place of lace veil,
> I peered from bandage gauze. And if,
>   in rage, some suitor
> tore that off, the red sun was a scald, and I felt
>   scalped and rocket shot
> onto the nearest flight. So everyone I kissed
>   left hurt.[54]

Yet on the other hand, she also will celebrate those times when "I opened up my shirt to show this man / the flaming heart he lit in me," when

> I was scooped up
> like a lamb and carried to the dim warm.
> I who should have been kneeling
> was knelt to by one whose face
> should be emblazoned on every coin and diadem.[55]

The two examples, both taken from her book *Sinners Welcome*, not only illustrate the ways violence and joy have colored her relationships but also indicate Karr's determination to explain the "hurt" and "heart" with religious allusions and imagery. It is no coincidence that, in the first poem, Karr is both the head-bandaged victim and the one who delivers the Judas kiss.[56] Nor is it by chance that she describes her happiness in terms that are rife with religious connotations—the kneeling lover, the lamb being carried, the flaming heart and blazing diadem—and that these connotations are specifically Catholic in their references. After all, it is Catholicism that is best known for its liturgical "movements," especially kneeling; since the publication of the Book of Hours during the late Middle Ages, Catholics have embraced and popularized the story of Saint Christopher with visual images of either the Christ child or the lamb across the saint's shoulders; they have advocated a devotion to the Sacred Heart and filled worship spaces for centuries with pictures of saints topped with blazing diadems.

In Karr's poetry, of course, such references comprise more than mere allusions to her faith. Together, they explain the violence and joy she has known and suggest a context for understanding her experiences. This context does more than just refer to God, it actually places God at the center of Karr's life and writings, and it attempts to justify God's ways to us and of us toward one another. Complicated by Christian ironies and Catholic forms of expression, the context nevertheless constitutes a theological position in Karr's poetry that should not be dismissed by serious Catholic Christians willing to listen for words and a message amid the "chatter" of our time.

It was in her 1998 book of poems titled *Viper Rum* that Karr first suggested a theological foundation to her writing. In that collection, two poems, "The Grand Miracle" and "Christ's Passion," pointed readers to the most important element of her theology, the body of Christ. Both poems were about the crucifixion, and both explored the torments Jesus suffered. "The Grand Miracle" directed attention to the physical sufferings: to the "long spike . . . centered," the skin torn, the bones "split." "Christ's Passion" drew more explicitly upon the psychological pain; thus Karr wrote of the crucified Christ: "Think of all we don't see in an instant. / Cage that in one skull."

But though Karr's theology begins with echoes of Paul's words to the Church at Corinth, "I resolved to know nothing while I was with you but Jesus Christ and him crucified" (1 Cor. 2:2), it develops rapidly along lines established by her Catholicism. Karr betrays the basic optimism that many have associated with a Catholic theological tradition steeped in experiences of God incarnate. Though the body of Christ "hung heavy, a carcass— / in carne, the Latin poets say, in meat," it nevertheless becomes for Karr the source of expectation and hope. "That some creator might strap on / an animal mask to travel our path between birth / and ignominious death— now that / makes me less lonely," she writes. But it is not just the historical fact of incarnation that amazes Karr; it is the present reality of God in the ritual activity of the Roman Catholic Mass that sustains her and shapes her thinking. It is not only the resurrection of 33 C.E. but "the rising up at the end into glory," specifically "into the white circle of bread on the meat of each tongue that God / might enter us" that takes readers to the center of the poet's understanding. For "2000 years," she writes, "my tribe has lined up at various altars"; so, Karr admits, "I dumbly open this mouth for bread and song."

"Dumbly." That choice of words betrays Karr's faith but also hints at the theology by which she maintains it. Like Sister Aloysius in Shanley's drama, Karr too has "such doubts." But a theology that takes the crucifixion seriously never escapes those doubts, just as Sister Aloysius could not escape them in the midst of her need to act decisively. Why did the crucifixion have to happen? Was it, Karr wonders, a "torment Jesus practically begged for, / or at least did nothing to stop?" Did it hurt less because "He was a god, after all," and "an eternal light swarmed in his rib cage / no less strong than the weaving nebulae?" In the end, was it all a mistake or, worse, a trick? Recall that "History," she points out, "is rife with such hoaxes. (Look at Herodotus.)"

Perhaps one of the reasons to begin a theological reflection with the crucifixion is so that believers never lose sight of their doubt, that they approach the world with the kind of critical realism that calls for inquiry, reflection, and, at times, intense suspicion. As Benedict says in his encyclical, "Our crying out is, as it was for Jesus on the Cross, the deepest and most radical way of affirming our faith in his sovereign power."[57] The greatest Catholic theologian of the twentieth century, Karl Rahner, puts the matter this way:

> We Christians can be bound by a feeling of brotherhood and sisterhood, not to the militant atheists, but quite certainly to those who are agonized by the question of God, those who are silent, reserved, averse to noisy conviction: all of us have called upon the silent incomprehensibility of God with or without the name, both in us and in them the question of the most exact picture of the universe as a whole is not one that answers itself; they and we have experienced something of what we read in the scriptures: "My God, why have you forsaken me?"[58]

For Karr, the body of Christ serves to link her to God and to others. "That's why I pray and poeticize: to be able to see my brothers and sisters despite my own (often petty) agonies, to partake of the majesty that's every sinner's birthright."[59] As Karr's choice of words reminds us, these are not necessarily distinct experiences. Our "birthright" gives us to our creator and to one another, just as the heavenly body of Christ comes quite specifically to our earthly bodies. Moreover, as Karr reminds us, the arrival of Christ's body to one who has made a habit of "swatting" Christ away can be as harsh and blunt as our experiences with our neighbor. When the speaker in her poem "Disgraceland" decides that she has "lurched out to kiss the wrong mouths, / get stewed and sulk around," she finds herself hungry for a different existence. The response she receives, which is a paraphrase of the words spoken at the Roman Mass during the moment of consecration, is striking: "You are loved, someone said. Take that / and eat it."

The mingling of the natural and supernatural that is crucial to a theological term and concept like "body of Christ" is perhaps the most persistent theme in the collection of poems that constitute *Sinners Welcome*. Karr uses the theme in a particular way, however, for the body occupies a unique position in her poetry: it becomes the site where God enacts a cosmic drama. Five poems in the collection *Sinners Welcome* illustrate this point, each one suggesting the interaction by developing the New Testament story within a context Karr (like Benedict XVI) calls "Descending Theology." In the first poem, "Descending Theology: The Nativity," Karr presents Mary's body as the original site of this grand drama. The key to the poem is the connection Karr fashions between Mary's swollen womb and the image of the earth's orb. She holds "in her belly's globe that desert night / the earth's full burden," and the child curled in this "muted womb-world with its glutinous liquid" knows nothing "of its own fire." From this fundamental connection between cosmos and womb, Karr draws Biblical imagery directly upon the flesh of mother and child. In this way, the "star of Bethlehem" shines not only as a sign to travelers but also as "a blade point" upon the flesh of this babe—and those other innocents—who eventually will fall prey to Roman authority. The manger that provides shepherds with their angelic clue about the child's whereabouts also holds real animals, whose "tails sweeping side to side" are the external signs of a struggle played out on Mary's body "between contractions," those times when "her skin flinched / with the thousand animal itches that plague / a standing beast's sleep."[60]

This pattern of theological descent, where the supernatural is clearly inscribed upon the natural body, is repeated in the other poems that share the common title. "Theology Descending: The Garden" connects the parched, "cracked earth" of Gethsemane with the "tear-riven face" of Judas and insists that "This / was our doing, our death."[61] "Theology Descending:

Christ Human" points out that "the human frame" itself "is a crucifix" and that

> Any wanting soul lain
> prostrate on a floor to receive a pouring of sunlight
> might—if still enough,
> feel your cross buried in the flesh.[62]

According to Karr, the cross is deep within us, like bone. It is the new life promised in "Theology Descending: The Resurrection," where the breath that "spilled back into that battered shape" now seeks us. "It's your limbs he longs to flow into," Karr writes, "from the sunflower center in your chest / outward—as warm water / shatters at birth, rivering every way."[63]

For this poet of Christ crucified, however, the most poignant example of the cosmic drama unfolding within the body appears where readers might expect: in a poem titled "Descending Theology: The Crucifixion."

> Once the cross props up and the pole stub
> sinks vertically in an earth hole, perhaps
> at an awkward list, what then can you blame for hurt
>   but your own self's burden?

Resurrection may find its complement in the drama of birth, the warm water of the uterus "rivering every way" both outside and inside the body. But it is the cross and the type of death it demands that illustrate for Karr's readers just how profound this association between cosmic and human drama can be.[64] Victims of crucifixion did not die from the wounds inflicted by their persecutors but by suffocation, the weight of their bodies too much for them to bear. Who can the victim "blame for hurt" but himself and the carcass he must heave with each breath? Karr's description, however, is brilliant in what it evokes: to locate blame is to single out the "own self's burden," and with that phrase the poet taps the rich vein of theological reflection on the nature of that self and its burden: full man and fully God; sinless yet bearing the sin of the world.

But the burden is also (and, for the crucified human, most importantly) a body. That which holds God's breath chokes it from us. "In a breath," Karr writes of Christ, "we can bloom and almost be you."[65] The terrible irony is that this involves such risk; God may require of our bodies what God asked of Jesus. And so, while at times we long for the source of our breath—like Karr, who "thirsted / for your breath to come / easing down my lungs"—at other times we find ourselves in the position of the infant Jesus, who was left in the grain bin:

> Some animal muzzle
> against his swaddling perhaps breathed him warm
> till sleep came pouring the first draught
> of death, the one he'd wake from
>   (as we all do) screaming.

To pull the "other" into our lungs, therefore, is both to find joy and to risk death.

Yet this is what Karr, like Benedict XVI, calls believers to do, for it is the inevitable consequence of linking *eros* and *agape*. Benedict opens *Deus Caritas Est* with a quote from the first letter of John: "God is love, and he who abides in love abides in God, and God abides in him" (4:16).[66] For the Pope, that claim expresses "with remarkable clarity the heart of the Christian faith," and for that reason he goes on to organize his thoughts around it. By his own description, the encyclical examines "the intrinsic link between [God's] love and the reality of human love," a link that Benedict asserts with his closing charge to pray. In prayer, "those who draw close to God do not withdraw from men," writes Benedict, "but rather become truly close to them."[67] Helping humans recognize this fact is essential to the life of the Church, for "the entire activity of the Church," writes the Pope, "is an expression of a love that seeks the integral good of man."[68]

The tragedy of all sexual abuse, but perhaps especially of those who have been abused by a member of the clergy, is the rift that prevents the victim from accepting a link between *eros* and *agape*. Benedict describes the true dilemma when he writes: "Anyone who wishes to give love must also receive love as a gift."[69] The problem is that victims of abuse are unable to accept the gift, a point dramatized when Robert Cooperman leaves Mary McCormick alone with the fissure that now defines her life: a chasm opened yet unfilled. The horror of sexual abuse is that it prevents victims from seeing their bodies as receptacles for the "other"—in sacred or secular manifestation. In this way, it also inhibits the ability to see with the eyes of those who are other; not because victims cannot position themselves to "know . . . about the needs of others" as Benedict says, and thereby "share their situation and their difficulties," but because they cannot accept that anyone would stand in their shoes.[70]

In part, this is a call for Catholic theology to find the words and experiences necessary to revive a sense of inner oneness with God's love. But it is also a call to the Catholic imagination, for the plight of sexual abuse victims depends upon their ability to imagine themselves worthy of God's gift. For many victims, Catholicism can hold no solutions, for it remains one source of the problem, perhaps even the deepest source. But for others, the willingness of Catholic theology to find value in the complex reality of bodily existence is a source of hope and a reason to persevere. For Catholic poetry to give us a Christ child with "sticky eyes smeared blind" and head "lolling" as its "sloppy mouth / found that first fullness" in its mother's breast is a remarkable accomplishment.[71] If only Mary McCormick could hear the words as she stands before the cracked ground of the Grand Canyon. Ultimately, the Catholic poet might be the one who reconciles Mary to her life, helping her see how the earth draws together and heals in the same moment that the young mother lifts a child to her bosom to drink.

6.   The Body "As It Was": On the Occasion of Mel Gibson's The Passion of the Christ

On 22 January 2004, Peggy Noonan, columnist and contributing editor to the *Wall Street Journal*, recounted her efforts to report accurately papal reaction to the year's most popular artistic work about the human body by a Catholic: Mel Gibson's film *The Passion of the Christ*. "My December 17 column," Noonan wrote, "reported that Pope John Paul II had seen Mel Gibson's movie on the crucifixion of Christ, *The Passion*, and had offered a judgment on it: 'It is as it was.'" That quote," Noonan went on to explain, "came from the film's producer, Steve McEveety, who told me that it was given to him by the Pope's longtime private secretary, Archbishop Stanislau Dziwisz."[1]

Although Noonan may have been the first to report papal reaction to Gibson's drama about Jesus' last hours, she was not alone. Both the *National Catholic Reporter* and the Reuters news service published similar stories, independent of one another. In their respective accounts, both *NCR* and Reuters claimed that John Paul II had seen the film, and both referred to sources within the Vatican to confirm the papal pronouncement that the film showed the Passion "as it was" for Jesus. Such verification would prove to be important, because within weeks other Vatican sources would come forward to deny the papal quotation. Vatican spokesperson Joaquin Navarro-Valls, for example, would attempt to clarify the situation by describing Gibson's work in different terms. "The film," he said, "is a cinematographic transposition of the historical event of the Passion of Jesus Christ according to the accounts of the Gospel." As *NCR* correspondent John L. Allen noted shortly after Navarro-Valls' statement: "There's some Vatican-speak here, but the thrust seems clear. Navarro is saying the film depicts what's in the Gospel." That claim, as Allen went on to point out, "was the essence of the 'It is as it was' remark" all along. Thus, even though the terminology changed, the Vatican position did not: according to an institutional hierarchy that reportedly included the Pope, Gibson's film remained historically accurate and true.[2]

This was a greater claim for the movie than Gibson himself dared to make; repeatedly during interviews surrounding its release he referred to the film as the product of his "belief." The rush to *laud* it therefore says much more about the Church that watched it than it does about its director, and in fact the apparent need to see it as a true report about what happened to Jesus is remarkably consonant with the ideological moment in which much of the current Church hierarchy has chosen to live. In this age of "certainty" for members of the Roman Catholic hierarchy, the Church, as Francis Cardinal George of Chicago has pointed out, may be "a mystery of communion because it arises from and is centered in the mystery of God," but there is no mystery surrounding either the source of its authority or how that authority is to be asserted. The "Church's authority," writes the Cardinal, "is not the authority of secular power but the authority of truth emanating from God." In exercising that authority, "Regrettably," he continues, "an ecclesiology of communion is sometimes presented as an alternative to ecclesial hierarchy. No such opposition exists."[3] God's intentions, according to the Cardinal, are clear.

This sense of certainty, which characterizes so much of the new Catholic apologetic, is echoed in other voices from the teaching authority of the Church. For example, Archbishop Raymond Burke of St. Louis has written that Catholics "are obliged to inform our conscience with the knowledge of God's law, both the natural law inscribed in our hearts and the law revealed in God's Word taught with authority by the Church."[4] Once informed by the hierarchy, the Catholic course of action is prescribed. Thus important voices within the United States Conference of Catholic Bishops insisted during the 2004 U.S. Presidential election, for instance, that there is only one way to vote. According to Charles Chaput, Archbishop of Denver, "Real Catholics," must vote exclusively for candidates who support the current position of the Catholic Church on the issue of abortion. To do otherwise, as Chaput said at a breakfast honoring President George W. Bush, would be to engage in a "habit and rhetoric of cowardice."[5]

The source or rationale for this remarkable certainty seems to be twofold. First, it appears to stem from a new understanding of the "universal" quality of the Church. The laudatory rhetoric of Vatican II documents had sought to describe this universal dimension by equating the Church with an ideal: "the entire holy people." "Growth in insight into the realities and words" of the tradition occurred not only through "the episcopate" but also "through the contemplation and study of believers" and the "experience" of those who possess an "intimate sense of spiritual realities."[6] Rhetoric and ideal coalesced in an adage followed by John XXIII: "In necessary matters, unity; on doubtful issues, liberty; but in all things, love."

In the closing decades of the twentieth century, the Church seemed to have changed its description of what it means by the term "universal." The idealism that motivates the epideictic statements by the Council receded into the background to make room for claims that focused more tightly upon the recipients of one sacrament, the ordained clergy, and specifically one set of officeholders, the bishops. Thus, in his Prologue to the 1994 *Catechism of the Catholic Church*, John Paul II insisted that the *Catechism* "testifies to the Church's catholicity" precisely because it "reflects the collegial nature of the Episcopate." By shifting attention to the local bishop, Vatican II had opened the door to a line of argument that would seek to foster unity through the Episcopal office. But in practice, that unity increasingly developed into an exercise in authority. Thus the recent *Catechism* was "addressed to redactors of catechisms, to priests, and to catechists," but the diversity of their witness would remain indirect at best because, as the document asserts, the Episcopate controls the catechetical process. In fact, the *Catechism* declares that no members of its intended audience should feel entirely confident to read and use the document on their own; their access should come "through the bishops."[7]

The second source of confidence within Catholic hierarchy comes from the peculiar way the Church of the late twentieth and early twenty-first centuries has tried to explain its relationship to history. The claim in paragraph 770 of the *Catechism* that "The Church is in history, but at the same time she transcends it" is, of course, not new. Augustine introduced the Church to the possibility of viewing itself both in and out of history by dividing the course of human events into periods with and without Christ. As Peter Brown demonstrates, for Augustine the "power of the demons" showed itself in "centuries of misdirected habit" (primarily sacrifice and all its trappings). That power was broken by Christ, who not only ended certain practices but also altered the temporal framework in which those practices occurred. Put simply, "the past remained a pagan place": "*Antiquitas*, 'antiquity, mother of all evils,' was," Brown reminds us, "the last enemy of all true Christians." The problem with those who entered the Church from that era was that they risked maintaining an association with a "past once ruled by the *dei buggiardi*." They were suspicious, for they "brought with them the shadows of an untranscended, ancient way of life."[8]

But even Augustine cautioned that such division led to restlessness, not certainty. Indeed, as David Tracy reminds us, "Augustine's demand that we face the dialectical bondage of our distorted and disoriented wills" stood as a "destructive force toward ancient pagan self-confidence."[9] In *Gaudium et Spes: The Church in the Modern World*, the authors followed Augustine and refused to allow the Church to rest comfortably in its position as an entity living both within and without the world. Specifically, it rejected the notion that the Church should engage the world exclusively or even primarily from a position of transcendent authority. For that reason, the document states:

> Although the Church has contributed much to the development of culture, experience shows that, for circumstantial reasons, it is sometimes difficult to harmonize culture with Christian teaching. These difficulties do not necessarily harm the life of faith, rather they can stimulate the mind to a deeper and more accurate understanding of the faith. The recent studies and findings of science, history and philosophy raise new questions which affect life and which demand new theological investigations. Furthermore, theologians, within the requirements and methods proper to theology, are invited to seek continually for more suitable ways of communicating doctrine to the men of their times. . . .[10]

Among those cultural activities that can promote a more active and (what the Council goes on to call) "mature" faith are literature and the arts, for these two

> strive to make known the proper nature of man, his problems and his experiences in trying to know and perfect both himself and the world. They have much to do with revealing man's place in history and in the world; with illustrating the miseries and joys, the needs and strengths of man and with foreshadowing a better life for him. Therefore they are able to elevate human life, expressed in multifold forms according to various times and regions.

Far from asserting an ideal of transcendence, *Gaudium et Spes* encouraged the Church to explore its role within the historical reality. Its rationale was simple: when the Church demonstrates a commitment to living "in history," when it "shows itself to be relevant to man's actual conditions of life," its "knowledge of God is better manifested and the preaching of the Gospel becomes clearer to human intelligence."[11]

The Passion of the Christ *and Vatican II*

The rush to declare *The Passion of the Christ* to be history "as it was" appears to challenge the dialogical imperative between faith and culture called for in *Gaudium et Spes.* In various announcements, papal spokesmen seemed to declare that one work of art could accompany the Church out of the exigencies of historical change and into a transcendent realm. Moreover, Gibson's film acquired this privileged position in the early twenty-first century not only because it offered a narrative that was, as Archbishop Chaput extolled, "extraordinarily faithful to the Gospels" but, more specifically, because it was faithful to that portion of the narrative that dealt explicitly with the body.[12]

Vatican II invited an extended theological reflection on the metaphor that named the Church the "Body of Christ." As we saw in Chapter 1, that invitation included a challenge to Catholics to see the Church as a "body" that was both individual and social, a combination that, among other things, grounded the metaphor in the realities of everyday life. The Council suggested that the Church, as a social body, must begin with the fact of pluralism and with all of the complexities that accompany that fact, including the way society negotiates differences. Though such a combination is frustrating, it illustrates one of the most enduring features of religious discourse: namely, tension.[13] St. Paul was a master of this tension, exercising it most succinctly in that sweeping passage from Romans 12:4–5 that Vatican II authors valued so deeply: "For as in one body we have many parts, and all the parts do not have the same function, so we, though many, are one body in Christ and individually parts of one another." The authors of *Lumen Gentium* took very seriously that portion of Paul's pronouncement that others often neglect, namely its final clause, that we are "individually parts of one another." Despite their impulse to panegyric statements, ultimately the conciliar authors were prepared to challenge the Church to conceive of an ideal that not only included all bodies but also called for participation in the lives of "neighbors" who are far from ideal. As Sebastian Taggart asks himself while he ponders the possibility of entering the seminary:

> Could he endure celibacy? Could he say Mass every day? Could he care for people who would bring him all their grubby, insoluable problems, and to whom, if he were a good priest, he would listen? To the gay in the laundry whose lover has AIDS? To the floozy in the Sevens with incipient alcoholism? To the lonely old ladies in the nursing home? To the homeless and neglected? To people like himself?[14]

This sense of the body as a participant in a social reality that has a history is almost entirely lacking in a work like *The Passion of the Christ.* Gibson's

Jesus moves through the world of his day without acknowledging any connection to it. In a film that relies almost exclusively on images of Jesus' body to tell its story, there is virtually no connection between that body and the world that has supported it for approximately thirty years by the time the story opens. Gibson's Jesus simply does not belong to history "as it was."

This is not to say that Gibson's protagonist does not live within a historical context; review after review has called attention to historical details included in *The Passion*. But as Biblical scholar Margaret Mitchell points out, the real context for Gibson's Jesus is not the history that surrounds him but one that is yet to be written, a world that will be, not the one already existing at the time of the tale. Though Gibson's Christ "may have walked around in some hazily distant East," Mitchell says, he "is not 'one of them.'" Rather, "he is the inventor of Western culture," the prophet who not only announces Western hegemony but who, in the same breath, also establishes the otherness of the East, a place forever damned by its rejection of the Western savior.[15]

Mitchell's insightful analysis of the film begins with the explication of a scene where Jesus flashes back to his life as a carpenter. Sweaty from his work, the Nazarene shows his mother his latest creation, a table that, as Mitchell says, "looks like something one might find in the weekend rustics section of a Crate and Barrel catalogue." He explains to his mother that people will sit at it when they eat, and she replies with humor that it will never catch on. Although the scene, as Mitchell rightly says, is a "throwaway" moment in the film, it nevertheless reveals a tremendous amount about the filmmaker's agenda. "The vignette," as Mitchell points out, "is emblematic of the misleading, half-turn orientalism that drives the film." According to her argument, examples of this bias mount quickly and are evident in the most fundamental aspects of the movie, its setting and language. Gibson, as she reminds us, chose to shoot the account of Jesus' passion "as it was" not in Israel but in Italy, at the Cinecitta Studios outside Rome. His much publicized choice of vernacular subtitles is the result of his decision to make his actors speak in languages that would be foreign to most of his audience. Unfortunately, his choices included neither the language of the Gospels nor of the dominant Hellenistic culture; instead, with the help of Father William Fulco, S.J., Gibson's script opted for Aramaic translations of English texts and for Ecclesiastical Latin.[16]

In setting, language and, as many viewers have said, in numerous editorial decisions, *The Passion of the Christ* takes its audience "not to the roots of Christianity in the East, but to its late medieval heritage in Europe."[17] This is the historical world in which Gibson's Jesus lives and moves, a world that contributes to the film both a fascination with Jesus' suffering and an eagerness to blame Jews for it. Like the figure of the savior in a Byzantine work of art, Gibson's Jesus is two-dimensional, painted upon a scene that depicts historical figures who woodenly interact with him. He is the *corpus* that hangs upon the famous San Damiano crucifix, surrounded by images from his biography and bleeding from wounds to his tangible flesh, yet ultimately belonging to another history entirely. With remarkable consistency, *The Passion of the Christ* does not give viewers history "as it was" but, instead, a moment within contemporary Catholic theology.

Theology of the Body

As an artifact of late-twentieth-century Catholicism, *The Passion* is not a history of Jesus' body but a dramatization of a "theology of the body," similar in its message to a collection of occasional works by the most prominent Catholic figure of the period, Pope John Paul II. In his *Theology of the Body: Human Love in the Divine Plan*, which contains a series of pieces originally delivered as weekly addresses between September 1979 and November 1984, the Pope reflects on the proper understanding of the human body in Catholic teaching. Prompted originally by an "assembly of the Synod of Bishops" that took place in the Fall of 1980, these addresses evolved into first one and then three books, which were collected by the Daughters of St. Paul and published together in 1997, along with a fourth set of reflections by the Pope on *Humanae Vitae*.[18]

John Paul's *Theology of the Body* gives Gibson's film its central metaphor: the body as sacrament. "In some way," the Pope writes, "the body enters the definition of being a sacrament, being 'a visible sign of an invisible reality.'" That claim for Catholic sacramentality flows from the long-standing and remarkably hopeful theological assertion that grace abounds in a fallen world. What is striking for both the Pope's theology and Gibson's dramatization of it is the rush to identify that invisible reality with a sacred realm that transcends an otherwise grace-filled world. In this understanding of the Catholic theological tradition, the sacramental status of an entity like the human body depends upon its ability to, in a sense, shed its skin and reveal what the Pope calls a "transcendent truth," a "spiritual, transcendent, divine reality."[19] Although John Paul insists that "the meaning of the body is not just something conceptual," his analyses continue to speak of it in this manner.[20] The "original and fundamental manifestation of mankind" becomes, in the Pope's interpretation, the ability of "Man" (the text resists any language that would acknowledge gender differences) "to express, through self-definition, his own self-knowledge." Human "consciousness," he goes on to say, "reveals man as the one who possesses a cognitive faculty as regards the visible world." We are created primarily to think, and thinking involves making distinctions. Thus the Pope finds in the first story of creation from Genesis 1 not the liturgical document so many scripture scholars have posited but "a solid basis for a metaphysic." And in the second story, specifically in the naming episode of Genesis 2:19–20, he chooses not to recognize any grounds for intimacy between humanity and the creatures Adam names (a common presupposition still for Jewish parents when they set about naming their children); instead, the Pope interprets this passage as "a specific test or examination which man undergoes before God." By "means of this test," John Paul continues, "man becomes aware of his own superiority. . . ."[21]

According to the Pope's *Theology of the Body*, the first Adam is the perfect template for Gibson's version of the second in *The Passion of the Christ*. Both are essentially solitary figures, and their solitude is presented as ideal. The "Yahwist text" of Genesis 2, John Paul insists, "enables us to link man's original solitude with consciousness of the body." The Pope will go on to develop this link throughout his theology, even to the point of describing the physical relationship between Adam and Eve as a "double solitude."[22] This image of the body as separate—both alone and solitary—allows John Paul to apply certain distinctions. Considered in isolation from the rest of creation, the body can be compared first to itself, with certain distinctions implying a corresponding set of evaluations. The Pope prefers metaphors of surface and depth both to distinguish dimensions of the solitary self and to evaluate those dimensions. Important qualities of the self possess "deep roots" and have a "deep significance."[23] The fact that "man is a 'body,'" for instance, belongs "more deeply" to his life than the corresponding fact that "he is also male or female."[24]

But John Paul also extends this principle for making distinctions, and the corresponding method of evaluation, to written texts that take as their topic bodies. In his analysis, meaning belongs to a sphere of "deeper content" and, in the case of scripture, for example, is buried "under the layer of the ancient narrative." Like a disembodied spirit, the "condensation of truths" within a text becomes available once readers are able to remove the troubling presence of writing itself. Because texts are like bodies, his preferred metaphor can apply: "meaning" is deep and "writing," by contrast, is superficial. "We always take man's historicity into account," the Pope insists, but only "because we start from his theological prehistory."[25] The same can be said of textual analysis, which seeks motives for creativity that transcend historical circumstance.

This surprising disregard for the historical, embodied quality of physical reality, and the parallel disregard for the value of narrative in stories, are just two of the issues that separate the ideals of John Paul's *Theology of the Body* from the work of contemporary Catholic authors discussed in preceding chapters. As Catholics, these writers fashion a literature that explores, among other things, the relationships between texts and bodies. As such, they inherit a tradition that stretches back to the community that wrote John's Gospel, a group that, as Karmen MacKendrick points out, gave us in five short verses first the metaphor of the Word incarnate and then the metaphor of the incarnate as light.[26] In both metaphors, MacKendrick argues, the body is key.

> These three, then, are interrelated, infolded, neither distinct nor identical. The Word will be incarnate as flesh; without incarnation, it remains inaudible, spoken to no one. The light becomes flesh, too; without this becoming, it remains invisible, its shining indistinguishable from darkness. Flesh is not simply that which blocks the light but that which makes possible the very fact of illumination, as both medium and object of luminosity.[27]

Novelists and poets from Ron Hansen to Mary Karr hold the body to be valuable precisely because it is a body, not in spite of that fact. Their guide is nothing less than the resurrected body of a man who repeatedly is mistaken (in the narratives people tell) for someone whose flesh is still quite profane: a gardener tending a tomb, a figure on the shore calling instructions to fishermen, a traveler seemingly out of touch on the road to Emmaus. As Hansen says: "A faith-inspired fiction has a fondness for humanity and finds cause for celebration in the beauties of the natural world," including its human bodies.[28] Cardinal Newman was more direct, anticipating the concerns that motivate John Paul's *Theology*. "It is a contradiction in terms," Newman wrote, "to have a sinless Literature of sinful man."

Pearl

Read against the backdrop of John Paul's *Theology of the Body* and Mel Gibson's *The Passion of the Christ,* Mary Gordon's novel *Pearl* offers an interesting response to both texts. Published just one year after the release of

Gibson's film, *Pearl* tells the story of Pearl Meyers, an American student studying in Dublin who has begun a protest that she plans to end with her own death.[29] Refusing food for six weeks, Pearl has chained herself to a flagpole outside the U.S. embassy. She intends her presence on the embassy lawn to bear witness to the death of a young Irish friend named Stephen Donegan, who was killed in the aftermath of a contested Irish peace accord. She also believes her slow suicide will testify to her personal role in that death and to her profound need to atone for her actions.

This is a book about Pearl's body, about what starvation does to the flesh and what that flesh means to others. When we meet Pearl, she is being cared for against her wishes, "lying on the freezing ground" while embassy staff and Irish officials try to keep her warm. They have set up propane lamps around her and every few minutes they cover her with blankets that she quickly kicks off. The reaction to her plight is mixed. Some connected with the Irish and American embassies are concerned about the way her death will reflect on their diplomatic efforts. Others are more blunt: "If she wants to freeze to death on top of everything else," one observer notes, "it's her funeral."[30] Still others read her efforts in the light of past acts. They speak of "Civil disobedience," "Gandhi and Martin Luther King," of "May 1970: Kent State" and of course: "Bobby Sands."[31]

"Reading" Pearl correctly is crucial to understanding what she hopes to accomplish. As she lies upon the hard stone of the embassy walk, she describes the essence of her actions as "making of her life only the essential sentence, the one she can know to be true."[32] It is a metaphor that she returns to later, when she is in the hospital arguing with the attending physician about her goal. "You seemed to think that action, your taking your life, was the only way to communicate what you believed," Dr. Morrisey states. "As if your body were stronger than words."[33] Pearl believes it is stronger than words, but only because words have shaped it, provided contexts for understanding it, and finally transformed it into something it is not. "Don't you see what I was doing?" Pearl asks. "Turning my body into a sentence, a sentence that everyone would have to understand."[34]

The comparison between words and flesh is natural for Pearl, who is a student of language, studying, among other things, Gaelic at Trinity College. She even muses at one point that "on her passport where country of origin is written she should put: *language*."[35] Pearl's interest in language is part of a much broader fascination with the topic maintained by Gordon throughout the novel. The most obvious set of examples comes from the repeated references to other "writings": to emails in the bland Tom Hanks/

Meg Ryan romance *Sleepless in Seattle*; to the text of George Herbert's poem "Prayer"; to the title of the book itself—an allusion to Matthew 13 and the parable Jesus tells about the pearl of great value. But there is also the narrative structure Gordon employs, which includes sections where a narrator speaks directly to readers, introducing himself or herself as a "godfather" of sorts, perhaps a "midwife"—someone who was "present" at Pearl's naming, at "the speaking of the most important word."[36] Occasionally this voice will speak to us with questions and notes. "Do these words help you understand?" it asks readers. "Now I must tell you about a strange episode," it begins. "We will leave Pearl for a little while," it concludes.[37]

The effect of these narrative intrusions makes us self-conscious of our role as readers.[38] As we become more conscious of language in the narrative, so too do the characters. Pearl's mother, Maria, for example, becomes aware that doctors in Dublin are "using language in a way that muffles the truth" about Pearl because they do not wish to cause alarm. Though she is frustrated by the tactic, she understands that the physicians report to her in a "language that is born not of the impulse to tyranny but of the impulse to kindness."[39] Maria's lifelong friend and close companion, Joseph Kasperman, who travels to Dublin to support both Maria and Pearl, "can't get over" a waitress's "colloquial use of . . . words or their cognates."[40] At one point he is struck by Maria's choice of the word "Timbuktu." "No one uses that word anymore, no one even thinks of it," he says. "What happened to Timbuktu, he wonders? Was it only a place in the mind?"[41]

In fact, one of the claims in the novel is that, if something like "Timbuktu" is only a place in the mind, then language has created it. Joseph's simple, offhand musing takes readers to the heart of what Gordon proposes about the remarkable qualities of words: they really do alter reality. Perhaps the notion comes to Maria first when she reads another Herbert poem, "The Collar," and begins to feel its words, with their "chafing" and "restriction," "on her skin."[42] Joseph, who is perhaps the most perceptive character in the novel, realizes it throughout the text. He notes that Maria never uses the name of Pearl's father in conversation for fear it might change their own relationship, which has involved their affections for one another as well as the love they both felt for Joseph's deceased wife. He says of Pearl's actions that they constitute "atonement," and he laments that others have trouble seeing them that way because we generally have lost the word from our vocabulary. "Would anyone have imagined that an impulse so deep," he wonders, "so ancient, would evaporate because it had not been nourished by the proper word?"[43]

Although Joseph acknowledges that the impulse to "atone" has its roots in Judaism, even he understands that it comes to characters in the novel, and to readers, primarily through the interpretive lens of Catholic tradition. Gordon's novel is steeped in Catholicism. There are, of course, the obvious references: to priests ("Father Lynch") and nuns ("Sister Berchmans"), to the Catholic school Maria and Joseph attended as children (Saints Cosmas and Damian), and even to the figure who came to define the Church for a generation, John XXIII. Beyond a collection of names and places, however, Catholicism in *Pearl* constitutes a motive to insight and a principle of interpretation. The tradition provides characters and readers with a "hermeneutic" to make sense of what they experience.

This Catholic hermeneutic is "embodied" in Pearl, but before she is born it is present in the love between Maria and Pearl's father. Unnamed to Joseph, the father is a Cambodian refugee called "Ya-Katy," who meets Maria in 1977 while part of a tour designed to protest Pol Pot and the atrocities practiced by the Khmer Rouge. Although Ya-Katy does not like Catholicism, he nevertheless cannot escape its influence. Educated by Jesuits, he knows when he passes St. Patrick's Cathedral in New York on August fifteenth that it is the Feast of the Assumption. He recites the Song of Solomon to Maria, and during their love-making he laughs and sings "Salve Regina" and "Pange Lingua," a "little obscene" version of "Sing, My Tongue."[44]

Though her father was a convert from Judaism, Maria was raised close to the faith. As she matures and seeks to be free of its influence, Ya-Katy provides her with incentives to dissolve the bond. Yet even when she is with him, she cannot resist the framework Catholicism has established for her life. Ya-Katy, for example, delights in the anticipated child of their love, Pearl, precisely because the baby will be "very impure: Jewish, Russian, Cambodian, Catholic, Buddhist. A real mess." He is "in love with the idea of the mess," he tells Maria, because it provides "our only hope against the tyranny of the pure," a kind of tyranny Pol Pot systematically forces upon Cambodia.[45] By contrast, Maria cannot abandon the ideal of purity. More specifically, she cannot abandon her Catholic understanding of this value. In response to his attack on "the pure," for example, her impulse is "to tell Ya-Katy about her First Communion." When "he speaks of the dangers of purity, against her will the image of herself in her white dress enters her mind." When he talks about the image of "a closed circle, impenetrable, impermeable," with the ability to signify "one thing fully, with no contradictions," she thinks immediately of "the White Circle of the Host and her

First Communion."[46] Catholicism comprises Maria's interpretive paradigm for human experience. It is, as one of her later lovers asserts, "her 'religious default setting.' "[47]

The paradigm has certain features. For instance, it is sacramental, and its sacramentality is dramatized through actions that involve the presence of a human body. In the very important scene where Maria recalls her first Communion, purity and the Eucharist come together in a memory that is focused specifically on her body. They join as she describes what it felt like to experience the tangible reality of the bread on her tongue and in her stomach.

> Inside her body: the Host, an illuminated circle; her ribs incandescent; the bones of the crucified Jesus visible to her through the stretched skin of his torso, ribs like her own incandescent ribs, illuminated by the Host. She was glorified, transfigured, shining like the whitest snow. In her heart, an oval flamed, like the light of a lamp in a dark room, and she knew of course she would be one of the children willing to die in the name of this, this thing that was only one thing, the body of Christ, the thing she too had become: illumined, without blemish, without contradictions.[48]

Maria's description emphasizes the most outstanding claim made by Roman Catholicism about the sacraments it administers: that they operate *ex opere operato*, "by the very fact of the action's being performed."[49] Like the burning torso of Annie Dillard's moth, which becomes the flame it carries, the action of sharing communication does not just signify what the Kingdom of God is like, it actually promotes the presence of the Kingdom in those who receive the physical realities of the bread and wine. Furthermore, the elements of the "meal" also enact this understanding. The bread and wine are more than signifiers of the divine; the sacramental structure of the liturgy causes the elements to change into body and blood. Maria's description of her First Communion, therefore, illustrates a Catholic understanding with both beauty and clarity. The sacrament "illumines" her. Her ribs become the ribs of the one crucified. To carry Karmen MacKendrick's reflections on John 1:1–5 one step further, his light becomes her light. She too is "transfigured."

The Eucharist not only "purifies" Maria, it also empowers her to act upon the convictions that God's grace instills in her as she swallows his body. The scene goes on to relate that, when Maria becomes unexpectedly pregnant with Pearl, she has the child despite the fact that "most of her friends had had at least one" abortion.[50] With an apparent allusion to 1 Peter

3:15, she gives birth to her daughter specifically "in the name of hope."[51] In this scene—with its particular configuration of ideas and events—the primary consequences of Maria's reception of the sacrament are physical because, as the sacramental experience insists, God's grace touches us through the physical world. In fact, grace abounds in tangible realities: bread, wine, water, oil, touch. According to a hermeneutic grounded in Catholic tradition, the physical world reveals—and the Church "dispenses"—the fullness of God's presence, which is both spirit and incarnated body.[52]

Crucial in this process is the role of language, which does far more in the Catholic understanding than simply refer us to reality. Consider, for example, the Roman liturgical experience, the very one that offers Maria her first "Host." "A sacramental celebration," the *Catechism* notes, "takes the form of a dialogue, through actions and words."[53] In the case of the Mass, "At the heart of the Eucharistic celebration are the bread and wine that, by the words of Christ and the invocation of the Holy Spirit, become Christ's body and blood."[54] Anyone attending a Catholic liturgy recognizes that the moment of transubstantiation is signaled primarily through language with the words of consecration spoken by the priest. This is exactly what Maria's memories confirm: that every time the Church celebrates the Mass it demonstrates the power of words to change reality beyond our cognitive faculties, to transform with a sentence bread and wine so that they never lose their physical attributes yet become body and blood. The act is what Maria calls "the potential of language" for "forcing the miraculous."[55]

In Gordon's novel, the body of Pearl dramatizes precisely this fact. Her physician recognizes it when she says she "is interested in this girl whose language is the body and yet not the body." What fascinates Dr. Morrisey is the way Pearl has been transformed by what the doctor later calls "the power of language."[56] She now is something that is fully a body but also more than a body. Clearly Pearl is not experiencing what she earlier called "one of those moments when a cliché becomes lived out in the body."[57] In this case, her situation is much more dire and relevant to those around her. By no means a cliché, Pearl has become, in short, a sacrament.

Such a claim cannot be grasped (let alone appreciated) apart from a Catholic perspective or model of interpretation that makes room for the transformative power of words. Despite its debt to that long tradition, however, the claim remains radically different from those contained in the writings of John Paul II, especially his *Theology of the Body*. Unlike the dramatic role for language that Gordon provides in *Pearl*, for the Pope the purpose of words is strictly representational. In *Theology of the Body*, for example, the source of linguistic authority comes from the second chapter of Genesis, where Adam uses language to "name" a reality that already exists. For John Paul, words are simply the by-product of "one who possesses a cognitive faculty" strong enough to enable him to attach certain verbal signs to objects around him.[58] In the Pope's rendering of the Genesis story, the names that Adam gives to items in the world do not place him in a relationship to those items; rather, they constitute the means by which he "distinguishes himself" and "becomes aware of his own superiority."[59] According to the Pope's understanding, nothing new is created by these encounters; nothing is transformed.

In fact, John Paul argues that the "human body speaks a language which it is not the author of." He goes on to explain this fundamental break between language and body in terms of the marriage covenant: "male and female, husband and wife" grasp the significance of language only after they "reread" it in the light of "the content and principle of their new life in Christ and the Church."[60] One can argue whether this claim by John Paul II constitutes a theological insight or simply a misunderstanding of the way metaphor works; the more general point, however, is that the Pope is unwilling to acknowledge that the human body *as a body* is instrumental in the formation of a system of words that empowers us to name truth, indeed, even to utter a thought.[61]

The Pope perhaps is more direct when he is not constrained by the rigors of theological argument. His own poem "Thought's Resistance to Words," written when he was still Father Karol Wojtyla, makes plain his skepticism about language.

> Sometimes it happens in conversation: we stand
> facing truth and lack the words

The problem in this situation, Wojtyla's poet explains, is that, when we turn to the body for assistance, it fails us.

> we fight with the likeness of all things
> that inwardly constitute man.
> But when we act, can our deeds surrender
> the ultimate truths we presume to ponder?[62]

For the future Pontiff, the answer is no, for as one of the characters in his play *The Jeweler's Shop* puts it:

Body—thought passes through it,
is not satisfied in the body—
and love passes through it.[63]

Given this attitude toward the body, it should be clear why John Paul II praised *The Passion of the Christ* for its historical veracity (or at least why so many at the Vatican assumed he did). The overwhelming violence done to the body of Jesus in Mel Gibson's film, and the director's refusal to show any image of that body resurrected, leads viewers to see the flesh as dispensable, a vessel for what really matters, which is the idea of divinity. Stripped not only of his garments but also of much of his skin, Gibson's Jesus has few remaining ways to communicate his message. The director's decision to rely heavily on what he considered to be the language of the day, a move that could have reasserted the value of the body as a historical reality, serves only to reinforce the distance between the historical period that sustained Jesus' body and the reality of the Godhead. As many scholars have noted, Gibson ignored virtually all archeological evidence in and around Jerusalem to produce a vision of the region where commoners spoke Aramaic, colonizers spoke Latin, and Hebrew was all but dead. The result may be exactly what Gibson intended, but it certainly is not historically accurate. Rather, as Seth Myers points out, what the vocabulary of *The Passion of the Christ* portrays is Gibson's own "visceral religious experience," one that actually "transcends language."[64] The film constitutes, in other words, a cinematic presentation of what John Paul tries to convey in *The Jeweler's Shop*: thought and love passing through the body on their way to someplace else.

This remarkable corollary between Gibson's art and John Paul's theology finds no match in what Mary Gordon dramatizes in *Pearl* about the value of the body. Gordon's understanding of the relationship between words and bodies is different. Certainly all three agree that the Word became flesh and dwelt among us and, conversely, that we can utter words and thereby transform substances into flesh and blood. For John Paul and Gibson, as for Gordon, the body is a sacramental sign of invisible grace. But in the end they interpret this sign differently. For John Paul and for Gibson, the meaning of the sign is grasped principally at the cognitive level, and thus the body begins to appear as a repository of ideas, a container to be spurned once the concepts have been understood. For Gordon, on the contrary, the body itself helps to teach us about the sacramental life. The narrator of *Pearl* gives readers a remarkable example of how the body instructs us in the essential mysteries of the sacramental experience.

> I must tell you something strange, strange yet a scientific fact. The paradox: as a starving person is given nutrition, she becomes aware of hunger, an awareness that was blocked when the starvation progressed to a critical state. Like other starving people, Pearl had not felt hunger; now, fed, she has begun to crave.[65]

Has not "everything we've experienced taught us to believe," the narrator asks, "that nourishment diminishes hunger rather than increasing it?" For those who have experienced the sacraments, the answer must be "no," for if the sacraments effect the grace they represent, then they must lead us back to their source. According to a sacramental logic, each meal makes us hungry for more. The foundations of such a notion are not only intellectual—the product of a metaphysic—they are physical as well. That makes their correlation at best complicated and at worst inconsistent, what Gordon's character Ya-Katy might call (with ironic reference to the visible signs of sacramental meaning) "a real mess."

Conclusion: The Body Plural

The distrust of purity that Ya-Katy holds during the novel involves his opposition to Pol Pot but begins, he insists, with his academic background in science. "I am a scientist," he notes, "and I know that nothing alive is pure. To be pure is to be impervious to change, to mixture. Change and mixture is our lot, our lot as living things."[66] Maria applies his insight to herself as she flies nervously to Dublin.

> She thinks of all the bodies she has had: the little girl's body, the desiring and desirable body, the childbearing body, the body that moved through space, that swam and danced and ran and ran, and now the aging body, feeling the first bites of the inevitable bad news. None of the bodies lost, all contained in the same envelope, reliving their histories, sometimes insistently, sometimes muted for long periods, dormant but not quite asleep.[67]

Aboard the plane, she wonders about "the state of Pearl's body" and thinks of all the ways she has known her daughter, of "all the bodies [Pearl] has been": infant, child, woman, and now starving adult.[68]

What Maria sees in the bodies of herself and her daughter, her friend Joseph recognizes in the long tradition of the Church, what Catholicism calls "the body of Christ." At the same time Maria is flying to Dublin thinking about herself and Pearl, Joseph is leaving his hotel in the Piazza Minerva,

Rome, and passing the Church of Santa Maria Sopra Minerva. The collection of statues in front of the Church, which includes an elephant by Bernini and an ancient Egyptian obelisk dedicated to Isis, constitutes a vivid reminder of just how complex Christian history is.

> Santa Maria Sopra Minerva: the Virgin mother atop the Roman goddess of wisdom and, on top of that, the Egyptian goddess of fertility. A mishmash, a mix-up, no pure statement possible; contradictions stacked one on top of the other, no structure, no hierarchy: just a pile. A pile of history, a pile of understandings. Chockablock.[69]

The commitment of an artist like Mary Gordon to the creative power of Catholic "chockablock" is testimony to her relentless pursuit of what is "classic" about the tradition.[70] Like the other writers in this study—Annie Dillard, Ron Hansen, Alfred Alcorn, Louise Erdrich, J. F. Powers, John Patrick Shanley—she reminds us that Catholic history is too diverse for any one interpretation; that, despite fervent denials by many in the contemporary Church, fundamental claims made by the postmodern age we inhabit are relevant. The moment Church authorities invoke "tradition," their claims begin to deconstruct themselves, for tradition is not a final word. It is, rather, what permits us to negotiate a series of contradictions that never disappear.

John Paul II's successor, Benedict XVI, can look to the Catholic heritage and assert that, during the Roman liturgy, the "elements of the earth are transubstantiated, pulled, so to speak, from their creaturely anchorage."[71] Mel Gibson can resist the image of a God who is both wholly transcendent and fully social. But in doing so they eventually must respond to contrary interpretations and practices from deep within the very body of literature and practice that they scrutinize. If transubstantiation finally pulls the elements of bread and wine away from the historical moment they share with the bodies of those who kneel before them, then what does one make of the earliest Church practice of eating a full meal with those sacramental objects?[72] How does one explain the early paintings of bread and fish that adorn second-century Christian catacombs? What do we make of the practices described by Egeria in *The Peregrination* of fourth-century Christians who celebrated the Passion in Jerusalem not by proclaiming Jesus to be the ultimate idea of God but by inserting themselves bodily into liturgical movements that began at Bethany and ended days later at Golgotha? What does one do with virtually all of Augustine's early writings, or with his startling claim in *De Musica* vi.11.29 that "Delight orders the soul"?

With these questions in mind, we might agree that Gordon's novel fails to dramatize notions of the tradition held by John Paul II, Benedict XVI, and certainly the production staff involved in preparing *The Passion of the Christ*. But we cannot deny that, despite its failure, *Pearl* nevertheless does resonate with chords from within Catholic history and imagination, traditions themselves as old as Ephraim the Syrian's fourth-century poem, also titled "The Pearl." In that work, the poet holds the valuable gem in his hand and sees "in its pureness a great mystery / Even the body of Our Lord which is well refined." This strange mixing of the tangible and the intangible in the objective world before us is met with a corresponding mixture in ourselves. "Prayer and prying from one mouth" come, the poet notes: "From the tongue / The incense of praise riseth / Along with the fume of disputation." We are called, the poet says, to reside within "the mystery of truth," a place where "Searching is mingled with thanksgiving," beauty is "shadowed forth," and an "awl" in the flesh establishes a most potent "reign."[73] Here, it seems, is an intersection of word and body that is trans-substantial, not because it slips its earthly anchor, but because the ground holds it fast, tethering its remarkable otherness to the sand and clay that summon both pearls and people.

Conclusion: The Body Mutinies

In a collection of poems from her book *Decreation*, the Canadian Catholic poet and essayist Anne Carson reflects on time spent with her elderly mother, who suffers from both an aging body and mind. In the course of fourteen pieces that constitute the opening pages of Carson's complex text, the poet's mother appears in various guises: from a woman who worries about running up the bill on long-distance phone calls to one who no longer remembers to pick up the phone at all; from a bedridden lady "gripping a glow-in-the-dark rosary" to a frail body looking for all the world like "bent twigs."[1] The "speaker" in these poems—one assumes it is Carson herself—is unabashed about her feelings for the person who binds these different figures together. Her mother is, quite simply, the "love of my life."[2] Yet we cannot help seeing how each manifestation of Carson's mother differs from the next, a phenomenon that the poet underscores by crafting links across her texts that highlight both the similarities and differences in this otherwise consistent figure.[3]

Ultimately, what binds these images of the poet's mother together is the very aspect of her life that separates them in the first place: the body. When the shared love between mother and daughter—*"that halfmad firebrand"*—is loosed from its tether and left to "race once around the room / whipping everything," what brings it to rest are the bodies that also share a common space, each of them "living moving mourning lamenting and howling incessantly."[4] When the jumbled thoughts of the aging mind echo the "sound of oars drawing away from shore," it is, the poet admonishes her mother, "time to fly back to where they keep your skin," to the flesh that provides some harbor for the memories and thoughts that otherwise drift aimlessly.[5] In this cycle of poems, as in the entire text of *Decreation*, Carson repeatedly explores uneven dualities or pairings of concepts and then views them from the unexpected perspective of the term less used. Thus, in this opening series (a "start" ironically called "Stops") Carson initiates a discussion of the dualism between her mother's mind and body from the perspective of the woman's flesh. In a later series entitled "Gnosticism," she will explore the ancient dualistic model of the tangible and intangible from the side of material existence, challenging a long history of privileging the spirit. These perspectives will open for Carson a *via negativa* wherein the poet favors the things of this world both for their substance and for the traces they leave behind: "a dust / an indentation, stain / of some guest / centuries ago."[6] Even the title of her collection, *Decreation*, invites readers to take more seriously the interplay between the promising beginning of a spiritual Genesis and the final threat posed by the vivid imagery of Revelation.

The body plural—youthful and weary, tangible and intangible and, as Mary Gordon's *Pearl* might say, ordered and chockablock—both evolves and comes undone. The generation of Catholic writers to which Carson belongs discovers, even celebrates, God in the midst of this plurality. But because these writers encourage readers to think about the human body as a site, in fact *the* site, where God and human beings interact, the divine presence carries the traces of its medium: it is known through the tensions, conflicts, and complexities that define physical existence. Although they represent the body in different ways, these writers all insist upon its inherent value and authority; in so doing they dramatize a crucial reality for Catholic theology: namely, that the body will not yield readily to intellectual categories or paradigms that do not acknowledge its foundational role. For this reason, these writers use ideas and terminology from the rich tradition of Catholic sacramentality, especially as it was articulated in the documents of the Second Vatican Council, to describe their insights.

In this way, each of these authors challenges the Church to take its own tradition very seriously. All would agree with Elizabeth Johnson, for example, when she refers to *Gaudium et Spes* and argues that Vatican II considered as "basic doctrine" the call for "equal dignity of both women and men created in the image of God, redeemed by Christ, and graced by the Spirit."[7] That doctrine and the "social obligations" it advanced constitute nothing less than (in the words of the Council) a network of "sacred duties."[8] The problem for contemporary Catholics, as Johnson goes on to explain, is that discrimination contrary to this doctrine is deeply engrained in our lives, that it is even "part of the heritage of the church both in theory and practice, continuing to the present moment."[9] Taking the body seriously from within the tradition, therefore, is to raise the specter of discrimination, to witness the Church as the body of Christ turned at times against itself.

It is the contention of these authors that the most honest and meaningful way to address dilemmas such as this is to enter more deeply into communion with the body—not only as a concept or symbol but also, indeed principally, as flesh, blood, and bone. It is here that we discover the kind of alterity that the works of Carson and others proffer.[10] Taking seriously metaphors of the body that the Church herself adopted in its conciliar documents, Catholics can discover in their reflections on physical existence ways to embrace challenges and change, to grow and develop—perhaps age and falter—yet still remain Catholic. What they can know is similar to what an often-neglected twentieth-century pontiff had to say shortly before his brief tenure as Pope. In 1976, Cardinal Albino Luciani, who would become Pope John Paul I for thirty-three days in 1978, published a book of his sermons—homilies given in the form of letters addressed to historical figures and even to fictional characters.[11] These "letters" are remarkable for the large heart they show their audience—an expression of hope contained within the epideictic orations and panegyric forms that mark so much Vatican II writing. They speak of human dilemmas, in particular of the need to understand youth, who, in their rapidly changing bodies, often require our patience. But the texts also are adamant about what young men and women have to offer. To the character of Figaro the Barber, for example, Luciani writes that "we can learn from youth." "Priests," he insists, "must admit that we have committed mistakes of method and that we have not paid enough attention to young people. It is necessary to start again with a spirit of humility and true service, to get ready for a meticulous work. . . ." Rather than introduce the codes and canons by which adolescent behavior should be measured, these letters advocate the type of kindness shown by St. Francis de Sales, and they take to task a Church that, as Luciani points out, burned de Sales' work *On the Devoted Life* from the pulpit because certain clergy found it too lax.[12] In perhaps the most famous of these correspondences, the future pontiff addresses the character of Pinocchio on the occasion of his becoming not only "a real boy" but one whose body soon will enter manhood. "You will see for yourself," the Cardinal writes, that this is a "*difficult* age, as much for you as for your educators. You are not a child any more," he admits, "and you will reject the company, the readings, the games of the little ones; but you are not a man either, and you will feel misunderstood and almost rejected by adults."

Luciani is very direct about the changes that will come to Pinocchio with the onset of puberty, but his directness yields to a pastoral sensibility that accepts these changes for what they are: the inexorable growth and development of the youthful body. "And while you are going through the strange experience of a fast physical growth, you will have the feeling of finding out that you suddenly have mile-long legs, Briareo's arms and a strangely changed, unusual, unrecognizable voice." The impulse of the future pope is to reassure, to ease the burden carried not by the fictional Pinocchio, of course, but by those in the pews who hear his words and translate them to their own bodies or, just as important, to the bodies of their teenage children. To those parents, for example, who would insist upon the certainty of fixed rules and regulations for young people, the Cardinal offers a different perspective. Remember, he says, that although "certainty deserves esteem . . . it does not share the evidence of mathematics. The existence of Napoleon, Caesar or Carlomagnus," Luciano points out, "does not enjoy the certainty as 2 + 2 = 4, but for that reason it does not stop being true with a human, historical certainty." In the place of a mathematical certainty, the future pope introduces the "sense of mystery. *From anything we know everything*, Pascal said. I know many things about myself, but not all. I do not know exactly what is my life, my intelligence, the degree of my health, etc. Then, how can I try to understand and know all about God?"[13]

When John Paul I describes this sense of mystery in terms that emphasize its anthropological origins in life, intelligence, and health, he introduces the body as an important source of its power and influence. For the contemporary Catholic poet Lucia Perillo, who was a junior in college when Luciani was named pope, the notion of the body as a locus of both the marvelous and the paradoxical provides a compelling motive to write. This sense of mystery is captured in the title of her 1996 collection of poetry, *The Body Mutinies*, which explores the challenges all humans face in learning to live within the confines of their flesh. In Perillo's case, the phrase assumes a special significance for, as someone who suffers from multiple sclerosis, Perillo knows firsthand what it means to discover the body in mutiny against itself, consuming itself by becoming, as it does in one of her poems, its own breakfast—"poor eggshell heart / poor lungs made of toast."[14] In the piece that gives her book its title, the speaker inhabits a body from which she feels separated yet to which she knows she is intensely connected, a body that is both as hard and unfamiliar as the shop windows that surround it displaying "dusty bedpans [that] glint like coins," and tender as the fir trees that lay a "lean" shadow across a wet courtyard and beckon bodies to "struggle in then out" of their cover.[15]

Into this seam between hardness and tenderness Perillo introduces a faith that is the product of her Catholic heritage and upbringing, and in this way she helps to summarize the ethos and practices of Catholicism experienced by writers included in this study. For example, when Perillo recalls the bobby pins that fix "the scrap of black lace to her head," readers can hear the echoes of Mary Gordon describing her years growing up in her preconciliar parish. When she recalls her mother's choice of pews in church— "midway back where we did not sing loudly"—one can recall Annie Dillard's imaginative flights from her own seat and onto ice floes filled with the sounds of strumming guitars. When Perillo goes on to note that "for mass" her mother "drove the Cadillac . . . / the kind of car / we'd take to heaven because its chrome would suit the brightness there," we can recollect the long, dark Buicks of Father Joe Hackett or of his predecessor in J. F. Powers' fictional worlds, Father Urban.[16]

Despite references to all of these memorable items and places, the faith Perillo describes is decidedly not the kind of conviction that is born of following blindly the outward signs of Catholic practice. Like Gordon, Dillard, and Powers, and in a manner similar to Erdrich, Shanley, and Karr, Perillo's faith is meaningful because it connects her more deeply to a body that is always negotiating its identity amid these signs. Thus, in the poem "The Believers," the poet, her mother, and sister leave Mass with their bobby-pinned hair and Cadillac car and drive until they "stop at the deli for roast beef."[17] Earlier in the poem, we heard how once bobby pins are fastened together they "made the sign of the cross." But now we discover what this sign signifies. At the end of the poem, we find the delicatessen owner, Mr. Albanese, slicing meat for Perillo's mother "from the rare, pink heart." The flesh in this last line suddenly clarifies all that precedes it. We attend Mass, Perillo seems to claim, because of desires that come from the body, a need for Christ that is no less physical than spiritual. The rare heart symbolizes love both divine and human, coming from God and Mr. Albanese, who perhaps is the reason Perillo's mother races out of church each Sunday "without pausing for the greeting and consolation that reigned on the steps."[18]

Positioned precariously between the human and divine, Perillo's faith reflects a deep admiration for figures within the Catholic tradition whose lives help define it: the Communion of Saints. These saints, as Perillo asserts in her poem "Retablo with Multiple Sclerosis and Saints," bear connections not only to the body generally but, specifically, to our bodies.

Saint Joseph for the good death.
Camillus for protection against sickness of the feet.
And Saint Liberata, whose miraculous beard
sprouted to save her from being married to a king . . .[19]

These and others in her poetry such as Veronica, Raphael, and Juan do not reveal an other-worldly God at their core but rather a profound humanity defined principally by the most basic of bodily functions and experiences. Elizabeth Johnson describes the Communion of Saints as a "communion of memory" that "gains its character in the course of a certain history."[20] To this description, Perillo would add that such history is remembered not only cognitively but also through the body. Consider, she says, the example of "Saint Rita: our lady of the last ditch, impossibility's patron." For Perillo, the name conjures not an ideal to which we aspire but a person we recall, perhaps "a waitress in the only diner left in town." Such embodiment does not supplement an intangible sacred presence, it constitutes the sacramental reality we name when we speak of being "in Christ." "What we need" from this Communion, Perillo insists,

is that Rita kind of salvation, a miracle
trapped by the crudest grace.
No need for shapeliness or color.
No need for lines converging at a point in space—

just the saint
and the body
and the story that ends with the body raised.[21]

Elsewhere Perillo explicates more fully the sources of salvation that become available within a community of bodies bound together. Her poem "On the Sunken Fish Processor *Tenyo Maru*" invites readers to reflect upon a historical event, the 1991 sinking of the Japanese fishing vessel that went down off the coast of Cape Flattery. Its collapse into the ocean becomes a metaphor for what lay hidden in our own human depths, not some kernel or nugget washed clean by words like "soul" and "spirit" but a hold full of "a secret depth charge": "a quarter million barrels of crude oil" and "tons of fish." As the boat rocks precariously on the ocean floor, threatening to crack open and spill its cargo, Perillo wonders what it would be like if, as the saints before us, we released the inner core of our lives into the world, "breaching the social contract."

For what might happen if we lift
the codicils on belching?
If sex were permitted in the shopping malls? If people
were allowed to sing arias
from Don Giovanni, loudly and out of tune, waiting in line
at Department of Motor Vehicles?

Her reflections become more personal when she goes on to describe how a former supervisor, "Dr. Daniel Thompson at the Denver Wildlife Research Center, whose hair was pale as a baby's," spoke to her about the odor her body emitted and the way that her shirt, with its "greasy half- / moon under each sleeve," seemed to hold the aroma within its fabric. Dr. Thompson, "who, after telling me about / his being born again / and consequent belief in all men being created in the image / of Christ, / said that I'd better get some new clothes or I'd be fired."[22]

The memory of this incident for Perillo, which is occasioned by the image of the deep-hulled *Tenyo Maru*, leads the poet to develop the metaphor of the ship's hold further. Should the sunken hull burst, would it resemble what happens when the body breaches social convention? On the one hand, yes, for what is released by both would be reviled. But on the other hand, no, for as the metaphor goes on to demonstrate, what is reviled in the ocean's depths becomes a reason for Christian love among human beings. Like Ruby Turpin, the protagonist of Flannery O'Connor's short story "Revelation," who witnesses a parade of strange and exotic souls bound for heaven, Perillo's poet goes on to recall her own cast of characters who lead her to confront the divine presence. The first is "a black woman whose hair stood in the high / crocheted hat of poverty."[23] The woman sings too loudly on the subway, moving other passengers away with the presence of a body huge and fleshy, "her legs bare from the thighs to purple sneakers, even though / the December cold was breaking records." The second figure is more troubling: a woman "who resembled Simone Weil" with hair pulled tight and "stick limbs clothed / in a nurse's tunic and yellowed slacks." She marches up and down empty library aisles emitting "rankness / an order of magnitude removed / from the gamy hobos who live beneath the railroad trestle / and make their living collecting cans." As she moves, the poet notes that she walks between placards upon which she has written letters from the word "Leviticus." Her "stink [is] from the parishes of women," the poet says, and her odor belongs to the world—to women and the "frank incense / of all our druid witchery" and to men who would rest complacent and secure among the social rules and regulations of a code like the Biblical book that prods her steps.[24]

For Perillo, these two women are members of God's kingdom, perhaps saints, wearing on their exterior what in fact permeates the being each of us claims for ourselves, that is, the ripeness of our physical existence. Just as the ocean can be found "scrubbing" clean those "tons of fish / dead in their hold," so the body vindicates the soul and not only invites but mediates God's presence. This is what another Catholic poet, Denise Levertov, finds when she examines the incarnation throughout her small but powerful collection entitled *The Stream and the Sapphire*. The physical nature of Levertov's Christ is more than merely a dimension of his otherwise divine being; it is the opportunity for divinity. "To be absolute," Levertov points out, the "sublime acceptance" of Christ in the garden "had to have welled / up from those depths where purpose / drifted for mortal moment." Without the human decision made amid the "taste" of "humiliation," the "torture of the body," and the "desire to renege," there is no genuine acceptance; there is only the unmediated presence of God. This will not do, Levertov insists, for many of the same reasons Anne Carson's poet claimed it would not suffice. To know the divine we must be "convinced of its ground, / its roots / in bone and blood. / We must feel," in Levertov's words, "the pulse of the wound / to believe."[25]

Carson, Perillo, and Levertov—in fact all of the writers discussed here—likely would find a compatriot in the protagonist created by one more author, Andre Dubus. In "A Father's Story," Luke Ripley is an old stable owner who wakes alone every morning to "talk with God" before he heads to the barn to feed his horses.[26] His conversation with the Lord is as heavy as his footsteps, for when the story begins Luke has known sin. Just weeks earlier his twenty-year old daughter, Jennifer, had visited and, one night while drinking and driving, she strikes a young man who is walking alone along a country road. The man dies, and Luke helps Jennifer cover the accident—even to the point of disguising the damage done to the car by running it into a tree in the yard of his local parish. When Luke is finished destroying the evidence, he enters the Church for morning Mass and receives communion.

In his morning conversations with God, Luke ponders his sin, peeling back the layers of his identity until he comes to an essence that helps him understand all others: "not a stable owner or a Catholic or any other Luke Ripley . . . but the father of a girl." As a father, he accepts his actions and "the cup" of punishment that follows. As a father, he admits to differences between how he has treated his daughter and how he would treat his son in a similar situation. "And if one of my sons had come to me that night," he admits, "I would have phoned the police and told them to meet us with an ambulance at the top of the hill." Finally, it is as a father that Luke forges his deepest and most compelling connection with God, for in admitting that "I could bear the pain of watching and knowing my son's pain, could bear it with pride as they took the whip and nails," he knows what God also knows: that neither of them could ever bear the "passion" of a daughter. God's response to Luke, that "you love her more than Me," initiates an exchange that welds the two speakers together in the fires of a parental care that aches for flesh and bone.

> "I love her more than truth," Luke answers.
> "Then you love in weakness," He says.
> "As You love me. . . ."

It is the joy and sorrow of this bond, the mixed feelings of holding the vocation of parent in the Kingdom of God, that Luke carries with him at the end of the story as he makes his way "with an apple or carrot out to the barn."[27]

From Sebastian Taggart's concern that he might not be able to rise each day to minister to the bodies of those who need help, to Father Modeste's decision to do so; from Mariette Baptiste's humility at the pain in her hands as she washes dishes in her kitchen sink—now an old lady who tutors neighborhood children in French, to Annie Dillard's confidence in her vocation as a "nun" in a world where grasses grow, "tides slack and ebb," and "people buy shoes"; from the wracking doubts entertained by Sister Aloysius to the weariness of apostles in Mary Karr's poetry who sleep peacefully "wrapped in old hides," to finally the mutinous bodies of Anne Carson's mother and Lucia Perillo's poet: taken together, this is the literature of bodies finding their way. The path leads them through a world they dare not take for granted because, finally, it is all any of us knows of heaven. And so we wash, serve, doubt, sleep, and buy shoes hoping that, as Catholics, respect for the world that our bodies inhabit betrays a corresponding respect for God and God's mystery. After all, as David Tracy and Stephen Happel point out in their book *A Catholic Vision*, "in this matter of God's kingdom, ours is only the trying, the attempts at achievement. The rest is none of our business."[28]

Notes

Introduction: The Body, Flesh and Bone

1. Ron Hansen, "Writing as Sacrament," in *A Stay Against Confusion: Essays on Faith and Fiction* (New York: HarperCollins Perennial, 2002), 166.

2. Alfred Alcorn, *Vestments* (Boston: Houghton Mifflin, 1988), 167.

3. Louise Erdrich, *The Last Report on the Miracles at Little No Horse* (New York: HarperCollins, 2001), 69.

4. Aidan Kavanaugh, *Liturgical Theology* (New York: Pueblo Publishing, 1984), 73.

5. Peter Steinfels, *A People Adrift: The Crisis of the Roman Catholic Church in America* (New York: Simon and Schuster, 2003).

6. See Joseph Cardinal Ratzinger, *Principles of Catholic Theology: Building Stones for a Fundamental Theology* (San Francisco: Ignatius Press, 1987), 371–72.

7. John W. O'Malley, S.J., "Vatican II: Did Anything Happen?" in *Theological Studies* 67 (March 2006). O'Malley's skill as an interdisciplinary scholar capable of explicating an array of texts and trends has been amply demonstrated in two studies that received strong reviews: John W. O'Malley, *Trent and All That: Renaming Catholicism in the Early Modern Era* (Cambridge, Mass.: Harvard University Press, 2002); and O'Malley, *Four Cultures of the West* (Cambridge, Mass.: Harvard University Press, 2006).

8. O'Malley, "Vatican II: Did Anything Happen?": 19. O'Malley points out that Vatican I issued eighteen canons; Trent, 130.

9. Ibid., 23.

10. O'Malley argues that, thanks to the publication of *Sources chretiennes* by Danielou and de Lubac, an edition that began as early as 1943, the epideictic style of oratory was "at hand" during the Council. He also points to the work of Jacques-Paul Migne, who had finished publishing *Patrologia latina* in 1865, a decade before the papal encyclical on Aquinas by Leo XIII; ibid., 24.

11. The claim here is similar to Mark Bosco's analysis of the way Catholicism influenced the writings of Graham Greene. "From the beginning," Bosco asserts, "Catholicism for Greene was never a system of laws and dogmas or a body of belief demanding assent or dissent but rather a system of concepts, a reservoir of attitudes and values, and a source of situations with which he could order and dramatize his intuitions about human experience." I would describe the difference between

Greene and the writers considered here—those who followed his generation—as one of degree. These more recent writers negotiate their relationship with a Church that they understand as "pilgrim," as finding its own way in the "modern world." Mark Bosco, S.J., *Graham Greene's Catholic Imagination* (New York: Oxford University Press, 2005), 18.

12. The writer Jon Hassler reports that, during Powers' funeral Mass at St. John's Abbey in Collegeville, Minnesota, people refrained from engaging in one of the liturgical reforms introduced by the Council: shaking hands before Communion. They resisted "out of respect for Jim's disdain for the practice." See http://www.csbsju.edu/english/misc/TheEnglishWeb/january2000.

13. Annie Dillard, "An Expedition to the Pole," in *Teaching a Stone to Talk* (New York: Harper & Row, 1982), 18.

14. Few items were more hotly contested than the " 'modest and pastoral literary style' " that came to shape both presentation and content of the documents. See O'Malley, "Vatican II: Did Anything Happen?": 22.

15. Ibid., 26.

16. Mary Gordon, "More Catholic Than the Pope," in *Good Boys and Dead Girls and Other Essays* (New York: Viking, 1991), 179.

17. Ron Hansen, "Eucharist," in *A Stay Against Confusion: Essays on Faith and Fiction*, 260.

18. Annie Dillard, *For the Time Being* (New York: Knopf, 1999), 105.

19. He also would invite to opening night his first-grade teacher from the Bronx school he attended, a nun who shares with one of his characters the name "Sr. James."

20. Lynn Neary, "*Doubt* Looks at Child Molestation in Catholic Schools," an interview with John Patrick Shanley, National Public Radio (31 March 2005). Found at www.npr.org/templates/story/story.php?storyId4568827.

21. Pope John Paul II, *Encyclical Letter Fides et Ratio* (15 September 1998), par. 13.

22. Ibid.

23. Ibid., 12.

24. The Eucharistic liturgy of the Mass insists upon this kind of physical action and interaction. Recall that, at the words "a reading of the Holy Gospel according to . . . ," the priest touches his thumb to the book, makes a small cross, and then traces that same symbol upon his forehead, mouth, and chest (while he asks God silently to cleanse his heart and lips). The congregation imitates his actions, and in this way they collectively embody a quality of worship that distinguishes Catholicism from so many of its Christian peers. For Catholics, the end or purpose of the word is to feel it and act upon it, to "experience" it physically as well as intellectually. By referring ritually to the physical presence of a "body" during the otherwise cerebral process of hearing and thinking about the Gospel message, the Catholic liturgy prepares congregations for what follows in the Eucharist.

25. Mary Karr, "Facing Altars: Poetry and Prayer," afterward to *Sinners Welcome* (New York: HarperCollins: 2006), 86.

26. Ibid., 31.

27. John Dominic Crossan, *In Parables: The Challenge of the Historical Jesus* (New York: Harper & Row, 1974), 64.

28. *Lumen Gentium: Dogmatic Constitution on the Church* (21 November 1964), par. 48.

29. Mary Gordon, *Pearl* (New York: Pantheon: 2005), 343.

30. Ibid., 348.

31. Alcorn, *Vestments*, 275.

32. Karr, *Sinners Welcome*, 31.

33. Annie Dillard, *Holy the Firm* (New York: Harper & Row, 1977), 64–65.

34. Fahey goes on to identify "the other" in the physical shape of those living on the margins, in particular "Christian women" and "the poor and persecuted of this world." He continues the spatial metaphor implied by a term like "marginalization" by contrasting this movement of oppressed groups to an imagined perimeter with the efforts of others to "recenter" the Church. For Fahey, if an important theological spokesperson for the former is a liberation theologian like Leonardo Boff, an equally impressive figure for the latter is then-Cardinal Joseph Ratzinger. According to this contrast, Boff values "the other" as "a variety of disparate cultures" wherein the Gospel message flourishes, "especially among the poor," while Ratzinger recoils from such a concept of otherness. For Ratzinger, Boff's attention to those living "on the margins" threatens to undermine the larger project called for by the powerful Vatican office of the Congregation for the Doctrine of the Faith, namely, the "'recentering'" the Church "intellectually and liturgically within its ancient homeland (Europe)." Michael A. Fahey, S.J., "Church," in *Systematic Theology, Roman Catholic Perspectives*, vol. 2, Francis Schussler Fiorenza and John P. Galvin, eds. (Minneapolis: Fortress Press, 1991), 9–10.

35. Richard R. Gaillardetz, "Do We Need a New(er) Apologetics?" *America* (2 February 2004): 29. See also Rosemary Luling Haughton's discussion of the following point: that "Catholic theology, recently, has been haunted by the fear that Catholics would become too concerned with immanence. . . ." Haughton, "Transcendence and the Bewilderment of Being Modern," in *A Catholic Modernity? Charles Taylor's Marianist Lecture*, James L. Heft, ed. (New York: Oxford University Press, 1999), 75.

36. Ibid., 30.

37. Bishop Thomas G. Doran, "Assignment of Priests," *The Observer Newspaper* (13 July 2007), Sec. A, 5. Doran and many other Christians who espouse evangelical positions would do well to acquaint themselves with the recent work of that Protestant ethicist, who has done much to promote serious theological dialogue between Christian traditions. See James M. Gustafson, *An Examined Faith: The Grace of Self-Doubt* (Minneapolis: Fortress Press, 2004).

38. Gaillardetz, "Do We Need a New(er) Apologetics?": 29.

39. Hopes to become as "she goes on her pilgrim way, to that continual reformation of which she always has need. . . ." *Decree on Ecumenism: Unitatis Rendintegratio* (12 November 1964), par. 6.

40. Robert Sokolowski, *Christian Faith and Human Understanding: Studies on the Eucharist, Trinity, and the Human Person* (Washington, D.C.: Catholic University of America Press, 2006), 1.

41. Miguel de Unamuno, *Tragic Sense of Life*, trans. J. E. Crawford Finch (New York: Dover, 1954), 3.

42. On describing and using the philosophical resources that challenge assumptions about the capacity of human rationality to know the ways of God, no one is better than Merold Westphal in *Toward a Postmodern Christian Faith: Overcoming Onto-Theology* (New York: Fordham University Press, 2001).

43. Ibid., 258, 6.

44. As S. de Madariaga explains in his preface to *Tragic Sense of Life*, Unamuno "refuses to surrender life to ideas, and that is why he runs shy of abstractions, in which he sees but shrouds wherewith we cover dead thoughts." Unamuno is more deliberate in identifying Catholicism as the source of his allergy to abstractions, and Chapter 4 of *Tragic Sense of Life* asserts his preference with his usual trenchant brand of insight. "And I have read in a Protestant theologian, Ernst Troeltsch," he begins, "that in the conceptual order Protestantism has attained its highest reach in music. . . . This then," he continues, "is what Protestantism dissolves into—celestial music!" On the other hand we may say that the highest artistic expression of Catholicism, or at least of Spanish Catholicism, is in the art that is most material, tangible, and permanent—for the vehicle of sounds is air—in sculpture and painting, in the Christ of Valasquez, that Christ who is forever dying, yet never finishes dying, in order that he may give us life. Miguel de Unamuno, *Tragic Sense of Life*, xvi, 70.

45. John Paul II, *Theology of the Body: Human Love in the Divine Plan* (Boston: Pauline Books and Media, 1997), 314. The Pope's analysis of Ephesians 5 strains to develop the metaphors of Christ and Church, head and body, husband and wife. He would have done well to take more seriously the summary statement that the author of Ephesians gives to the passage, namely, that within this great mystery of God's relationship to us, love and respect are essential (Eph. 5:33).

46. Paul's instruction is echoed in a passage from the much later letter to the Ephesians that John Paul II does not quote: "Be subordinate to one another out of reverence for Christ" (5:21).

47. As a result, all of them are likely to agree with Walter Cardinal Kasper that "Ecumenical dialogue does not mean that we abandon the convictions of our own faith, but rather (as with the doctrine of justification) that we penetrate these more deeply, until we reach the point at which they are compatible with the convictions of the faith of the other church. This requires serious theological work: laity, clergy, and bishops must all be trained in the ecumenical spirit, not least because the fruits of the preparatory work achieved in our various dialogues remain largely unknown. They must be 'received' by the church as a whole." Walter Cardinal Kasper, *Leadership in the Church: How Traditional Roles Can Serve the Christian Community Today*, trans. Brian McNeil (New York: Herder and Herder, 2004), 204.

48. As Neil Ormerod argues, recent appeals to an ecclesiology based on notions of "*communio*" serve to enforce authority. "Symbolically the notion of *communio* has an integrative function. It stresses values of harmony and integration. Such a function resists change, because change introduces stresses into the community that threaten to disrupt communal harmony. Thus, the recognition of communion ecclesiology by the 1985 Synod of Bishops as the central and fundamental idea of the documents of Vatican II was not just a theological stance; it can be read as an expression of anxiety over potentially disruptive forces of change within the Church. This is why communion ecclesiology has been so rapidly adopted by more conservative bishops seeking to put a halt to forces of change." Neil Ormerod, " 'The Times They Are a Changin' ": A Response to O'Malley and Schloesser," *Theological Studies* 67 (2006): 853.

49. Considering a range of patristic reformers, but especially Augustine, Christopher M. Bellitto distinguishes the phenomenon of reform in the Latin Church this way. "So, unlike the Greek fathers' primary emphasis on a reform that turns backward to Eden, the Latin fathers looked forward. The western idea of reform entailed a return to a past state plus a renewal of that former state aimed at a future existence in the fullness of Christ's resurrected life. In the west, the movement of reform looks both backward to Eden and forward to Christ's second coming and heaven. The future state will return to the prior existence, but remake it anew." Referring to the work of Phillip Stump, Bellitto compares western reforms to the Roman God Janus and concludes that, "like Janus, the church will often be at odds with herself as she seeks to follow the Latin patristic tradition of considering past and future at the same time." Christopher M. Bellitto, *Renewing Christianity: A History of Church Reform from Day One to Vatican II* (New York: Paulist Press, 2001), 25. See also Phillip H. Stump, *The Reforms of the Council of Constance (1414–1418)* (Leiden: E. J. Brill, 1994), 206.

50. Peter Brown, *The Body and Society: Men, Women, and Sexual Renunciation in Early Christianity* (New York: Columbia University Press, 1988), 32.

51. Mary Karr, "The Toddler as Cathedral," in *The Devil's Tour* (New York: New Directions, 1993), 45.

1. Discovering the Body: Catholic Literature after Vatican II

1. Throughout I will use the term "rhetoric" to mean "a comprehensive, total way of using discourse." As Renato Barilli points out, this means that rhetoric is different from "a dense and specialized discourse that privileges the intellectual moment of the signified over the sensual pleasure of the signifier." Such a specialized and nonrhetorical form of speaking and writing narrows the audience considerably; it "takes the right to judge from the hands of the demos and gives it over to the experts." Renato Barilli, *Rhetoric*, trans. Giuliana Menozzi (Minneapolis: University of Minnesota Press, 1989), ix.

2. "The Tridentine Profession of Faith," in *Creeds and Confessions of Faith in the Christian Tradition,* vol. II, Jaroslav Pelikan and Valerie Hotchkiss, eds. (New Haven, Conn.: Yale University Press), 874, par. 8.

3. "Dogmatic Decrees of the Council of Trent," session 3 (4 February 1546), in ibid., 821.

4. *Lumen Gentium: Dogmatic Constitution on the Church* (21 November 1964), par. 1–8.

5. Before he became pope, Cardinal Ratzinger was perhaps the most important spokesman for this claim, insisting that Vatican II misunderstood the responsibility of the Church to answer "the fundamental biblical call for conversion and love of neighbor." According to Ratzinger, the Council led Catholicism "not only to uncertainty about the Church's own identity, which is always being questioned, but especially to a deep rift in her relationship to her own history, which seemed to be everywhere sullied." For Ratzinger, this amounted to a "naïve optimism" in Council participants. Joseph Cardinal Ratzinger, *Principles of Catholic Theology: Building Stones for a Fundamental Theology* (San Francisco: Ignatius Press, 1987), 372.

6. Clarke E. Cochran and David Carroll Cochran, *Catholics, Politics, and Public Policy: Beyond Left and Right* (Maryknoll, N.Y.: Orbis Books, 2003), 11.

7. Ross Labrie, *The Catholic Imagination in Modern Literature* (Columbia: University of Missouri Press, 1997), 268.

8. Ibid., 275.

9. Anita Gandolfo, *Testing the Faith: The New Catholic Fiction in America* (Westport, Conn.: Greenwood Press, 1992), 206.

10. The passage from Matthew 16 is as follows: "And so I say to you, you are Peter, and upon this rock I will build my church, and the gates of the netherworld shall not prevail against it. I will give you the keys to the kingdom of heaven. Whatever you bind on earth shall be bound in heaven; and whatever you loose on earth shall be loosed in heaven."

11. Ibid., 206–9.

12. J. C. Whitehouse, *Vertical Man: The human being in the Catholic Novels of Graham Greene, Sigrid Undset, and Georges Bernanos* (London: Saint Austin Press, 1999), xi. The same metaphors are used by Guiseppe Alberigo to distinguish between models of behavior in the Church at the time of the Second Vatican Council. He describes opposition to the idea for a Council this way: "Unless the initiative came from Rome, any attempt at horizontal coordination within this kind of vertical or pyramidal structure was for a long time regarded by the Vatican as a potential threat." Guiseppe Alberigo, ed., *History of Vatican II, Volume I: Announcing and Preparing Vatican Council II: Toward a New Era in Catholicism,* English version by Joseph A. Komonchek, ed. (Maryknoll, N.Y.: Orbis, and Leuven, Netherlands: Peeters, 1995), 67–68.

13. Ibid., 207.

14. Ibid., 208, 211.

15. Gandolfo, *Testing the Faith,* 206.

16. Whitehouse, *Vertical Man,* 210.

17. Ibid., 212.

18. In Guiseppe Alberigo, ed., *History of Vatican II, Volume II: The Formation of the Council's Identity, First Period and Intersession, October 1962–September 1963.* English by

Joseph A. Komonchek, ed. (Maryknoll, N.Y.: Orbis, and Leuven, Netherlands: Peeters, 1997), 14.

19. Quoted in Alberigo, *History of Vatican II, Volume I: Announcing and preparing Vatican Council II, Toward a New Era in Catholicism*, English by Joseph A. Komonchek, ed. (Maryknoll, N.Y.: Orbis, and Leuven, Netherlands: Peeters, 1997), 1.

20. *Gaudium et spes: Pastoral Constitution on the Church in the Modern World*, par. 25.

21. *Lumen Gentium*, par. 10.

22. *Sacrosanctum Concilium: The Constitution on the Sacred Liturgy*, par. 48.

23. *Acta Synodaliia Sacrosancti Concilii Vaticani II*, volume III/8, 913. Quoted in Alberigo, ed., *History of Vatican II*, volume IV, 633–34.

24. As I have said elsewhere, the ability to hold two apparently contradictory ideas in tension and to promote action because of the contradiction, not despite its consequences, is typical of language associated with religious experience. Readers can discover it in virtually all the key statements about Christianity, from the parables of Jesus, which use examples of individual life and action to illustrate a social reality (the Kingdom of God), to the claim by the First Vatican Council that those who have accepted their individual "faith under the guidance of the church can never have just cause for changing this faith or for calling it into question." *Dogmatic Constitution on the Catholic Faith (1870)*, in *Creeds and Confessions of Faith in the Christian Tradition*, vol. III, Jaroslav Pelikan and Valerie Hotchkiss, eds. (New Haven, Conn.: Yale University Press), 348. For a more detailed discussion, see John Waldmeir, *Poetry, Prose and Art in the American Social Gospel Movement, 1880–1910* (Lewiston, Me.: Edwin Mellen Press, 2002), 119.

25. Labrie, *The Catholic Imagination*, 270.

26. Jacques Dupuis, "The Synod of Bishops 1974," appendix to *Living Vatican II, the 21st Council for the 21st Century*, by Gerald O'Collins (New York: Paulist Press, 2006), 200.

27. Erasmo Leiva-Merikakis, forward to *The Heroic Face of Innocence: Three Stories of Georges Bernanos* (Grand Rapids, Mich.: William B. Eerdman's, 1999), xi. Publisher's Note, ibid., 39.

28. Whitehouse, *Vertical Man,* 182.

29. Ron Hansen, *Mariette in Ecstasy* (New York: HarperCollins, 1991), 99.

30. Ibid., 113.

31. In this way Mariette is like Bernini's famous Baroque statue of Saint Theresa above the altar in the church of Santa Maria della Vittoria in Rome. Touched by a happy-looking cherub, Theresa reels in the throes of a passion that clearly depicts an orgasm.

32. *Dogmatic Decrees of the Council of Trent*, Session 6 (13 January 1547), in *Creeds and Confessions of Faith in the Christian Tradition: Volume III, Reformation Era*, Jaroslav Pelikan and Valorie Hotchkiss, eds. (New Haven, Conn.: Yale University Press, 2003), 830. Chapter 4 of this volume examines how post–Vatican II writers use a similar image of "clothing" the body but draw very different conclusions about the relationship between garment and flesh.

33. *Baltimore Catechism*, Lessons 2:8–9 and Lesson 7:81, 86–88. As C. Stephen
Evans points out, there are good reasons to think about Jesus in terms of "kenotic
Christology"—a Christological approach that begins with notions of *kenosis* or self-
emptying as described first in Paul's letter to the Philippians. One appeal, as Evans
shows, is that the kenotic approach addresses more completely the New Testament
figure of Jesus as fully divine and fully human: spiritual and physical, intangible and
tangible. To help make his point, Evans contrasts the kenotic approach with the
"two minds view," which tries to account for the incarnation by describing Jesus
not as a physical presence but as an intellect—as having two minds, both divine and
human. See C. Stephen Evans, "The Self-Emptying of Love: Some Thoughts on
Kenotic Christology," in *The Incarnation: An Interdisciplinary Symposium on the Incarnation of the Son of God*, Stephen T. Davis, Daniel Kendall, S.J., and Gerald O'Collins, S.J., eds. (New York: Oxford University Press, 2002), 249–51.

34. *Lumen Gentium*, par. 7.

35. Christian sacraments—seven or two—have not fallen into this world
untouched by historical influences. In fact, the opposite is true. The sacraments as
rites have developed because of the commitment Christianity has made to the value
of historical existence. Nowhere in Christianity is this clearer than in the Catholic
tradition. For Catholics, the seven sacraments are expressions of a fundamental way
of looking at and living in the world. These rites have taken form because the Catholic tradition sees the world and God's interaction with it as sacramental. This is a
theological insight based on an interpretation of scripture and experience that
extends backward into the Latin patristic writers. The current *Catechism* demonstrates this point by citing Augustine's *Epistulae* to make its point that "Christ himself is the mystery (*mysterium*) of salvation: 'For there is no other mystery of God
except Christ.'" Augustine, *Epistulae*, par. 187, 11, 34; quoted in *Catechism*, par. 774.
This insight is developed most fully by those theologians who, in the spirit of Vatican II, explore studiously the role of the Catholic Church in the modern world.
For the likes of Karl Rahner and Edward Schillebeeckx, for example, Jesus "in his
humanity" is a fundamental sacrament, even "the primordial sacrament." This
"fact" is what creates for Catholics a sacramental paradigm and with it a corresponding insistence that the entire world is charged with God's grandeur, a wonder and
presence that, in the words of Gerard Manley Hopkins, "shines forth like shook
foil." Hopkins of course underscores an important point, namely, that certain Catholic authors bear witness to and employ this sacramental paradigm in ways that both
confirm and challenge the tradition.

36. Hansen, *Mariette in Ecstasy*, 120.

37. Ibid., 121.

38. Ross Labrie argues that the "doctrine of the Incarnation can be seen as the
axis on which Catholic American literature in general rests and from which variances between particular authors can be measured"; *The Catholic Imagination in
American Literature*, 270.

39. Ibid., 173.

40. Ibid., 97. See also the scene when Mariette first enters the convent and the nurse asks her if it was "awkward" being examined medically by her father; ibid., 20.

41. Georges Bernanos, *Dialogues of the Carmelites*, in *The Heroic Face of Innocence, Three Stories by Georges Bernanos* (Grand Rapids, Mich.: Wm. B. Eerdman's, and Edinburgh: T & T Clark, 1999), 59.

42. Ibid., 62.

43. Ibid., 76.

44. Ibid., 76, 71.

45. Ibid., 101.

46. Ibid., 100, 113.

47. Ibid., 126–29.

48. Ibid., 81–81.

49. Ibid., 109.

50. Furthermore, to draw wide conclusions based on a study of just two works would be unfair. Nevertheless, I would contend that *Mariette* and *Dialogues* are in many ways representative. Hansen commits a good deal of his art to depictions of the body. From the opening scene in *Nebraska*, his 1989 collection of short stories, which narrates the movement of a train conductor and a young boy as they negotiate a gunnysack filled with the body of an old man down the train aisle and between the seats; to the 1991 tale of Mariette's stigmata; to the 1996 publication of the novel *Atticus*, which is set primarily in the Mexican city of *Resurreccion* and turns on the bodily relationships between father, son, and a mistakenly identified corpse: throughout this period, Hansen repeatedly uses images of the body to explore relationships between flesh and spirit, self and other. The fact that his explorations employ such a subtle analogical imagination is the basis of several critical assessments that tend to praise Hansen as a consummate stylist. By contrast, Bernanos is far more concerned with representing the internal if not intellectual life of his characters. The protagonist of his famous novel *The Diary of a Country Priest*, for instance, is a complex character who shares a great deal of his physicality with the reader, but almost exclusively in the form of an internal monologue, captured by the diary genre. Bernanos makes this point early in the book when he draws the contrast between his "country priest" and his fellow clergyman, Curé de Torcy, whose attitude toward the priesthood, parish, and the Church springs from his awareness of the human foundations of faith.

51. Paula M. Cooey, *Religious Imagination and the Body: A Feminist Analysis* (New York: Oxford University Press, 1994), 11. Michel Foucault will claim that "what the discourse of sexuality was initially applied to wasn't sex but the body, the sexual organs, pleasures, kinship relations, interpersonal relations, and so forth." Michel Foucault, "The Confession of the Flesh" in *Power/Knowledge: Selected Interviews and other Writings, 1972–1977*, Colin Gordon, ed. (New York: Pantheon, 1980), 210.

52. Jacques Derrida, *Writing and Difference* (Chicago: University of Chicago Press, 1978), 129.

53. Mark Taylor, *Disfiguring: Art Architecture, Religion* (Chicago: University of Chicago Press, 1992), 9.

54. Ibid.

55. Ibid., 318–19.

56. Ron Hansen, "Writing as Sacrament," in *A Stay Against Confusion* (New York: HarperCollins, 2001), 9.

57. Hansen, "Eucharist," in ibid., 258–60.

58. Irenaeus, *Against Heresies*, Book 1, 9:3, 59; Boethius, *On the Catholic Faith*, c. 517–22 C.E., in *Creeds and Confessions of Faith in the Christian Tradition: Volume I, Early Eastern and Medieval*, Pelikan and Hotchkiss, eds. (New Haven, Conn.: Yale University Press, 2003), 701; *The Canons of the Lateran Synod*, 649, ibid., 709; *The Doctrinal Decree of the Fourth Lateran Council, The Lateran Creed*, 1215, ibid., 741; The Council of Vienne: *Decree on the Foundation of the Catholic Faith*, 1311–12, ibid., 749–50.

60. Pius X, *Sacrorum antistitum* (1910) in *Creeds and Confessions*, Pelikan and Hotchkiss, eds., vol. 3, 420.

61. *Lumen Gentium*, par. 2.

62. *Sacrocanctum Concilium*, par. 5.

63. Ibid., 5; *Lumen Gentium*, par. 13.

64. *Gaudium et spes*, par. 16.

65. Pope Benedict XVI develops this notion in his first encyclical, *Deus caritas est*, when he writes of "a heart which sees"; Benedict XVI, Encyclical Letter *Deus Caritas Est: On Christian Love* (25 December 2005), par. 31.

66. Ibid., par. 10.

67. *Dei Verbum*, par. 1–6.

68. *Lumen Gentium*, par. 1.

69. *Sacrocanctum Concilium*, par. 1.

70. Ibid., par. 18.

71. Joseph Ratzinger, *Theological Highlights of Vatican II* (New York: Paulist Press, 1966), 5; quoted in Alberigo, *History of Vatican II, volume II: The Formation of the Council's Identity, First Period and Intersession October 1962–September 1963* (Maryknoll, N.Y.: Orbis, 1997), 88.

72. Gerald McCool places Rousselot, along with Joseph Marechal, "at the head of the stream of theological and philosophical thought" that has come to be known as Transcendental Thomism. McCool, *From Unity to Pluralism: The Internal Evolution of Thomism* (New York: Fordham University Press, 1989), 34.

73. Pierre Rousselot, *The Eyes of Faith*, trans. Joseph Doncel, introduction by John M. McDermott (New York: Fordham University Press, 1990).

74. Maurice Nedoncelle, introduction to *Sermons universitaires*, by John Henry Cardinal Newman, in *Textes Newmaniens*, vol. 1 (Bruges: Desclee De Brouwer, 1955), 35.

75. Such a unified concept of the human being helped theologians at the Council transcend the dichotomy that opened this chapter: the split between the rhetoric of individuality and that of social action that so many have emphasized. As Fogarty

claims, under Rousselot's influence the Council accepted an anthropology where "man was appreciated not only in his individuality but also in his constitutively social character."

76. In Rousselot, *The Eyes of Faith*, 17.

77. Ibid., 22–23.

78. Ibid., 28–29.

79. *Lumen Gentium*, par. 9.

80. *Dei Verbum*, par. 9

81. *Lumen Gentium*, par. 1–3, 8.

82. Ibid., par. 51.

83. Rousselot, *The Eyes of Faith*, 34.

84. *Sacrosanctum Concilium*, par. 47–49.

85. *Lumen Gentium*, par. 7.

86. *Gaudium et Spes*, par. 14.

87. *Sacrosanctum Concilium*, par. 12; the document refers to 2 Corinthians 4:10–11.

88. Rousselot, *The Eyes of Faith*, 34.

89. Erasmo Leiva-Merikakis, Foreword to *The Heroic Face of Innocence*, by Georges Bernanos, ix.

90. John XXIII, *Gaudet Mater Ecclesia*, quoted in *Nothing Beyond the Necessary: Roman Catholicism and the Ecumenical Future*, by Jon Nilson (New York: Paulist Press, 1995), 72. Available at www.saint-mike.org/Library/Papal_Library/JohnXXIII/Opening_Speech_Vati ca nII.html; accessed 1 May 2006.

2. Writing and the Catholic Body: Mary Gordon's Art

1. Kathryn Hughes, review of *The Rest of Life*, by Mary Gordon, in *New Statesman and Society* 28 (January 1994):39.

2. Anita Gandolfo, *Testing the Faith: The New Catholic Fiction in America* (Westport, Conn.: Greenwood Press, 1992), 165, 173.

3. James Wolcott, "More Catholic than the Pope," *Esquire* 3 (March 1981):21. Gordon is a writer whose work has long drawn mixed critical reception. "Literary critics either love or hate Mary Gordon's work," Stacey Lee Donohue writes in the *Encyclopedia of Catholic Literature*. "She is either praised for being relentlessly honest in her portrayal of the cold Irish Catholic family, or she is accused of being superficial and angry in her depiction of anything Catholic. Stacey Lee Donohue, "Mary Gordon," *Encyclopedia of Catholic Literature*" vol. 1, Mary R. Reichardt, ed. (Westport, Conn.: Greenwood Press), 296–97.

4. Mary Gordon, "Flannery O'Connor," in *Good Boys and Dead Girls* (New York: Viking, 1991), 38.

5. Ibid., 42.

6. Ibid., 42–43.

7. Ibid., 44.

8. Ibid., 41.

9. Kenneth Burke, *Permanence and Change: An Anatomy of Purpose* (Berkeley: University of California Press, 1954), 69.

10. O'Connor, *The Habit of Being: Letters of Flannery O'Connor*, Sally Fitzgerald, ed. (New York: Farrar, Straus and Giroux, 1979), 411.

11. To explain this process of understanding one object by looking at another, one could use a term typically associated with T. S. Eliot and the school of New Critics who followed him, "objective correlative." Gordon in fact does use it to describe a prayer book that represents the various attributes and attitudes of the Passionist order. See Mary Gordon, "The Architecture of a Life with Priests," *Seeing Through Places, Reflections on Geography and Identity* (New York: Simon and Schuster, 2000), 146.

12. Richard A. Rosengarten, "The Catholic Sophocles: Violence and Vision in Flannery O'Connor's 'Revelation'"; part of the University of Chicago Divinity School Marty Center Religion and Culture Web Forum; available at http://marty-center.uchicago.edu/webforum/112003/comentary.shtml; accessed 7 July 2007.

13. Gordon, "The Architecture of a Life with Priests," 176–77.

14. Mary Gordon, "More Catholic than the Pope," *Good Boys and Dead Girls and Other Essays*, 184–85.

15. Ibid., 181, 185, 177.

16. Ibid., 186.

17. Ibid., 183.

18. Ibid., 193.

19. Ibid., 186–87.

20. Ibid., 175

21. Ibid., 160.

22. Ibid.

23. Mary Gordon, "The Architecture of a Life with Priests," *Seeing Through Places: Reflections on Geography and Identity* (New York: Simon and Schuster, 2000), 179.

24. Gordon, "Getting Here from There," *Good Boys and Dead Girls*, 161.

25. Mary Gordon, *Immaculate Man*, in *The Rest of Life: Three Novellas* (New York: Penguin Books, 1993), 29.

26. Mary Gordon, "I Can't Stand Your Books: A Writer Goes Home," *Good Boys and Dead Girls*, 206–07.

27. Gordon, "Getting Here from There," *Good Boys and Dead Girls*, 174.

28. Gordon, *Immaculate Man*, 104.

29. Ibid.

30. Gordon, *The Company of Women* (New York: Random House, 1980), 49.

31. Gordon, "Temporary Shelter," in *Temporary Shelter* (New York: Ballantine, 1988), 18–21, 29.

32. Gordon, "The Architecture of a Life with Priests," *Seeing Through Places*, 158.

33. Gordon, *Final Payments* (New York: Random House, 1978), 167.

34. Ibid., 9.

35. Ibid., 33.

36. Ibid.

37. Ibid., 2.

38. Ibid., 16–17.
39. Ibid., 5.
40. Ibid., 7.
41. Ibid., 114.
42. Ibid., 167.
43. Ibid.
44. Ibid., 116.
45. Ibid., 172–73.
46. Ibid., 209.
47. Ibid., 227.
48. Ibid., 203.
49. Ibid., 204–05. Twenty-two years after the publication of *Final Payments*, Gordon continued her interest in the connection between location and the self by collecting her essays around "geography and identity" in *Seeing Through Places*. In this collection, she explores the connections between people and various locations, beginning with her grandmother's house. Of that particular confluence, Gordon writes that "Her house was her body, and like her body was honorable, daunting, reassuring, defended, castigating, harsh, embellished, dark." This essay establishes an approach for much of what follows in the book, for in it Gordon allows the intersection of body and space to imply a series of additional connections. For example, she points out that neither her grandmother nor the house had anything "to do with America." They were anachronisms, out of place amid the "prosperity" of "postwar life." Both are related to "Old World" roots and, as such, they exude "righteousness" in their common "refusal to accept the modern world"; Mary Gordon, "My Grandmother's House," *Seeing Through Places*, 15–17.
50. Mary Gordon, *Final Payments*, 1.
51. Ibid.
52. Ibid., 21–22.
53. Ibid., 249.
54. Ibid., 297.
55. Ibid., 242.
56. Ibid., 258, 242.
57. Ibid., 254, 248.
58. Ibid., 265.
59. Ibid., 306–07.
60. Ibid., 307.
61. Thirty years after Vatican II, the Catholic body in Gordon's writing still struggles to find a home and, as such, it mirrors mainstream Catholic life since the Council. If sociologist Andrew Greeley is right when he asserts that the Church has always been torn between a belief "that the sexual union is sacramental, an image of the union between Jesus and the Church" and a fear that it also is "something shameful," then Catholicism since the Council bears witness to that rift in unprecedented ways. Greeley has documented the consequences of this split in Vatican II faith more extensively than any other observer. He has shown that its postconciliar

manifestation coincided with a "change in sexual attitudes [that] occurred in every age cohort." In many respects, priests were in the forefront of this change among Catholics. In 1968, writes Greeley, "the majority of priests were no longer ready to enforce the ban on artificial birth control by denying absolution. Given the almost universal insistence on the ban before 1963," he continues, "this decision by the priests strongly suggested that the rules structure of the Church was in serious trouble." Catholic congregations concurred, refusing to believe that what was sinful a decade before was still a cause for penance. This massive shift in attitudes leads Greeley to conclude that the changing beliefs of Catholics "in the wake of" the Council "represent what is probably the most drastic change in Catholic attitudes and behavior in the history of the Church." Such tremendous change introduced an equally remarkable sense of Catholic uncertainty that Gordon chronicles long after she completes *Final Payments*. The ambiguity constitutes a persistent topic in her writing, but it also comes to shape the narratives she creates. See both Andrew Greeley, *The Catholic Imagination* (Berkeley: University of California Press, 2000), 17, and Greeley, *The Catholic Revolution: New Wine, Old Wineskins, and the Second Vatican Council* (Berkeley: University of California Press, 2004), 35.

62. Anita Gandolfo, *Testing the Faith*, 197.

63. Gordon, *Final Payments*, 152.

64. Ibid., 275.

65. Ibid., 298.

66. Ibid., 42.

67. The sense of an ending to Gordon's memoir operates in the manner Frank Kermode describes in his book by that same title; it "gives each moment [of the narrative] its fullness." As Kermode argues, whether we imagine endings exclusively as literary creations or more broadly and historically as apocalyptic events, the stories we "plot" toward our conclusions tend to unfold "under the shadow of the end." Frank Kermode, *The Sense of an Ending: Studies in the Theory of Fiction* (New York: Oxford University Press, 1967), 5–6.

68. Mary Gordon, *The Shadow Man: A Daughter's Search for Her Father* (New York: Vintage, 1996), 261.

69. Ibid., 261.

70. Gordon, "Getting Here from There," *Good Boys and Dead Girls*, 165.

71. Gordon, *The Shadow Man*, 127.

72. Gordon, *Final Payments*, 165.

73. Gordon, *The Shadow Man*, 195–202.

74. Ibid., 195.

75. Ibid., 194.

76. Gordon, "Getting Here from There," *Good Boys and Dead Girls*, 173.

77. Ibid., 162–63.

78. Mary Gordon, "Women of God," *Atlantic Monthly* (January 2002):58; Gordon, "Getting Here from There," *Good Boys and Dead Girls*, 161.

79. Gordon, "More Catholic than the Pope," *Good Boys and Dead Girls*, 176; see also *Shadow Man*, 10.

3. Preserving the Body: Annie Dillard and Tradition

1. Annie Dillard, "An Expedition to the Pole," in *Teaching a Stone to Talk: Expeditions and Encounters* (New York: Harper & Row, 1982), 27.

2. Grace Suh, "Ideas Are Tough, Irony Is Easy: Pulitzer Prize Winner Annie Dillard Speaks," *Yale Herald* 4 (October 1996):3.

3. Dillard, *Teaching a Stone to Talk*, 18.

4. Ibid., 27.

5. Ibid.

6. Ibid., 31–32.

7. Ibid., 177.

8. Ibid., 34.

9. Ibid., 32.

10. Ibid., 34–35.

11. Ibid., 43.

12. It would be possible to explore connections between Dillard's twin themes of being and time and that philosopher whose work is synonymous with those two concepts in the postmodern era: Martin Heidegger. But Dillard never invites this comparison and, although it would be fruitful, so is the one she does suggest, which this chapter examines in detail.

13. Ibid., 31.

14. Ibid., 20.

15. Ibid., 74.

16. Ibid., 75.

17. Ibid., 76.

18. Ibid.

19. Annie Dillard, *For the Time Being* (New York: Knopf, 1999), 164.

20. Ibid., 111.

21. Ibid., 164.

22. Ibid., 39.

23. Ibid., 91.

24. Ibid., 38.

25. Ibid., 36.

26. Ibid., 6–7.

27. Ibid., 153.

28. Ibid., 110.

29. Ibid.

30. Ibid., 119.

31. Ibid., 154.

32. Ibid., 5.

33. Ibid., 8.

34. Avery Dulles, *The Catholicity of the Church* (Oxford: Clarendon Press, 1985), 37.

35. Dillard, *For the Time Being*, 13.

36. Ibid., 14.

37. Ibid., 15.

38. Ibid., 160.

39. Pierre Teilhard de Chardin, *The Vision of the Past*, trans. J. M. Cohen (New York: Harper & Row, 1966), 131.

40. Pierre Teilhard de Chardin, *The Divine Milieu*, trans. Wm. Collins' Sons (New York: Harper & Row, 1965), 46–47.

41. Ibid.

42. Dillard, *For the Time Being*, 15.

43. Ibid., 203.

44. Ibid., 17–18.

45. Ibid., 166–67

46. Pierre Teilhard de Chardin, *Hymn of the Universe* (New York: Harper & Row, 1964), 20.

47. Teilhard de Chardin, *The Divine Milieu*, 123; see also Dulles, *The Catholicity of the Church*, 152.

48. Dillard, *For the Time Being*, 202.

49. Teilhard de Chardin, *The Divine Milieu*, 46.

50. Teilhard de Chardin, *The Vision of the Past*, 240–41.

51. Ibid., 238.

52. Teilhard de Chardin, *The Divine Milieu*, 55.

53. Ibid., 58.

54. Ibid.

55. Dillard is fully aware of Teilhard's unhappy relationship with Church hierarchy during his career, just as she knows that, over the years, some of his followers have comprised "nutty . . . vague-brained new agers." Nevertheless, her admiration is sincere and well-informed. A theologian no less orthodox than Avery Dulles has noted that Teilhard's ideas, which clearly were far advanced of his time, have become basic to "many representative theologians." According to Dulles, Teilhard's efforts to see all creation as redeemed by God's actions through Jesus, what Teilhard called the *omnipresence of christification* and what Dulles refers to as Teilhard's "pan-Christic universalism," actually has "become the official Catholic teaching in Vatican II's Pastoral Constitution on the Church in the Modern World"; Avery Dulles, *The Catholicity of the Church*, 37–38.

56. Ibid., 57–58, 122.

57. Ibid., 122.

58. Dillard, *For the Time Being*, 200.

59. Ibid., 105.

60. Ibid., 128.

61. Teilhard de Chardin, *The Divine Milieu*, 126.

62. Ibid., 124.

63. Dillard, "An Expedition to the Pole," 19.

64. Ibid., 44.

65. Ibid., 40.

66. *Dei Verbum: Dogmatic Constitution on Divine Revelation,* par. 10.

67. Ibid.

68. Ibid.

69. Annie Dillard, *Holy the Firm* (New York: Harper & Row, 1977), 48, 64.

70. "Annie Dillard: Holy the Firm," Vincent Casaregola, in *Encyclopedia of Catholic Literature*, vol. 1, Mary Reichardt, ed. (Westport, Conn.: Greenwood Press, 2004), 170.

71. Dillard, *Holy the Firm,* 25.

72. Ibid., 18.

73. Ibid., 14.

74. Ibid., 15, 18.

75. Ibid., 17.

76. Born at Pentecost, the Church becomes a sacrament that in turn "communicates" its sacramental nature to its faithful. According to this understanding, the Church acts in a manner that is remarkably like the moth: in effect, it "wicks" God's presence to us, "giving off" that presence as the moth illumines the darkness around it; see *The Catechism of the Catholic Church,* par. 1076.

77. Ibid.

78. Ibid., 35.

79. Ibid., 43.

80. Ibid., 39.

81. Ibid., 41.

82. Ibid., 49.

83. Ibid., 48.

84. Ibid., 61.

85. "There is one church here, so I go to it," Dillard explains. The "minister is a Congregationalist" and "knows God," she notes. But by section three it is clear that Dillard has developed a sacramental outlook that owes a deep debt to Catholicism; ibid., 57.

86. Ibid., 60.

87. Ibid., 65.

88. *The Catholic Catechism,* par. 1108.

89. Dillard, *Holy the Firm,* 67.

90. Ibid., 68.

91. Dillard, *Holy the Firm,* 73.

92. Ibid., 71.

93. Teilhard de Chardin, *The Divine Milieu,* 124.

94. Dillard, *Holy the Firm,* 71.

95. Ibid.

96. Casaregola, "Holy the Firm," 174.

97. Ibid.

98. *Dei Verbum,* par. 7.

99. Dillard, *For the Time Being,* 201.

*4. Clothing Bodies/Making Priests: The Sacramental Vision
of J. F. Powers, Alfred Alcorn, and Louise Erdrich*

1. J. F. Powers, *Wheat That Springeth Green* (New York: Knopf, 1988), 238. Although he published only two novels and three collections of short stories in a life that ran from 1917 until 1999, Powers' work remains for many the quintessential example of Catholic American fiction. Few writers have grasped so thoroughly and demonstrated such a command of those principles that define Catholic identity, especially the principle of sacramentality—a perspective on life that sees the world and all its mundane details charged with God's presence. His two novels explore the lives of priests on either side of the Second Vatican Council. The first (and surely his most famous work) is *Morte d'Urban* (1962); the second is *Wheat That Springeth Green*.

2. Katherine A. Powers, introduction to *Wheat That Springeth Green,* by J. F. Powers (New York: New York Review of Books, 2000), xi–xii.

3. J. F. Powers, *Wheat That Springeth Green*, 10.

4. Ibid., 6, 21.

5. *Catechism of the Catholic Church* (Washington, D.C.: U.S. Catholic Conference, 1997), 875, 76.

6. Ibid., 875.

7. Ibid., 1548, 1583.

8. Ibid., 1597.

9. Ibid., 881.

10. Alfred Alcorn, *Vestments* (Boston: Houghton Mifflin, 1988), 21. Of all the writers in this study, Alcorn is the one least known. Born in 1941, Alcorn has spent a career as a museum curator; when he wrote *Vestments*, his second novel, he was curator of the Museum of Comparative Zoology at Harvard. Born in Cheshire, England, Alcorn was raised Catholic and identifies himself as such.

11. Ibid., 5.

12. Ibid., 59.

13. Ibid., 162.

14. Ibid., 80.

15. Ibid., 49.

16. Ibid., 72.

17. Ibid., 70–71.

18. Ibid., 136.

19. Thomas Aquinas, *Summa Theologiae* 1A: 4, 1.

20. Ibid., 1A: 3, 1.

21. Ibid.,

22. Ibid., 1A: 3, 2.

23. Ibid., 1A: 3, 1.

24. Ricouer admits that his most relevant response to this issue, his 1986 Gifford lectures published as *Oneself as Another,* is largely an answer to the work of Emmanuel Levinas. In Levinas, Ricouer asserts, "the identity of the Same is bound up with

an ontology of totality that my own investigation has never assumed or come across." Unlike Levinas, Ricouer refuses to posit "the identity of the Same, to which the otherness of the Other is diametrically opposed"; Paul Ricouer, *Oneself as Another*, trans. Kathleen Blamey (Chicago: University of Chicago Press, 1992), 335.

25. Ibid., 318.

26. Ibid., 315.

27. Ibid., 318.

28. Alcorn, *Vestments*, 89. Alcorn actually made this trip, dressing as a priest and wandering through various sections of the city, including the so-called "combat zone." A full description can be found in the audio interview he gave to Don Swaim; see http://wiredforbooks.org/alfredalcorn/.

29. Ibid., 75.

30. Ibid., 169.

31. Ibid., 177.

32. Ibid., 213.

33. Ibid., 267.

34. Ibid., 269.

35. Ibid., 271.

36. Ibid., 273.

37. Ibid., 275.

38. Ibid., 276.

39. Ibid., 274.

40. Louise Erdrich, *The Last Report on the Miracles at Little No Horse* (New York: HarperCollins, 2001). Erdrich leaves little doubt about the seriousness with which she takes her Catholicism. "Once you are a Catholic you are never not a Catholic," she asserts. "You may lapse, but you are never free of it; it informs the way you look at the world. Even if you are not a believer, you have some wistful urges that you can't quite control, like imagining you have a soul"; quoted in Joan Dupont, "Scenes From a Marriage Made in Literature," *International Herald Tribune* (23 October 1993), at www.iht.com/articles/1993/10/23/louise.php.

41. Ibid., 213.

42. Ibid., 213–14.

43. Alcorn, *Vestments*, 275.

44. Erdrich, *The Last Report*, 45.

45. Ibid., 43.

46. Ibid.

47. Ibid., 67.

48. Ibid., 68.

49. Ibid., 69.

50. As the classic Catholic definition contends, sacraments function *ex opere operato* and "confer the grace they signify"; *Catechism of the Catholic Church*, par. 1127, 1128. According to this formula, the bread, *as bread*, confers God's grace. When this administration of the sacrament concludes and Father Damien looks

more closely at the world to discern God's presence—in this case to the Church that institutionalizes God's name and message—he demonstrates that he recognizes the true significance of what has just transpired. By turning to the Church, he actually fulfills one of the intended purposes of the ritual.

51. Alcorn, *Vestments*, 274.

52. Erdirch, *The Last Report*, 215–16.

53. Ibid., 135.

54. Ibid., 157.

55. Ibid., 45.

56. Ibid., 307.

57. Ibid., 350.

58. Ibid., 108.

59. Ibid., 127.

60. Ibid., 206.

61. Ibid., 108.

62. Ibid., 273.

63. Ibid., 161.

64. Ibid., 50.

65. Ibid., 129.

66. Ibid., 128.

67. Ibid., 207.

68. Ibid., 51. In a signal that Father Miller at first does not understand, Father Damien asks his visitor if he smokes by holding up "two fingers in a V." The signal becomes clear to Father Miller and he declines the offer of a cigarette. For Erdrich's readers, however, the motion contains a second, hidden meaning. It alludes directly to the shape of Leopolda's contorted body.

69. Ibid., 349.

70. Ibid., 351.

71. Ibid., 44.

72. Graham Greene, *Monsignor Quixote* (New York: Simon and Schuster, 1982), 35.

73. Ibid., 122, 124.

74. Ibid., 214.

5. *The Body in Doubt: Catholic Literature, Theology, and Sexual Abuse*

1. Paul Ricoeur, *The Symbolism of Evil*, trans. Emerson Buchanan (Boston: Beacon, 1967): 347–57. When this does happen, the symbol effectively "dies," leaving readers with the interpretation that explains the meaning. As Ron Hansen says, "To fully understand a symbol is to kill it"; Hansen, "Writing as Sacrament," in *A Stay Against Confusion* (New York: Perennial, 2002), 12.

2. Jesus' description is more than just physical; it is "bodily" because, as the central metaphor of the Church as the body of Christ reminds us, the graphic language

of hands and feet, of eyes and ears, applies easily to social entities as well as to individuals (think of the number of times the *Tanakh* personifies Israel, beginning with Jacob).

3. Robert Cooperman, *The Trial of Mary McCormick* (Niagara Falls, N.Y.: Slipstream Publishers, 1990). The style resembles Edgar Lee Masters' *Spoon River Anthology*.

4. Ibid., 30.

5. Cooperman is a good poet; poems from *The Trial of Mary McCormick* were published in major magazines and journals before they were collected, and together they won Slipstream Publishers' annual chapbook contest. Nevertheless, the limitations of this work should become apparent once it is compared to texts by others like Mary Karr.

6. Cooperman trained early in his career as a social worker, and although that background serves him in good stead as he fashions Mary and her abusers, it does not necessarily prepare him to navigate the intricacies of the Catholic tradition.

7. The reference in one of the poems, "Katie Sullivan Thinks of Mary McCormick's Lawsuit," to the actor Mel Gibson and the singer Madonna indicates that the poems are set in the relatively recent past.

8. Cooperman, *The Trial of Mary McCormick*, 16.

9. One way to address the complexity would be to apply various theological notions to the metaphor and the concepts of justice it raises. For example, from within the Catholic tradition, one could turn to the theological use Aquinas makes of analogy or to "modern" social teachings on peace and justice, beginning perhaps with *Rerum Novarum*. But, as two generations of scholars (beginning with Nathan A. Scott) have demonstrated, a fresh set of problems arises when the categories of one discipline are brought to bear indiscriminately upon another. Three classic examples would be: Scott, *Negative Capability: Studies in the New Literature and the Religious Situation* (New Haven, Conn.: Yale University Press, 1969); Giles Gunn, *The Interpretation of Otherness: Literature, Religion, and the American Imagination* (New York: Oxford University Press, 1979); and Robert Detweiler, *Breaking the Fall: Religious Reading of Contemporary Fiction* (San Francisco: Harper & Row, 1989).

10. John Patrick Shanley, *Doubt: A Parable* (New York: Theatre Communications Group, 2005).

11. Ibid., 48.

12. Ibid., 16.

13. Ibid., viii–ix.

14. Ibid., ix.

15. Ibid., vii.

16. Ibid., vii–viii.

17. Ibid., viii.

18. Ibid., x.

19. Ibid., ix.

20. Ibid., 25.

21. Ibid., 55.

22. Ibid., viii.

23. Ibid., 55.

24. *Optatum Totius: Decree on Priestly Training* (28 October 1965), par. 1.

25. Ibid., pars.2, 3, 11.

26. Ibid., par. 8.

27. Ibid., par. 56.

28. Ibid., par. 18.

29. Ibid., ix.

30. *Optatum Totius,* pars. 6, 8, 10.

31. Ibid., pars. 11, 9

32. Congregation for Catholic Education, "Concerning the Criteria for Discernment of Vocations (29 November 2005), www.zenit.org/article-14693?I = english (accessed 2.18.09).

33. Ibid.

34. Shanley, *Doubt,* 54.

35. Peter Steinfels, *A People Adrift: The Crisis of the Roman Catholic Church in America* (New York: Simon and Schuster, 2003), 43.

36. Ibid., 43, 52.

37. Ibid., 53.

38. Ibid., 63. For a more complete analysis of the way a wide range of Catholics—from George Weigel to Andrew Greeley—took American journalists to task, see David E. DeCosse, "Freedom of the Press and Catholic Social Thought: Reflections on the Sexual Abuse Scandal in the Catholic Church in the United States," *Theological Studies* 68 (December 2007):865–67.

39. Ibid.

40. Benedict XVI, Encyclical Letter *Deus caritas est, On Christian Love* (25 December 2005).

41. Ibid., par. 3.

42. Ibid., 5.

43. Ibid.

44. Ibid., 5, 6.

45. Ibid., 10

46. Ibid., 19, emphasis added.

47. *Gaudium et spes: Pastoral Constitution on the Church in the Modern World,* par. 40.

48. Mary Karr, *The Liar's Club* (New York: Viking, 1995), 160–61.

49. Mary Karr, "Facing Altars: Poetry and Prayer," afterward to *Sinner Welcome, Poems* (New York: HarperCollins, 2006), 70–71.

50. One of the discoveries she makes in the essay is how many fellow poets struggle to express some sort of religious or spiritual motive.

51. Ibid., 69.

52. David France, *Our Fathers: The Secret Life of the Catholic Church in an Age of Scandal* (New York: Broadway Books, 2004).

53. Ibid., 323.

54. Mary Karr, "Last Love," in *Sinners Welcome: Poems* (New York: HarperCollins, 2006), 49.

55. Mary Karr, "Sinners Welcome," in ibid., 40.

56. Significantly, it is the table of fellowship that breaks, not the bread of sacrifice.

57. Benedict XVI, *Deus caritas est*, par. 38

58. Karl Rahner, *The Content of the Faith: The Best of Karl Rahner's Theological Writings*, Karl Lehman, ed. (New York: Crossroad, 1992), 215.

59. Karr, *Sinners Welcome*, 93.

60. Karr, "Descending Theology: The Nativity," in *Sinners Welcome*, 9.

61. Karr, "Descending Theology: The Garden," in ibid., 38.

62. Karr, "Descending Theology: Christ Human," in ibid., 31.

63. Karr, "Descending Theology: The Resurrection," in ibid.,61.

64. "Rivering" also refers to the pierced side of Jesus, an image that Benedict also finds expressive of the union between *eros* and *agape*.

65. Karr, "Descending Theology: Christ Human," in *Sinners Welcome*, 31.

66. Benedict XVI, *Deus caritas est*, par. 1.

67. Ibid., 1, 42.

68. Ibid., 19.

69. Ibid., 7.

70. Ibid., 30.

71. Ibid., 31, 9. It is interesting that John XXIII chose for his opening remarks at the Council the rather graphic quote by St. Cyprian, who described our relationship to the Church this way: "We are born of her, are nourished by her milk, we live of her spirit" (*De Catholicae Eccles: Unitate,* par. 5).

6. The Body "As It Was": On the Occasion of Mel Gibson's The Passion of the Christ

1. Peggy Noonan, "Passion and Intrigue: The Story of the Vatican and Mel Gibson's Film Gets Curiouser, *The Wall Street Journal Opinion Journal* (22 January 2004); available at http://www.opinionjournal.com/columnists/pnoonan/?id = 110004587; accessed 1 June 2005.

2. John L. Allan, Jr., "Pope on Gibson's Movie: Was It As It Was?" *National Catholic Reporter* (30 January 2004); available at http://ncronline.org/NCR_Online/archives2/2004a/013004/013004s.php; accessed 15 June 2005.

3. Francis Cardinal George, "Magisterial Teaching," in *Together in God's Service: Toward a Theology of Ecclesial Lay Ministry* (Washington, D.C.: United States Conference of Catholic Bishops, 1998), 132–33. In an address delivered at Loras College, the Cardinal was much more succinct on this matter, stating simply: "Christ willed the hierarchy."

4. Archbishop Raymond Burke, "On Our Civic Responsibility for the Common Good," Pastoral Letter (1 October 2004).

5. Joe Feuerherd, "President Praises Benedict XVI, Chaput Warns of 'Cowardice' at D.C. Prayer Breakfast," *National Catholic Reporter* (26 May 2005); available at www.nationalcatholicreporter.org/washington/wnb2605.htm; accessed 3 March 2007.

6. *Dei Verbum: Dogmatic Constitution on Divine Revelation*, par. 8.

7. *Catechism of the Catholic Church* (Washington, D.C.: United States Catholic Conference, 1994), par. 12.

8. Ibid., 24.

9. David Tracy, *The Analogical Imagination: Christian Theology and the Culture of Pluralism* (New York: Crossroad, 1981), 349, 356.

10. *Gaudium et Spes: Pastoral Constitution on the Church in the Modern World*, par. 62.

11. Ibid.

12. Archbishop Charles Chaput, quoted in *Rocky Mountain News* (21 August 2003); available at www.passion-movie.com/promote/comments; accessed 5 May 2005.

13. For an analysis of this tension, see Wesley Kort, *Bound to Differ: The Dynamics of Theological Discourses* (University Park: Pennsylvania State University Press, 1992), 50–51.

14. Alfred Alcorn, *Vestments* (Boston: Houghton Mifflin, 1988), 157–58.

15. Margaret M. Mitchell, "*Aramaica Veritas* and the Occluded Orientalism of Mel *Gibson's Passion of the Christ*," *Criterion* 43 (Spring, 2004), 20.

16. Ibid., 20–21.

17. Ibid., 20.

18. John Paul II, *The Theology of the Body: Human Love in the Divine Plan* (Boston: Pauline Books and Media, 1997).

19. Ibid., 306.

20. Ibid., 124.

21. Ibid., 36–37. An interesting alternative to John Paul's interpretation comes from Jewish Studies scholar Jon Levenson, who points out that the word "man" in Genesis 1:27 (*ha'adam*) refers to the human species. Levenson points out that, by reading the passage this way, we discover "an alternative to both the pedestrian anthropomorphic interpretation and the vague, abstract theological reading" that characterize so many Christian interpretations; Jon D. Levenson, *Creation and the Persistence of Evil: The Jewish Drama of Divine Omnipotence* (Princeton, N.J.: Princeton University Press, 1988), 111–12.

22. John Paul II, *Theology of the Body,* 39, 46. Christopher West tries to explain the Pope's terminology by pointing out that a concept like "double solitude" describes the fact that, before a man and woman can join together as one, they must first acknowledge their individuality. The Genesis narrative dramatizes this point by giving us characters who are solitary before they are coupled together. According to West, John Paul's terminology affirms "all that it means to be a person" by "affirming everything that constitutes 'man' in solitude." West's explanation makes sense of the Pope's prose, but it does not account for the obvious: that the distinctive feature of Genesis 2:18–24 is its emphasis upon Adam's need to overcome his solitude. He does not "name" creation because he seeks to control it; he names it because he seeks a relationship with it; Christopher West, *Theology of the Body*

Explained: A Commentary on John Paul II's "Gospel of the Body" (Boston: Pauline Books and Media, 2003), 77–78.

23. Ibid., 27, 38.

24. Ibid., 43.

25. Ibid., 43, 124.

26. They share what John B. Breslin calls the "first and most general theme that runs through Catholic fiction . . . its incarnational bias: that the physical and the spiritual are inextricably bound up with one another, that our composite nature is the truest thing about us, and that all attempts to deny the body its intrinsic place in the human scheme run the risk of Gnosticism." Breslin goes on to identify this theme with an attitude of "inclusivity" among Catholic writers. His very good summary does not leave much room for the kind of critical perspective the writers treated here tend to adopt; John B. Breslin, " 'The Open-Ended Mystery of Matter': Readings in the Catholic Imagination," in *Examining the Catholic Intellectual Tradition*, Anthony J. Cernera and Oliver J. Morgan, eds. (Fairfield, Conn.: Sacred Heart University Press, 2000), 159.

27. Karmen MacKendrick, *Word Made Skin: Figuring Language at the Surface of Flesh* (New York: Fordham University Press, 2004), 27.

28. Ron Hansen, "Faith and Fiction," in *A Stay Against Confusion: Essays in Faith and Fiction* (New York: HarperCollins, 2001), 24.

29. Mary Gordon, *Pearl* (New York: Pantheon, 2005).

30. Ibid., 102–03

31. Ibid., 137, 53, 207

32. Ibid., 102.

33. Ibid., 236.

34. Ibid., 238.

35. Ibid., 84.

36. Ibid., 13. Recall John Paul II's discussion of Gen. 2:19–20, which finds in Adam's "naming" opportunities to assert hegemony.

37. Ibid., 19, 124, 37.

38. The fact that Gordon is so imprecise, even elusive, about this narrative voice indicates that she does not want readers to identify the voice directly with Gordon herself or, for that matter, with any "character" she has created. The omniscient quality suggests, of course, that the voice possesses divine attributes, but Gordon never develops that quality in ways that would lead readers to draw explicit, theological conclusions.

39. Gordon, *Pearl*, 247.

40. *Ibid.*, 232.

41. Ibid., 221.

42. Ibid., 86.

43. Ibid., 104.

44. Ibid., 98.

45. Ibid., 95.

46. Ibid., 96.

47. Ibid., 215.

48. Ibid., 97.

49. *Catechism of the Catholic Church*, 1128

50. Gordon, *Pearl*, 98.

51. Ibid., 99. "Always be ready to give an explanation to anyone who asks you for a reason for your hope"; 1 Peter 3:15.

52. *Catechism of the Catholic Church*, 1131.

53. Ibid., 1153.

54. Ibid., 1333.

55. Gordon, *Pearl*, 136.

56. Ibid., 198–99.

57. Ibid., 173.

58. John Paul II, *Theology of the Body*, 37.

59. Ibid., 36–37.

60. Ibid., 361.

61. Historians like Roy Porter have traced this relationship to certain attitudes toward the body that emerged with the Enlightenment; linguists like George Lakoff and Mark Johnson have identified even older sources in the history of Western philosophy. With his uncanny ability to compress the history of an idea into a single phrase or image, Ludwig Wittgenstein illustrates the relationship when he notes that part of what we "mean" by the word "chair" is the act of sitting in it; Roy Porter, *Flesh in the Age of Reason: The Modern Foundations of Body and Soul* (New York: Norton, 2003); George Lakoff and Mark Johnson, *Philosophy in the Flesh: The Embodied Mind and Its Challenge to Western Thought* (New York: Basic Books, 1999).

62. Karol Wojtyla (Pope John Paul II), *Easter Vigil and Other Poems*, trans. Jerzy Peterkiewicz (New York: Random House, 1979), 19.

63. Wojtyla, *The Jeweler's Shop*, trans. Boleslaw Taborski (New York: Random House, 1980), 22.

64. Seth Sanders, "Mystically Correct," *Criterion* 43 (Spring, 2004):37.

65. Gordon, *Pearl*, 229.

66. Ibid., 95.

67. Ibid., 132.

68. Ibid., 133–34.

69. Ibid., 57.

70. For an analysis of the relationship between the phenomena of religion and religious traditions and the role of the classic, see David Tracy, *The Analogical Imagination: Christian Theology and the Culture of Pluralism* (New York: Crossroad, 1981).

71. Joseph Cardinal Ratzinger (Pope Benedict XVI), *The Spirit of the Liturgy*, trans. John Saward (San Francisco: Ignatius Press, 2000), 173.

72. In her remarkable study of the body in Christian tradition, *The Word Made Flesh*, Margaret Miles notes that the scholar of ancient liturgies, Joseph Jungmann, said the "greatest change in the history of Christian worship was abandoning the meal in the mid-fourth century when congregations became too large to make a

meal feasible"; Miles, *The Word Made Flesh: A History of Christian Thought* (Oxford: Blackwell Publishing, 2005), 63.

73. Ephraim the Syrian, "The Pearl," trans. John Brand Morris, in *Christian Literature: An Anthology*, Alister McGrath, ed. (Oxford: Blackwell Publishing, 2001), 77–79.

Conclusion: The Body Mutinies

1. Anne Carson, *Decreation: Poetry, Essays, Opera* (New York: Vantage, 2003), 12.

2. Ibid., 5

3. For example, in one poem, "That Strength," Carson's mother is associated with images of "strength"—a "Knife un / bloodable in grindbones," in another, that "knife" reappears as an instrument that has pared away her life—"skinned off that hour. / Sank the buoys." In other sets of poems, the presence of "wind" has a similar role in unifying yet distinguishing aspects of character. Wind blows throughout this set of poems like the movement of spirit across a very personal landscape. At times it is abundant—"there is so much here stones go blank"—and at others it "goes thin, to shreds," only to reemerge as a "glassy wind" that "breaks on a shoutless shore." It is the spirit of one whose body is failing and, in its demise, establishing new relationships to the surrounding world; ibid., 10–13.

4. Ibid., 14–15.

5. Ibid.

6. Ibid., 88.

7. Elizabeth A. Johnson, *Friends of God and Prophets: A Feminist Theological Reading of the Communion of Saints* (New York: Continuum, 1999), 25. The full quote, as Johnson cites it, is: "Nevertheless, with respect to the fundamental rights of the person, every type of discrimination, whether social or cultural, whether based on sex, race, creed, social condition, language, or religion, is to be overcome and eradicated as contrary to God's intent"; *Gaudium et Spes*, par. 29.

8. *Gaudium et Spes: Pastoral Constitution on the Church in the Modern World*, par. 30.

9. Johnson, *Friends of God and Prophets*, 25.

10. See Chapter 1 for a fuller discussion of the term "alterity."

11. Written when he was Cardinal Luciani, these letters were collected and published in English when he became Pope John Paul I; see Albino Luciani, *Illustrissimi: Letters from Pope John Paul I* (New York: Little, Brown, 1978).

12. The reference appears in his "letter" to Maria Theresa of Austria; ibid., 21. Burning such a text would not have been uncommon, but doing so from the pulpit would have been odd. Yet the Cardinal describes the scene in this way, with the angry monk removing the text from his sleeve and burning it by the flame of an altar candle.

13. Ibid., 75–77.

14. Lucia Perillo, *The Body Mutinies* (West Lafayette, Ind.: Purdue University Press), 16. A neglected poet critically, Perillo's stature increased measurably when she won a MacArthur Foundation Award in 2000.

15. Ibid., 30.

16. Lucia Perillo, *Luck is Luck* (New York: Random House, 2005), 16.

17. Ibid.

18. Ibid.

19. Perillo, *The Body Mutinies*, 31.

20. Johnson's description comes in part from her reading of Robert Bellah's *Habits of the Heart*; for more details see Johnson, *Friends of God and Prophets*, 22.

21. Perillo, *The Body Mutinies*, 34.

22. Ibid., 16.

23. Ibid., 17.

24. Ibid., 18. The kind of odor Perillo describes lingers with a pungency that overpowers, "corrupting" all it touches. It is a smell that accomplishes physically what Ruby Turpin only envisions at the conclusion of O'Connor's short story "Revelation." Like Ruby's vision of the "vast, swinging bridge" to heaven that ironically reorganizes the transit of souls, this unmistakable physical "mark" transforms social outcasts into the most profound manifestations of God's kingdom while at the same time marking the lives of otherwise upright, "born again" citizens. These latter now resemble the least on Ruby's bridge, trailing behind the others with "even their virtues . . . burned away"; Flannery O'Connor, "Revelation," in *Three by Flannery O'Connor* (New York: Signet, 1983), 423.

25. Denise Levertov, *The Stream and the Sapphire: Selected Poems on Religious Themes* (New York: New Directions, 1997), 74.

26. Andre Dubus, "A Father's Story," in *A Celestial Omnibus: Short Fiction on Faith*, J. P. Mahoney and Tom Hazuka, eds. (Boston: Beacon Press, 1997). 33. For a more detailed analysis of the role of the body in Dubus's fiction, see Robert P. Lewis, "'No More Male and Female': Bodiliness and Eucharist in Andre Dubus's Stories," *Religion and the Arts* 6¹/₂ (2002), 36.

27. Ibid. A recent study of the Kingdom of God by John Caputo emphasizes the remarkable weakness of what Jesus enacts. "The kingdom of God is the rule of weak forces like patience and forgiveness, which, instead of forcibly exacting payment for an offense, release and let go"; see John D. Caputo, *The Weakness of God: A Theology of the Event* (Bloomington: Indiana University Press, 2006), 15.

28. David Tracy and Stephen Happel, *A Catholic Vision* (Philadelphia: Fortress Press, 1984), 190.

Works Cited

Alcorn, Alfred. *Vestments*. Boston: Houghton Mifflin, 1988.

Allen, John L., Jr. "Pope on Gibson's Movie: Was It as It Was?" *National Catholic Reporter* (30 January 2004). Available at http://ncronline.org/NCR_Online/archives2/2004a/013004/013004s.php. Accessed 15 June 2005.

Ashley, Benedict M., O.P. *Theologies of the Body: Humanist and Christian*. St. Louis: Pope John Center, 1985.

Bellitto, Christopher. *Renewing Christianity: A History of Church Reform from Day One to Vatican II*. New York: Paulist Press, 2001.

Benedict XVI. Encyclical Letter *Deus caritas est: On Christian Love* (25 December 2005).

Bosco, Mark, S.J. *Graham Greene's Catholic Imagination*. New York: Oxford University Press, 2005.

Breslin, John B. " 'The Open-Ended Mystery of Matter': Readings in the Catholic Imagination." In *Examining the Catholic Intellectual Tradition*. Edited by Anthony J. Cernera and Oliver J. Morgan. Fairfield, Conn.: Sacred Heart University Press, 2000.

Brown, Peter. *The Body and Society: Men, Women, and Sexual Renunciation in Early Christianity*. New York: Columbia University Press, 1988.

Burke, Archbishop Raymond. "On Our Civic Responsibility for the Common Good." Pastoral Letter (1 October 2004).

Burke, Kenneth. *Permanence and Change: An Anatomy of Purpose*. Berkeley: University of California Press, 1954.

Caputo, John D. *The Weakness of God: A Theology of the Event*. Bloomington: Indiana University Press, 2006.

Carson, Anne. *Decreation: Poetry, Essays, Opera*. New York: Vantage, 2003.

Casaregola, Vincent. "Annie Dillard: Holy the Firm." In *Encyclopedia of Catholic Literature*, vol. 1. Edited by Mary Reichardt. Westport, Conn.: Greenwood Press, 2004: 167–77.

Catechism of the Catholic Church. Washington, D.C.: U.S. Catholic Conference, 1997.

Congregation for Catholic Education, "Concerning the Criteria for Discernment of Vocations" (29 November 2005). Available at http://www.zenit.org/article -14693?I = english. Accessed 18 February 2008.

Cooey, Paula M. *Religious Imagination and the Body: A Feminist Analysis.* New York: Oxford University Press, 1994.

Cooperman, Robert. *The Trial of Mary McCormick.* Niagara Falls, N.Y.: Slipstream Publishers, 1990.

Crossan, John Dominic. *In Parables: The Challenge of the Historical Jesus.* New York: Harper & Row, 1974.

Crowley, Paul G., S.J. "Homosexuality and the Council of the Cross." *Theological Studies* 65 (2004): 500–29.

Davis, Stephen T., Daniel Kendall, S.J., and Gerald O'Collins S.J., eds. *The Incarnation: An Interdisciplinary Symposium on the Incarnation of the Son of God.* New York: Oxford University Press, 2002.

DeCosse, David E. "Freedom of the Press and Catholic Social Thought: Reflections on the Sexual Abuse Scandal in the Catholic Church in the United States." *Theological Studies* 68 (December 2007): 865–99.

Decree on Ecumenism: Unitatis Rendintegratio (12 November 1964).

Dei Verbum (18 November 1965).

Detweiler, Robert. *Breaking the Fall: Religious Reading of Contemporary Fiction.* San Francisco: Harper & Row, 1989.

Dillard, Annie. *For the Time Being.* New York: Knopf, 1999.

———. *Holy the Firm.* New York: Harper & Row, 1977.

———. *Teaching a Stone to Talk: Expeditions and Encounters.* New York: Harper & Row, 1982.

Donohue, Stacey Lee. "Mary Gordon." *Encyclopedia of Catholic Literature*, vol 1. Edited by Mary R. Reichardt. Westport, Conn.: Greenwood Press, 2001, 290–98.

Dubus, Andre. "A Father's Story," in *A Celestial Omnibus: Short Fiction on Faith.* Edited by J. P. Mahoey and Tom Hazuka. Boston: Beacon Press, 1997, 15–33.

Dulles, Avery. *The Catholicity of the Church.* Oxford: Clarendon Press, 1985.

Dupont, Joan. "Scenes From a Marriage Made in Literature." *International Herald Tribune* 23 (23 October 1993). Available at www.iht.com/articles/1993–10/23/louise.php. Accessed 24 November 2008.

Ephraim the Syrian. "The Pearl." Translated by John Brand Morris. In *Christian Literature: An Anthology.* Edited by Alister McGrath. Oxford: Blackwell Publishing, 2001, 378.

Erdrich, Louise. *The Last Report on the Miracles at Little No Horse.* New York: HarperCollins, 2001.

Fahey, Michael A., S.J. "Church," in *Systematic Theology: Roman Catholic Perspectives*, vol. 2. Edited by Francis Schussler Fiorenza and John P. Galvin. Minneapolis: Fortress Press, 1991, 1–75.

Feuerherd, Joe. "President Praises Benedict XVI, Chaput Warns of 'Cowardice' at D.C. Prayer Breakfast." *National Catholic Reporter* (26 May 2005). Available at www.nationalcatholicreporter.org/Washington/wnb052605.htm. Accessed 24 November 2008.

France, David. *Our Fathers: The Secret Life of the Catholic Church in an Age of Scandal.* New York: Broadway Books, 2004.

Gaillardetz, Richard R. "Do We Need a New(er) Apologetics?" *America* (2 February 2004).

Gandolfo, Anita. *Testing the Faith: The New Catholic Fiction in America.* Westport, Conn.: Greenwood Press, 1992.

Gaudium et Spes (7 December 1965).

George, Francis Cardinal. "Magisterial Teaching." In *Together in God's Service: Toward a Theology of Ecclesial Lay Ministry.* Washington, D.C.: United States Conference of Catholic Bishops, 1998: 132–33.

Godzieba, Anthony, Lieven Boeve, and Michele Saracino. "Resurrection—Interruption—Transformation: Incarnation as a Hermeneutical Strategy: A Symposium." *Theological Studies* 67 (2006): 777–815.

Gordon, Mary. *The Company of Women.* New York: Random House, 1980.

———. *Final Payments.* New York: Random House, 1978.

———. *Good Boys and Dead Girls and Other Essays.* New York: Viking, 1991.

———. *Pearl.* New York: Pantheon, 2005.

———. *The Rest of Life: Three Novellas.* New York: Penguin Books, 1993.

———. *Seeing Through Places: Reflections on Geography and Identity.* New York: Simon and Schuster, 2000.

———. *The Shadow Man: A Daughter's Search for Her Father.* New York: Vintage, 1996.

———. *Temporary Shelter.* New York: Ballantine, 1988.

———. "Women of God." *Atlantic Monthly* (January 2002): 58–91.

Greeley, Andrew. *The Catholic Imagination.* Berkeley: University of California Press, 2000.

———. *The Catholic Revolution: New Wine, Old Wineskins, and the Second Vatican Council.* Berkeley: University of California Press, 2004.

Greene, Graham. *Monsignor Quixote.* New York: Simon and Schuster, 1982.

Gunn, Giles. *The Interpretation of Otherness: Literature, Religion, and the American Imagination.* New York: Oxford University Press, 1979.

Gustafson, James M. *An Examined Faith: The Grace of Self-Doubt.* Minneapolis: Fortress Press, 2004.

Hansen, Ron. *A Stay Against Confusion: Essays on Faith and Fiction.* New York: HarperCollins Perennial, 2002.

Hassler, Jon. "J. F. Powers RIP." Available at http://www.csbsju.edu/english/misc/The EnglishWeb/january2000. Accessed 5 January 2008.

Haughton, Rosemary Luling. "Transcendence and the Bewilderment of Being Modern," in Kathryn Hughes' review of *The Rest of Life*, by Mary Gordon. *New Statesman and Society* 28 (January 1994): 39.

Imbelli, Robert P. "The Pope and the Poet." *America* 194 (13 March 2006): 8–10.

Isherwood, Lisa. *The Good News of the Body: Sexual Theology and Feminism.* New York: New York University Press, 2001.

Heft, James L., ed. *A Catholic Modernity? Charles Taylor's Marianist Lecture.* New York: Oxford University Press, 1999.

John Paul II. Encyclical Letter: *Fides et Ratio* (15 September 1998).

———. *Theology of the Body: Human Love in the Divine Plan.* Boston: Pauline Books and Media, 1997.

Johnson, Elizabeth A. *Friends of God and Prophets: A Feminist Theological Reading of the Communion of Saints.* New York: Continuum, 1998.

Karr, Mary. *The Devil's Tour.* New York: New Directions, 1993.

———. "Facing Altars: Poetry and Prayer," afterword to *Sinners Welcome: Poems.* New York: HarperCollins, 2006.

———. *The Liar's Club.* New York: Viking, 1995.

———. *Sinners Welcome, Poems.* New York: HarperCollins, 2006.

Kasper, Walter Cardinal. *Leadership in the Church: How Traditional Roles Can Serve the Christian Community Today.* Translated by Brian McNeil. New York: Herder and Herder, 2004.

Kavanaugh, Aidan. *Liturgical Theology.* New York: Pueblo Publishing, 1984.

Kermode, Frank. *The Sense of an Ending: Studies in the Theory of Fiction.* New York: Oxford University Press, 1967.

Kort, Wesley. *Bound to Differ: The Dynamics of Theological Discourses.* University Park: Penn State University Press, 1992.

Lakoff, George, and Mark Johnson. *Philosophy in the Flesh: The Embodied Mind and Its Challenge to Western Thought.* New York: Basic Books, 1999.

Levenson, Jon D. *Creation and the Persistence of Evil: The Jewish Drama of Divine Omnipotence.* Princeton, N.J.: Princeton University Press, 1988.

Levertov, Denise. *The Stream and the Sapphire: Selected Poems on Religious Themes.* New York: New Directions, 1997.

Lewis, Robert P. "'No More Male and Female': Bodiliness and Eucharist in Andre Dubus's Stories." *Religion and the Arts* $6^{1}/_{2}$ (2002): 36–51.

Luciani, Albino (Pope John Paul I). *Illustrissimi: Letters from Pope John Paul I.* New York: Little, Brown, 1978.

Lumen Gentium (21 November 1964).

MacKendrick, Karmen. *Word Made Skin: Figuring Language at the Surface of Flesh.* New York: Fordham University Press, 2004.

Miles, Margaret. *The Word Made Flesh: A History of Christian Thought.* Oxford: Blackwell Publishing, 2005.

Mitchell, Margaret M. "*Aramaica Veritas* and the Occluded Orientalism of Mel Gibson's *Passion of the Christ.*" *Criterion* 43 (Spring 2004): 20.

Moltmann-Wendel, Elisabeth. *I Am My Body: A Theology of Embodiment.* New York: Continuum, 1995.

Neary, Lynn. "*Doubt* Looks at Child Molestation in Catholic Schools." Interview with John Patrick Shanley, National Public Radio, 31 March 2005. Available at www.npr.org/templates/story/story.php?storyId4568827. Accessed 22 February 2008.

Nelson, James B. *Body Theology.* Louisville, Ky.: Westminster/John Knox Press, 1992.

Noonan, Peggy. "Passion and Intrigue: The Story of the Vatican and Mel Gibson's Film Gets Curiouser." *Wall Street Journal Opinion Journal* (22 January 2004). Available at http://www.opinionjournal.com/columnists/pnoonan/ ?id=110004587. Accessed 1 June 2005.

O'Connor, Flannery. *The Habit of Being: Letters of Flannery O'Connor.* Edited by Sally Fitzgerald. New York: Farrar, Straus and Giroux, 1979.

———. *Three by Flannery O'Connor.* New York: Signet, 1983.

O'Malley, John W., S.J. *Trent and All That: Renaming Catholicism in the Early Modern Era.* Cambridge, Mass.: Harvard University Press, 2002.

———. "Vatican II: Did Anything Happen?" *Theological Studies* 67 (March 2006): 3–33. October 1993. Available at www.iht.com/articles/1993/10/23/louise.php. Accessed 6 June 2007.

Optatum Totius (28 October 1965).

Ormerod, Neil. "'The Times They Are a Changin'': A Response to O'Malley and Schloesser." *Theological Studies* 67 (2006): 834–55.

Perillo, Lucia. *The Body Mutinies.* West Lafayette, Ind.: Purdue University Press, 1996.

———. *Luck Is Luck.* New York: Random House, 2005.

Porter, Roy. *Flesh in the Age of Reason: The Modern Foundations of Body and Soul.* New York: Norton, 2003.

Powers, J. F. *Wheat That Springeth Green.* New York: Knopf, 1988.

Powers, Katherine A. Introduction to *Wheat That Springeth Green,* by J. F. Powers. New York: New York Review of Books, 2000.

Prokes, Mary Timothy, F.S.E. *Toward a Theology of the Body.* Grand Rapids, Mich.: Wm. B. Eerdmans, 1996.

Rahner, Karl. *The Content of the Faith: The Best of Karl Rahner's Theological Writings.* Edited by Karl Lehman. New York: Crossroad, 1992.

Ratzinger, Joseph Cardinal (Pope Benedict XVI). *Principles of Catholic Theology: Building Stones for a Fundamental Theology.* San Francisco: Ignatius Press, 1987.

———. *The Spirit of the Liturgy.* Translated by John Saward. San Francisco: Ignatius Press, 2000.

Ricouer, Paul. *Oneself as Another.* Translated by Kathleen Blamey. Chicago: University of Chicago Press, 1992.

———. *The Symbolism of Evil.* Translated by Emerson Buchanan. Boston: Beacon Press, 1967.

Rosengarten, Richard A. "The Catholic Sophocles: Violence and Vision in Flannery O'Connor's 'Revelation.'" Available at http://marty-center.uchicago.edu/ webforum/112003/comentary.shtml. Accessed 7 July 2007.

Rousselot, Pierre. *The Eyes of Faith,* trans. Joseph Donceel, S.J. (New York: Fordham University Press, 1990).

Sacrosanctum Concilium (4 December 1963).

Sanders, Seth. "Mystically Correct." *Criterion* 43 (Spring 2004): 37.

Scott, Nathan. *Negative Capability: Studies in the New Literature and the Religious Situation.* New Haven, Conn.: Yale University Press, 1969.

Shanley, John Patrick. *Doubt: A Parable.* New York: Theatre Communications Group, 2005.

Sokolowski, Robert. *Christian Faith and Human Understanding: Studies on the Eucharist, Trinity, and the Human Person.* Washington, D.C.: Catholic University of America Press, 2006.

Steinfels, Peter. *A People Adrift: The Crisis of the Roman Catholic Church in America.* New York: Simon and Schuster, 2003.

Stump, Phillip H. *The Reforms of the Council of Constance (1414–1418).* Leiden: E. J. Brill, 1994.

Suh, Grace. "Ideas Are Tough, Irony Is Easy: Pulitzer Prize Winner Annie Dillard Speaks." *Yale Herald* 4 (October 1996): 3.

Swaim, Don. Interview with Alfred Alcorn. Available at http://wiredforbooks.org/alfredalcorn/. Accessed 2 January 2008.

Teilhard de Chardin, Pierre. *The Divine Milieu.* Translated by Wm. Collins' Sons. New York: Harper & Row, 1965.

———. *Hymn of the Universe.* New York: Harper & Row, 1964.

———. *The Vision of the Past.* Translated by J. M. Cohen. New York: Harper & Row, 1966.

Tracy, David. *The Analogical Imagination: Christian Theology and the Culture of Pluralism.* New York: Crossroad, 1981.

Tracy, David, and Stephen Happel. *A Catholic Vision.* Philadelphia: Fortress Press, 1984.

Unamuno, Miguel de. *Tragic Sense of Life.* Translated by J. E. Crawford Finch. New York: Dover, 1954.

West, Christopher. *Theology of the Body Explained: A Commentary on John Paul II's "Gospel of the Body."* Boston: Pauline Books and Media, 2003.

Westphal, Merold. *Toward a Postmodern Christian Faith: Overcoming Onto-Theology.* New York: Fordham University Press, 2001.

Wojtyla, Karol (Pope John Paul II). *Easter Vigil and Other Poems.* Translated by Jerzy Peterkiewicz. New York: Random House, 1979.

———. *The Jeweler's Shop.* Translated by Boleslaw Taborski. New York: Random House, 1980.

Wolcott, James. "More Catholic than the Pope." *Esquire* 3 (March 1981): 21–23. Available at http://www.nationalcatholicreporter.org/washington/wnb2605.htm. Accessed 3 October 2007.

Index